This is the first English edition of a treatise which influenced French thinkers from its publication in 1610 until the end of the *ancien régime*. Charles Loyseau's *Treatise of Orders and Plain Dignities* is the third of three major works in which he set out to harmonise with law his fellow citizens' values and behaviour in the crucial sphere of possession and exercise of public power. In attempting this he developed a thesis, calculated to justify the monarch's overriding role, which illuminates contemporary perceptions of the nature of the state.

Howell A. Lloyd's introduction outlines Loyseau's political thesis on the basis of all three of the author's treatises, and examines in relation to the *Treatise of Orders* Loyseau's use of literary, historical and legal materials within the philosophical framework that governed his approach. This edition thus not only makes available an important text, but also casts light upon the intellectual milieu of those who administered early-modern France.

CAMBRIDGE TEXTS IN THE
HISTORY OF POLITICAL THOUGHT

LOYSEAU
A Treatise of Orders and Plain Dignities

CAMBRIDGE TEXTS IN THE
HISTORY OF POLITICAL THOUGHT

Series editors

RAYMOND GEUSS

Political Sciences, University of Cambridge

QUENTIN SKINNER

Professor of Political Science in the University of Cambridge

Cambridge Texts in the History of Political Thought is now firmly established as the major student textbook series in political theory. It aims to make available to students all the most important texts in the history of western political thought, from ancient Greece to the early twentieth century. All the familiar classic texts will be included but the series does at the same time seek to enlarge the conventional canon by incorporating an extensive range of less well-known works, many of them never before available in a modern English edition. Wherever possible, texts are published in complete and unabridged form, and translations are specially commissioned for the series. Each volume contains a critical introduction together with chronologies, biographical sketches, a guide to further reading and any necessary glossaries and textual apparatus. When completed, the series will aim to offer an outline of the entire evolution of western political thought.

For a list of titles published in the series, please see end of book.

LOYSEAU

A Treatise of Orders and Plain Dignities

EDITED AND TRANSLATED BY

HOWELL A. LLOYD

Professor of History
University of Hull

CAMBRIDGE
UNIVERSITY PRESS

Published by the Press Syndicate of the University of Cambridge
The Pitt Building, Trumpington Street, Cambridge CB2 1RP
40 West 20th Street, New York, NY 10011–4211, USA
10 Stamford Road, Oakleigh, Melbourne 3166, Australia

First published 1994

Printed in Great Britain at the University Press, Cambridge

A catalogue record for this book is available from the British Library

Library of Congress cataloguing in publication data
Loyseau, Charles, 1564–1627.
[Traicté des ordres et simples dignitez. English]
A treatise of orders and plain dignities / Loyseau: edited by
Howell A. Lloyd.
p.   cm. – (Cambridge texts in the history of political thought)
Includes bibliographical references and index.
ISBN 0 521 40519 X (hardback)
1. Estates (Social orders) – France. I. Lloyd, Howell A.
II. Title.   III. Series.
KJV4089.L6913 1994
301'.0944 – dc20   93-23155 CIP

ISBN 0521 40519 X hardback
ISBN 0521 45624 X paperback

1001424333

for Tim

Contents

Acknowledgements

I gratefully acknowledge the British Academy's award of a grant which enabled me to carry out research for this project in various libraries. My thanks are due to the custodians of those repositories; they include the Cambridge University Library, London's British Library, Oxford's Bodleian Library, and especially Edinburgh's Advocates' Library, this last a private institution, the Librarian of which, Mr Brian Gill QC, showed me particular consideration. My greatest debt of this nature is, as always, to the hard-pressed members of staff of the Brynmor Jones Library, University of Hull. For a stimulating environment in which to work, remarkably sustained in trying times, I am indebted to colleagues in that university's Department of History. I received welcome assistance from Professors Francis Cairns of Leeds and Desmond Costa of Birmingham on certain of Loyseau's sources; from Dr J. P. Canning of Bangor on a point concerning Baldus de Ubaldis; and from Professor William Doyle of Bristol on Loyseau's continued significance in the eighteenth century. But my deepest obligations are to Professor J. A. Watt, formerly of Newcastle, for responding most generously to my appeal for help with matters especially of civil and canon law; and to Dr Lionel North of the Department of Theology, University of Hull, for cheerfully allowing me to draw at will upon his expertise in matters of Greek. Without these, and above all the two last-named scholars, I should not have been able to complete my task (though it goes without saying that I alone am responsible for all faults and insufficiencies that may remain). And without the certainty of support from my wife, Gaynor, I should not have ventured to begin it.

Introduction

Loyseau's life

Charles Loyseau's paternal grandfather was a husbandman of Nogent-le-Roi in the Eure valley, some thirteen kilometres south-west of Dreux. To the north of Dreux, in the same valley, lies Anet with the remains of its château which Diane de Poitiers, mistress of King Henry II, made into one of the masterpieces of French Renaissance architecture. The patronage wielded by *La Grande Sénéschalle* was instrumental in shaping the career of Loyseau's father, Regnauld. Trained as an advocate, he became Diane's regular legal representative when his predecessor in that role, the distinguished lawyer Christofle de Thou, was appointed through the same patroness's good offices to a senior judgeship in the Paris *parlement*. Regnauld Loyseau himself built a successful practice at the Paris bar, and it was probably in the capital that his son Charles was born in 1564. Diane de Poitiers stood godmother to him (*Offices* III.iii.45). Eclipsed in influence at court since Henry II's death in 1559, she was to die in 1567; but protégés of hers remained conspicuously in place. And with his father's own contacts to help him on his way, a brilliant future for the young Loyseau may well have been anticipated.

Such expectations were not entirely fulfilled. Doubtless Loyseau received the university education and qualifications in civil and in canon law which, as he states (*Orders* 8.15), were necessary for all aspiring advocates, hard though the statement is to reconcile with his later remarks on the minimum age for admission into the profession (*Orders* 8.44), and those remarks in turn with his own experience. While he hints that he was educated in Paris (*Offices* II.vii.15), the civil law was not taught there; his knowledge of it, evidently profound,

xi

seems to have been gained in part at Toulouse (*Orders* 11.15). At all events, he became an advocate at Paris at the age of twenty. Yet the time was not propitious. In a France rent since before Loyseau's birth by civil war, the year 1584 saw the revival of the noble-led Catholic League as well as the formation, in Paris, of a radical group known as the Sixteen and involving a number of advocates, attorneys and magistrates of the sovereign courts. Both movements aimed, *inter alia*, to exclude from the royal succession the Bourbon and Huguenot Henry of Navarre, heir presumptive through the death of Henry II's youngest legitimate son and the childlessness of the latter's brother, Henry III. In his writings Loyseau was to devote considerable space to unravelling the law governing succession to the throne (for example, *Orders* 7. 68–75). But for the time being the political and professional environment in Paris was scarcely congenial for a young advocate of a conservative cast of mind. Within four years he decided to withdraw in order to devote himself to study.

In 1593, however, Loyseau was appointed to the office of *lieutenant particulier*, or deputy to the presiding judge, in the presidial court at Sens, a town still resistant to the authority of the new king Henry IV. What role, if any, he played in bringing the town to terms is uncertain, though expedients to which Henry resorted for the purpose were not unknown to him (*Orders* 11.17). Whilst at Sens he began to publish technical treatises on the question of landed securities: an urgent question, as he declared, owing to the straits to which the civil wars had reduced so many French families, and owing to the 'confused' condition of 'our customary laws' to which 'Roman law must be linked' so as to supplement 'usage with reason' (*Garantie des rentes*, preface. 9; *Déguerpissement*, 1.i.9, preface. 1). He also married. His wife, Louise Tourtier, was the daughter of a master of requests in the royal household of Navarre and treasurer to the dowager duchess de Longueville, Louise's mother being from one of the leading families of Châteaudun. It was through de Longueville patronage that Loyseau gained in 1600 the office of *bailli*, or chief magistrate, in the county of Dunois. For the rest, his marriage yielded six children. His eldest son was to follow him into the legal profession; his elder daughter married an advocate and, upon being widowed, became a nun. His other four children all entered the church, three of them taking religious vows. Such commitment on the part of his family suggests that the prominence of religious and ecclesiastical considerations in Loyseau's own writings sprang as much from conviction as from convention.

In the decade which he spent at Châteaudun Loyseau's duties left him, by his own account, 'few enough hours of respite' for scholarly pursuits (*Orders*, dedicatory epistle). Even so, they brought him face to face with the inadequacy and corruption of local judicial administration which Parisian jurists had long since denounced. In 1603 he produced a polemical *Discourse on the Abuse of Village Justices* who, learned only in the ways of chicanery, 'proceed not by reason and justice but by a pure usurpation' (*Discourse* 2). Provoked by them and by what he saw as other dangerous deviations in contemporary French mores from the dictates of 'reason', he found respite enough to write the three substantial treatises upon which his reputation as a political thinker rests. His *Treatise on Seigneuries*, of which the tract against 'village justices' was planned as the tenth chapter, had appeared by 1608, to be followed by his *Five Books on the Law of Offices* which was licensed in 1609 and, in 1610, by his treatise *Of Orders and Plain Dignities*. From the rapidity with which they pursued one another into print, as well as from his prefatory remarks and numerous cross-references, it is evident that their author was engaged upon all three at approximately the same time and conceived of them as intimately related works. All three attracted interest and were soon reissued, not only severally, but also in collected form: at least nine editions of Loyseau's collected works, always including the three major treatises, were published by the end of the seventeenth century. His opinions, especially on the law governing appointment to offices, continued to be regarded as authoritative throughout the eighteenth century. Philosophers such as Montesquieu evidently knew his work well; and twentieth-century scholars have described him as 'by far the ablest jurist of the period ... superior even to Bodin' (Church, 1941, p. 315; cf. Gilmore, 1941, p. 122).

In 1610, owing possibly to a conflict between his judicial responsibilities and de Longueville interests, Loyseau left his post at Châteaudun and returned to Paris, ostensibly to resume his career at the bar. Despite the reputation which by then he had gained as an academic lawyer, his name figures infrequently as an advocate in the registers of the *parlement*. Perhaps Loyseau, like his predecessor Charles Du Moulin, widely acknowledged as the greatest jurist of mid sixteenth-century France, was an ineffectual pleader. Perhaps his practice was that of a consultant advocate which rarely involved appearance in court and yet commanded, as in ancient Rome, both influence and prestige (*Orders* 8.17, 28–9). Certainly his professional associates thought highly enough of him to elect him, in 1620, *bâtonnier*, or president, of the order of St Nicolas, the confraternity to which advocates and attorneys of the Paris bar belonged. But the likelihood is strong that Loyseau in his maturity chose by and large to live in the manner of a gentleman, accepting occasional consultancy fees as honoraria and otherwise following the 'very useful' English example of subsisting on the rents of his considerable accumulation of properties in Paris and the environs of Dreux (cf. *Orders* 5.108, 116; 8.28). He was the head of a family which in two generations had risen via noble patronage, office and the law, a family destined formally to attain in the next generation noble status in its own right (cf. *Orders*, 5.40, 44; *Offices* 1.ix.32). Whether or not content with that, he died in 1627, after a fit of apoplexy.

Loyseau's purpose and method

The position which Loyseau elaborated in his three major treatises was, up to a point, a *thèse de circonstance*, prompted by what he regarded as the dangerous condition of key elements in French public affairs. In *Seigneuries*, the problem was abuse and corruption in the exercise of judicial authority at the local level, a matter of which he had first-hand experience. In *Offices* it was the avidity with which Frenchmen sought public offices and, above all, treated them as vendible and heritable – a practice institutionalised in 1604 (edict of the *paulette*) by a government concerned at once to reduce the great nobility's power of patronage over the magistracy and to tap into sources of revenue other than the over-taxed rural commoners. As a jurist, Loyseau believed that the reason of the law must be brought to bear upon both these problems and even adjusted, in moderation, to accommodate their effects (*Offices*, preface). Yet both problems were phenomena manifesting the 'confusion and disorder which today pervert the eutaxy and good arrangement of this state' (*Orders*, dedicatory epistle). How to refurbish order in society at large was thus the subject of Loyseau's third treatise, somewhat less technical and more discursive than the other two, but no less political in its thrust. Its significance can be understood only by examining it in relation to its companion works.

All three treatises bore upon the well-being of the state which, in Loyseau's view, was indissociable from the values and behaviour of those who affected to possess and to exercise public power. In developing that view he built upon the insights of Jean Bodin. During the civil wars of Loyseau's youth, Bodin had arrived at a new concept of the state as the locus of public power at its supreme level: the level of sovereignty which was at once indivisible and a property of the state itself, unifying its otherwise disparate members. Yet, as Loyseau perceived all too plainly, to an alarming degree in the France of his day public power lay diffused and patrimonially in the hands of landed lords and venal office-holders. The task which he set himself was therefore to focus upon the actual mechanisms of public power and to show how and why control of these could and should rest ultimately with the sovereign prince. In undertaking that task he necessarily covered ground a great deal of which was already well trodden. Even so, it was the richness of his exposition as well as its expertise that ensured the abiding influence of his thesis: a thesis geared firmly to practical issues, structured with tolerable clarity, and blending a wide range of literary, historical and legal materials within a persuasive philosophical matrix.

For each of his three treatises Loyseau adopted broadly the same structure. Each proceeds from the general to the particular, beginning with an overall appraisal of its subject and then considering in turn a series of instances arranged, by and large, in descending order of importance, with ample interludes along the way for discussion of technical issues. Thus, *Seigneuries* begins with 'lordships in general' (chapter i) and proceeds via 'sovereign lordships' (ii) and 'interme diate lordships' (vii) to 'petty lordships and simple justices' (x), ending with 'justices appertaining to towns' (xvi). The five books of *Offices* are each arranged internally along much the same lines; and the pattern, though complicated by the attention paid to ancient Rome, is maintained in the treatise of *Orders*.

As an advocate Loyseau was accustomed to support his arguments with 'proofs', and he supplies these generously in the form of quotations and citations from supposedly authoritative sources. His deployment of his materials varies in accordance with the different subjects of his three treatises. Owing not least to the prominence of the Roman dimension in *Orders*, writers from classical antiquity account for 30 per cent of the author's citations from identified sources in that work; in *Seigneuries*, by contrast, the proportion of such citations falls to below 10 per cent. Cicero predictably takes pride of place, cited in *Orders* on no fewer than thirty-eight occasions and emulated even in Loyseau's habit of decorating his prose with superfluous scraps of Greek. This apart, the breadth of his acquaintance with classical literature is at first sight impressive and, coupled with his devotion to argument from etymology, suggests an immersion on his part in humanist scholarship as well as in works well established in the medieval canon. Yet the appearance may be deceptive: Loyseau's material, much of it the standard fare of contemporary learned discourse, seems in places to have been acquired at second hand, perhaps from one or other of the numerous compendia available to him. And, while his reading is studiously comparative and verbally sensitive, it is also indiscriminate. In search of historical information he turns far less often to Tacitus, whose reputation for discernment and 'prudence' was rising steadily in his lifetime, than to Livy or Suetonius, both of whom he quarries for anecdotes and does not hesitate to paraphrase or distort for his own purposes (for example *Orders* 2.6, 10.16). The fictions (as we now recognise them) of the alleged contributors to the *Historia Augusta* – 'Capitolinus', 'Lampridius', 'Spartianus', 'Vopiscus' – readily seduce him. Compilers of miscellanea such as Aulus Gellius and the latter's modern Italian imitators, Alessandri and Paolo Manuzio, bring welcome grist to his mill. Capable of appreciating the quality of Carlo Sigonio's researches into Roman institutions, Loyseau when it suits his purpose is equally capable of brushing aside debates over such striking issues as the authenticity of the Donation of Constantine, long since exposed as a forgery by that pioneer of critical humanist scholarship, Lorenzo Valla (*Orders* 2.62; 3.30).

In these and other respects Loyseau is typical of the educated readership of his day: omnivorous, enthused by rhetoric, fascinated by antiquity and critical only in spasms. Yet he also exhibits a sense of history. The space which he devotes in *Orders* to Roman institutions may suggest an intention on his part to present these simply as a model for the French society of his own day. This is not so: he warns explicitly of the dangers of anachronism, stressing that 'it is an abuse always to think of relating the ways of Rome to our own' (*Orders* 6.12). True, he finds much to be learned from the classical experience, and precedents – even origins – for French institutions are often discoverable in those of the ancient world. But French institutions have their own peculiar origins as well and, in common with those of Rome, have changed and evolved through time. Consciousness of chronological change, sometimes but by no means always in terms of decline from a pristine condition, is central to Loyseau's approach. To argue merely for a re-adoption of the 'ways of Rome' would be absurd. Rather, what Rome offers is a well-documented case-study in how institutions made by men and therefore imperfect and impermanent are none the less informed to some degree, and certainly ought to be informed, by an 'order', a divinely appointed system of values and behaviour, which is of universal application. In so far as French arrangements of his day exemplify order in their turn, they are sound and the well-being of the state is assured. In so far as they do not – and from the 'abuses' of seigneurial justices, the 'cacocthes' (*Offices* III.i.9) of office-seekers, the 'vainglorious' ambitions of the would-be upwardly mobile, it is evident that disorder is widespread – Loyseau's task is to show how they may be corrected. In this he shares the ethical purpose of 'exemplar' historians of the Renaissance world, and makes some use of the materials with which they and their contemporaries provided him.

Even so, Loyseau's main sources in all three of his treatises are legal materials. References to Roman law, canon law and French law in the shape of customs and royal ordinances account for 37 per cent of his citations in *Orders*, and almost 63 per cent in *Seigneuries*. In the latter work, dealing with an institution unknown to ancient Rome, citations from French law amount to 31 per cent of the whole; in *Orders* their contribution declines to below 5 per cent. Dependence upon commentators, and especially upon medieval commentators, is relatively rare; all in all, the jurist's principal reliance is directly upon statements in the *Corpus iuris civilis*. Those statements, so many of them uttered by the ancient jurisconsults who, like him, 'applied themselves to philosophising ... on the law' (*Orders* 8.23), are treated as axiomatic. While Loyseau again warns of the folly of approaching the citizens of the ancient world 'as if their laws and customs bound us in France' (*Orders* 10.41), he himself thinks of the laws handed down to him and his contemporaries from the Roman

Republic and the western and eastern empires as an integrated collection, amounting to 'our law' (for example, *Orders* 2.25) and pregnant with ethical guidance. In general, his use of legal materials is
markedly more scrupulous than is his handling of literary texts; his
quotations and references reach a relatively high standard of accuracy, though there are signs that – as he occasionally admits (*Orders*
1.55) – he is working at least in part from memory. Yet even this
high-minded legal devotee is capable of arbitrarily distorting his
authorities. An outstanding instance occurs in the course of his central argument for the monarch's exclusive power to confer ennoblement. Ostensibly quoting from the *Digest*, Loyseau silently substitutes
the phrase *princeps verbis* ('the prince by his words') for *suffragio populus* ('the people by its vote'), and thereby dramatically alters the
meaning of the passage. Neither contemporary editions of the *Digest*
nor the *glossa ordinaria* (standard gloss) printed in those editions
afford any justification for such a substitution. According to the gloss
at this juncture, several commentators have noted how at the time of
the law in question 'the people had the power of making laws', and
that 'today so much is done by the prince' (ed. Paris 1576, I, col. 82,
s.l. 'i'). But the observation figures only in the context of a discussion
as to whether custom overrides law, and it furnishes no warrant for
Loyseau's tampering with his source (*Orders* 4.41).

Trained as a lawyer, Loyseau had nevertheless received an earlier
training in philosophy, in common with all university students of
his day for whom passage through the arts faculty was a necessary
preliminary to entry into the higher faculties of medicine, law and
theology. And while law provided so much of the matter for his thesis,
it was from philosophy that he derived its form. *Pace* the neoplatonic
elements that figure in his exposition of 'order' and elsewhere too
(*Orders*, preface. 8; *Offices* I.vii.1–2, II.i.20, etc.), the framework as
well as key elements of his arguments are at bottom Aristotelian.
'Jurisconsults', he declares, 'are not tied down by the rules and form-
alities of dialectic' (*Offices* I.i. 98); yet Loyseau's thesis is in fact con-
structed on the basis of formal rules. These are the rules not so much
of rigorous scholastic logic with the syllogism as its centrepiece, as
of humanist logic developed for purposes of practical argument and
grounded upon principles which Aristotle, Cicero and the sixth-
century scholar Boethius in turn had adumbrated in their discussions
of 'topics'. Much simplified, the requisite procedure is first to estab-

lish the 'category' into which a given subject must fall and then to arrive, via successive stages of 'division', at its 'genus', its 'species', and ultimately its 'definition'. For purposes of 'division' the analysis depends upon 'differentiae'. These serve to identify the characteristics of a subject and to distinguish it from other subjects, for instance of the same genus. Thus, while man belongs to the genus 'animal', he is also rational – the differentia which renders him distinct from other animals and indicates his species. As we shall see, in Loyseau's thesis the key differentia is 'public power'. By proceeding in this way he brought coherence to his treatment of otherwise discrete subjects, and rendered his thesis as a whole persuasive to the minds of his similarly-schooled contemporaries.

Loyseau's thesis

The subjects with which Loyseau proposed to deal were lordship, office and order. His method required him to begin by placing each of them in its appropriate category. According to Aristotle there are ten of these of which only one, the category of 'substance', consists of members (such as a man, or a piece of land) that can exist independently. A member of any of the other categories – for instance, those of 'quantity', or of 'quality' or of 'position' – can exist not by itself, but only as an 'accident' in a subject which belongs to the category of 'substance'. By Loyseau's account, lordship and order both fall into the category of 'quality', and so neither 'can exist apart'. He therefore holds order to be predicable of individual persons, and lordship of particular heritages. Office, however, poses a difficulty: it seems in France to be transferable from person to person and so, apparently, can 'exist apart' from the individual officer. Office has therefore to be treated as a 'separable accident' predicable primarily of individuals and secondarily of the species to which they belong (*Offices* I.i.106; III.iv.15, ix.2; *Seigneuries* iv.4). The difficulty of categorising office in contemporary France greatly complicates Loyseau's treatment of that subject (cf. *Orders* 1.10, and below, p. xxi–xxii).

The 'genus' of lordship, office and order alike is 'dignity', as distinct from the genus of 'condition'. A man's condition 'restricts' his 'pure freedom', as when he is a minor. Dignity 'raises' him 'above freedom', making him 'more worthy' of respect by reason of the 'honourable quality' that it attaches to his name (*Offices* I.i.100–1).

The genus is divided in turn, by the differentia of 'public power'. 'Plain dignities' are qualities 'solely by honour' and lack the 'effect' of 'true orders, offices or lordships' (*Orders* 10.1). Public power attaches to the latter three, each of which is nevertheless differentiated from the rest and constitutes a 'species'. So Loyseau arrives at his preliminary 'definition' in respect of each. Lordship is 'dignity, with power in property'; office is 'dignity, with public function'; and order is 'dignity, with aptitude for public power' (*Orders* 1.6).

The 'power in property' that characterises lordship is, on the face of it, absurd. How can lords, who are 'private persons', have been allowed 'to filch the property of justice' and so 'to establish officers and public persons' empowered even to condemn men to death (*Offices* v.i.40)? Loyseau attacks the question by refining the terms of his preliminary definition. Both the term *propriété* and the term *seigneurie* have more than one meaning. The former can signify a relation or right, and an object or thing. Likewise, the latter can signify '*in abstracto* every right of property, or proprietary power, that one has in some thing', and '*in concreto* a seigneurial land' or fief (*Seigneuries* i.24). The definition applies to lordship *in abstracto*. By 'division' this 'has two species, namely public and private'. Private lordship is simply 'the right that every individual has in his thing'; it applies 'only to lands' and not to persons, for in France there is no longer 'any kind of slavery' (*Seigneuries* i.26, 28, 84). Public lordship applies to persons; it 'is called public because it concerns and signifies public command or power'. But of public lordship there are 'two degrees'. The one, 'which we call sovereignty', remains 'inseparably with the state'. For the other 'we have had to coin a special word, and to call it suzerainty' (*Seigneuries* i.27, 82). It is this latter degree of public lordship that Loyseau finds 'absurd'; and yet, the facts of its historical emergence and present existence are inescapable. The second public degree of lordship *in abstracto* attaches inexorably to seigneurial land, just as its first degree – sovereignty – 'is attached to the state'. And 'sovereignty is the form which gives being to the state', just as 'the fief is the matter and justice is the form which animates and gives being to the body of the lordship' (*Seigneuries* ii.6–7, iv.18).

Is the French kingdom, then, no more and no less than a feudal lordship writ large? Loyseau argues emphatically that this is not so, for two main reasons. First, sovereignty encompasses only public and not private lordship; unlike a possessor of the latter in relation to his fief, the sovereign prince has no proprietary right in the land of the realm (*Seigneuries* ii.53; *Offices* II.ii.30 *et seq.*). By the same token, he has no right to his subjects' goods and therefore cannot tax them without their consent, except in cases of 'extreme necessity' – though he may deal with them as with 'a sick person whom one purges against his will' (*Seigneuries* iii.47). What the sovereign prince does have is public power to the fullest degree – an 'absolute' power, 'perfect and whole in all respects', for 'the crown cannot be unless its circle is entire' (*Seigneuries* ii.8). The components of that power, as Loyseau schedules them, are strongly reminiscent of the 'marks of sovereignty' already described by Bodin (Bodin, 1992, pp. xvi, 46–88). Baldly stated, they consist of 'making laws, creating officers, deciding peace and war, exercising final judgement without appeal, and coining money' (*Seigneuries* iii.5). That power, as with Bodin, is none the less circumscribed by divine law, 'the rules of natural justice', and the 'fundamental laws of the state' (*Seigneuries* ii.9). Secondly, as Loyseau's definitions indicate, the kingdom differs from lordships in that the latter involve only 'power in property'. The limitation is strict. The 'power' of lordship encompasses no more than that of justice. Further, lords who have justice 'in property' do not have its exercise, for 'public function' appertains specifically to officers and not to them (*Seigneuries* iv.7–8). In this vital respect the position of the sovereign prince is altogether distinct from theirs. For kings 'perform the principal exercise of their power themselves and in person' (*Offices* II.ii.29).

In France, however, the king is far from alone in exercising public power. The realm is filled with officers who, moreover, handle their offices patrimonially. Loyseau therefore takes it upon himself to examine how far this may lawfully be done. In dealing with lordships he has stressed the importance of land to which public power can attach. A lordship combines both matter and form. But when he turns to offices he finds that in their case this is generally not so. While office 'seems to be in the category of substance', it is essentially 'incorporeal' (*Orders* 1.10, cf. *Offices* III.v.75). Some offices are associated with fiefs; others are 'domanial offices' and thus have a sort of material nature in terms of domanial rights. It is therefore admissible that such offices as these be heritable, vendible, and otherwise transmissible from one party to another (*Offices* II.ii, iii). But most offices lack the nature in question – and yet, the edict of the *paulette* seems to make 'the offices of France quasi-hereditary'. In Loyseau's view, that edict can give 'no assurance whatsoever to the particular acquirers' of those offices. By the fundamental laws of the realm, no king may prejudice his successors' rights, nor deprive the state of its essential property (*Offices* II.viii.8–11). From 'considerations of natural equity' rather than 'the principles and ratiocinations of the law', he contrives to unearth some incidental safeguards for investors in offices and their dependants. Even so, nothing can alter the fact that 'the function and the power' of office as well as its 'title and honour' remain, once bestowed and for the time of tenure, 'inherent to the person' of the officer himself (*Offices* III.ix.3, 45; x.16). To deal otherwise with offices, to treat them and thereby justice itself as vendible and heritable commodities, is 'a kind of madness', a symptom of the corruption of the times and profoundly dangerous (*Offices* III.i.9–11). Yet, given that the madness exists, Loyseau proposes remedies to control it. One is simply that the king take into his own hands the 'entire disposition' of offices of military command and the major judicial offices of the sovereign courts (*Offices* IV.iii.75; iv.61; vii.29, 58–63). The other is a pioneering analysis of four successive stages in the making of an officer – 'resignation', 'provision', 'reception' and 'installation' – such that the role of the 'sovereign prince' is fully acknowledged as 'sole collator' of public power which remains the property of the state itself (*Offices* I.ii–v). Of all the parts of Loyseau's thesis, this analysis was viewed as especially authoritative throughout the remainder of the *ancien régime*.

But that thesis involves far more than an exposition of procedural technicalities. It bears upon the nature of monarchy and of the society which the king controls. The king is not only sovereign lord, nor merely collator of offices to others. He is himself officer *par excellence*. The 'public function' or power which characterises offices is divisible in three: 'government, justice and finance'. And within the kingdom, the king alone has 'all these three functions conjoined in his person, and this in all sovereignty' (*Offices* I.i.120). Now in the Aristotelian metaphysical system 'function' is linked with the concepts of 'actuality' and of capacity, or 'potential'. Himself actual officer, the king is the source of the 'mystic energy and signal power' whereby the potential of becoming officers is actualised in those within his realm who have the capacity of functioning as such (*Offices* V.i.32). This is where order, defined as 'dignity, with aptitude for public power', comes into play. Of course, the doctrine that society consisted of three orders – *oratores* (those who pray), *bellatores* (those who fight) and *laborantes* (those who work) – was nothing new. Stated early in the eleventh century by Bishop Adalbero of Laon, widely canvassed and greatly elaborated throughout the Middle Ages and Renaissance, its origins were far older. Its serviceability as an ideology is obvious enough to monarchs engaged upon enlarging their power as well as to élites who enabled them to rule whilst simultaneously consolidating their own positions. The very idea of the monarch's combining the three functions in his person is traceable to the Carolingian era and beyond; and images of the king as 'ordained distributor' of virtues via the élites to his people at large occur strikingly in French Renaissance iconography. But Loyseau's distinctive contribution was to take this doctrine and apply it to underpin his systematic analysis of the proper deployment of public power in the dominant institutions of the realm.

His version of the doctrine may be examined in the translation that follows. After his opening review of 'order in general' followed by the touchstone of the 'Roman orders', he begins in the case of France with the clergy, ranked first among the three estates and the prime example of a clearly ordered social group despite certain historic disputes amongst them over precedence. For Loyseau's thesis the utility of ecclesiastical institutions with their reinforced hierarchical structure in the age of the Counter-Reformation is abundantly plain. Yet the church and its affairs lie outside that thesis's scope: in France 'religion has been quite separated from the state' (3.4). What matters, for the thesis, is the relation between order and public power. On this Loyseau reveals his position at an early stage: 'it is ordinarily necessary to have order before being an officer' (1.33). Central as the distinction is to his thesis, he finds its implications hard to sustain in dealing with the third estate. The inconveniences of history and of current arrangements compel him to recognise the existence of that alleged order which is 'not properly an order' at all (8.1). He has therefore to relax the terms of his analysis to the extent of allowing that order, like office a distinct 'species' of 'dignity', may signify 'a condition or occupation' even though these appertain strictly to a separate 'genus' (8.1; cf. above, p. xix). Even so, the disorder of the third estate is extreme, owing not least to venality of offices which has converted into public functions a range of activities that ought not to rank as such. Advocates, predictably, constitute a special case: they have ample academic qualifications, and moreover are admitted by 'magistrates' (8.15) whom the king in turn appoints. Attorneys have been erected into an order, but their concerns are with private litigation and 'they have no public function' (8.41). For the rest, some of the characteristics of order, including honour, are discernible in other groups within the third estate, given that they contribute to the public well-being and do not debase themselves with manual labour.

But the bulk of the treatise is devoted to the question of nobility. Here Loyseau considers himself to stand upon much firmer ground. He is confident of his view that the source of nobility is 'sovereign power' (5.37). Those who hold that nobility is genetically communicated and has its origin in some ancestral virtue are mistaken. So-called 'ancient and immemorial' nobility 'does not proceed from the right of nature . . . but from the ancient law and disposition of the state' (4.38). As for those ennobled at some identifiable point in time, their status 'derives in France from ennoblement by the prince' than whom no one else 'can confer nobility' (4.41, 6.62). It is upon the sovereign prince that both order and public power ultimately converge. Despite appearances to the effect that nobility is gained through possession of major offices and lordships, it is not 'the office nor the fief of dignity that ennobles, but the king, by his sovereign power' (6.65). Conversely, 'only gentlemen can hold principal offices'; and fiefs 'called noble' are 'assigned to persons already noble' (4.33, 6.66). Deviation from these principles causes grave confusion; but the argument for them is clinched by the case of France's princes. For the princes enjoy exceptional status precisely by virtue of their proximity to the sovereign prince himself and thereby 'aptitude' to attain public power in its highest form, sovereignty, in accordance with their 'degree of succession' (7.3). That degree is determined by considerations not so much of biology as of law. In so far as the laws of succession in this connection are observed, the constitution of the kingdom conforms to the will of God and, indeed, approximates to that of His chosen people (7.70).

The meaning of Loyseau's three treatises has occasioned considerable debate amongst historians. On the one hand he has been credited with composing 'a kind of anatomy of French society' (Mousnier, 1973, p. 67); on the other, with expressing and justifying the 'pretensions and aspirations' of the 'privileged French bourgeoisie' – and thereby, no doubt, his own – at the expense of the established nobility (Porchnev, 1963, p. 538). Neither of these interpretations seems acceptable. Far from offering an objective account of the society of his day, Loyseau pays scant attention to most of its members, and his observations on the rest are determined by the dictates of his legal lore and the exigencies of his political thesis. In developing that thesis he repeatedly berates the values and behaviour of his contemporaries, flagrant – as he believes – in their defiance of the rational norms which he espouses. As for his attitude towards his social superiors, Loyseau's denunciations of backwoods country gentlemen and the conduct of local lords ought not to be construed as an assault upon nobility as such. His treatise of *Orders* was dedicated to a cousin of Diane de Poitiers. Noble patronage was the route whereby he and his family had risen, and its continuance constituted the alternative to the arrangements of the *paulette* edict which he boldly attacked. His remained a conservative cast of mind – conservative even in his approach to the law and to the other varieties of learning that informed his dialectical position. And his conservatism was the surest guarantee of the impact of his ideas upon those with the capacity and inclination to read his works in the France of the *ancien régime*: a country where the ranks of jurists such as he supplied so many of the agents of government as well as the prime contributors to political thought.

Principal events in Loyseau's life

1564   Born, probably in Paris.

1567   Death of his godmother, Diane de Poitiers. Outbreak of second French civil 'war of religion' (September).

1568   Outbreak of third civil war (August).

1572   Massacre of St Bartholomew's night (24 August). Fourth civil war.

1574   Death of Charles IX (May). Accession of Henry III.

1576   Formation of Catholic League. Publication of Bodin's *Les six livres de la république* [Six books on the commonwealth]. Estates-general assemble at Blois (November).

1577   Dissolution of estates-general (March). Sixth civil war.

1580   Seventh civil war.

1584   Enters Paris *parlement* as advocate. Renewal of Catholic League, which proceeds to ally with Spain (December).

1587   Radical elements of League, later known as the 'Sixteen', perpetrate plots at Paris.

1588   Retires from *parlement*.

1589   Paris *parlement* split; royalist magistrates established at Tours. Assassination of Henry III (July). Succession of Henry IV, opposed by League and by Spain.

1591   'Sixteen' murder Barnabé Brisson, jurist and *président* of Paris (League) section of *parlement* (November).

1593   Appointed *lieutenant particulier* (deputy to the presiding judge) in the presidial court of Sens. Henry IV abjures protestantism (July).

1595   Publishes his *Traité de la garantie des rentes* [Treatise on security of revenues]. Henry IV declares war on Spain.

1597   Publishes his *Traité du déguerpissement et delaissement par hypothèque* [Treatise on surrender and cession by mortgage].

1598   Edict of Nantes (April) and Peace of Vervins (May) end France's civil wars and war with Spain.

1600   Appointed *bailli* (chief magistrate) in the county of Dunois, by Catherine de Gonzague, duchess de Longueville.

1603   Publishes his *Discours de l'abus des justices de village* [Discourse on the abuse of village justices].

1604   Edict of the *paulette* (December), giving security to venal office-holders and their heirs.

1608   Publishes his *Traité des Seigneuries* [Treatise on lordships].

1609   *Cinq livres du droit des offices* [Five books on the law of offices] licensed for publication.

1610   Publishes his *Traité des ordres et simples dignités* [Treatise on orders and plain dignities]; returns to Paris. Assassination of Henry IV (May).

1614   Estates-general assemble at Paris (October); call for abolition of venality of offices and of the *paulette*.

1620   Elected *bâtonnier* of the confraternity of Paris advocates and attorneys (Feast of St Nicolas, 9 May).

1627   Dies (November); buried in the Chapel of the Virgin, Church of St Côme and St Damien, Paris.

Bibliographical note

Loyseau: biography and appraisal

The only modern attempt at a biography of Loyseau, including information on his parentage, property and descendants, is J. Lelong, *La vie et les oeuvres de Loyseau (1564–1627)* (Paris, 1909). Some additional biographical details are provided by Brigitte Basdevant-Gaudemet, *Aux origines de l'état moderne: Charles Loyseau, 1564–1627, théoricien de la puissance publique* (Paris, 1977), a study which focuses mainly upon Loyseau's treatise on *Seigneuries* whilst making valuable observations on its subject's other works. For the political context of his career, to 1610, see J. H. M. Salmon, *Society in Crisis: France in the Sixteenth Century* (London, 1975). Salvo Mastellone provides an 'Introduzione al pensiero politico di Charles Loyseau', *Critica Storica*, vol. 4 (1965), pp. 446–82, and discusses him in connection with the problem of venality of offices in *Venalità e Machiavellismo in Francia (1572–1610)* (Florence, 1972). Overall appraisals are attempted by Graciela Soriano, *El pensamiento social de Charles Loyseau* (Caracas, 1968), and Howell A. Lloyd, 'The Political Thought of Charles Loyseau (1564–1627)', *European Studies Review*, vol. 11 (1981), pp. 53–82.

Intellectual context

Key aspects of intellectual history in the period immediately prior to Loyseau's *oeuvre* are surveyed in *The Cambridge History of Renaissance Philosophy*, eds. C. B. Schmitt, Q. Skinner and E. Kessler (Cambridge, 1988). The analytical approach which he adopted may be further explored in L. Jardine, 'Lorenzo Valla and the Intellectual Origins of Humanist Dialectic', *Journal of the History of Philosophy*, vol. 15 (1977), pp. 143–64; and in the text and accompanying essays of E. Stump's edition of Boethius, *De topicis differentiis* (Ithaca, 1978). Useful accounts of the history of the classical literary materials available to him will be found in E. R. Curtius, *European Literature and the Latin Middle Ages* (London, 1953); and, more succinctly, in L. D. Reynolds and N. G. Wilson, *Scribes and Scholars: a Guide to the Transmission of Greek and Latin Literature* (Oxford, 2nd edition 1974). 'Exemplar' history is discussed by George H. Nadel, 'Philosophy of History before Historicism', *History and Theory*, vol. 2 (1964), pp. 291–315.

Political thought

The most recent survey is *The Cambridge History of Political Thought, 1450–1700*, eds. J. H. Burns and Mark Goldie (Cambridge, 1991), which includes a valuable contribution by Donald R. Kelley on 'Law' (pp. 66–94). The standard work on the development of political ideas from the thirteenth to the end of the sixteenth century is Quentin Skinner, *The Foundations of Modern Political Thought* (2 vols., Cambridge, 1978). Dealing with the same period, M. P. Gilmore discusses some of Loyseau's leading ideas in the context of *Argument from Roman Law in Political Thought, 1200–1600* (Cambridge, Mass., 1941). An interpretation of Loyseau's position figures in W. F. Church, *Constitutional Thought in Sixteenth-Century France* (Cambridge, Mass., 1941), and more briefly in Nannerl O. Keohane's account of *Philosophy and the State in France: the Renaissance to the Enlightenment* (Princeton, 1980). A recent study of an important influence upon Loyseau's views, Jean Bodin with his seminal re-interpretations of 'sovereignty' and the 'state', is Simone Goyard-Fabre, *Jean Bodin et le droit de la 'République'* (Paris, 1989). A volume in the present series prints translated extracts from Bodin's major work: *Jean Bodin, On Sovereignty*, ed. Julian Franklin (Cambridge, 1992). Both Bodin and Loyseau figure in an attempt to place French political thought in a broad political and social context, by Howell A. Lloyd, *The State, France and the Sixteenth Century* (London, 1983). Comment upon iconography as a means of monarchical propaganda will be found in R. W. Scheller, 'Ensigns of Authority: French Royal Symbolism in the Age of Louis XII', *Simiolus*, vol. 13, no. 2 (1983), pp. 75–141.

Social thought

Given the prominence of Rome in Loyseau's treatise, Roman attitudes merit attention: see, in particular, Matthias Galzer, *The Roman Nobility*, trans. R. Seager (Oxford, 1969), which comments on 'the development of the concept of *nobilitas* from "notability" to "nobility founded on office"; and Peter Garnsey, *Social Status and Legal Privilege in the Roman Empire* (Oxford, 1970). A brief account of the doctrine of 'orders' in medieval thought with a revaluation of its significance will be found in Alexander Murray, *Reason and Society in the Middle Ages* (Oxford, 1978). Jacques Le Goff furnishes an illuminating 'Note sur société tripartie, idéologie monarchique et renouveau économique dans la Chrétienté du IXe au XIIe siècle', in his *Pour un autre Moyen Age: temps, travail et culture en Occident – 18 essais* (Paris, 1977), pp. 80–90. Georges Duby, *The Three Orders: Feudal Society Imagined* (Chicago, 1981) provides a fuller exploration of the theme, which is examined afresh in relation to early-modern France by Arlette Jouanna, *Ordre social: mythes et réalités dans la France du XVIe siècle* (Paris, 1977). But the most determined application of the doctrine in general and Loyseau's version of it in particular to the France of that period has been Roland Mousnier's: see especially his 'Problèmes de stratification sociale', in *Deux cahiers de la noblesse*, eds. Mousnier, J.-P. Labatut and V. Durand (Paris, 1965), pp. 25–33; his *Social Hierarchies: 1450 to the Present* (London, 1973); and his *La vénalité des offices sous Henri IV et Louis XIII* (2nd edition, Paris, 1971). An adoption of Loyseau for ideologically very different socio-analytical purposes, denounced by Mousnier, may be found in Boris Porchnev, *Les soulèvements populaires en France de 1623 à 1648* (Paris, 1963), especially pp. 538–45. Finally, Peter Burke reviews their and others' contributions to debate over 'The Language of Orders in Early Modern Europe', in *Social Orders and Social Classes in Europe since 1500: Studies in Social Stratification*, ed. M. L. Bush (1992), pp. 1–12.

Note on translation and citations

Loyseau is a vigorous user of the French language, and – as his dedicatory epistle immediately illustrates – he has some pretensions as a literary stylist. His sentences, however, are often very lengthy, and his syntax is sometimes convoluted to the point of obscuring his meaning. My aims in this translation have been to render what he wrote as accurately as possible whilst making it acceptable to twentieth-century readers. With the latter aim in view I have not hesitated to break up his sentences nor to vary their opening phrases as seemed appropriate. Except in a very few instances, all terms, titles and passages in Greek have been translated into English; so, too, have French technical expressions, such as *amende honorable* or *substitution graduelle*, elucidations of which are silently incorporated into the body of the text. In dealing with Loyseau's extensive Latin quotations, I have translated these from his own versions even when they differ markedly from modern or even early-modern editions of his sources.

The translation is based upon the first edition of the *Traité des Ordres* printed at Châteaudun in 1610 for the publisher Abel l'Angelier, and bound into the first collected edition of Loyseau's three major treatises, published in the same year. Subsequent editions contain a number of additions and amendments, generally minor and in most cases very likely the corrections and afterthoughts of Loyseau himself. Where such additions seemed worth recording, I have taken them from the last (1701, Lyon) edition of Loyseau's *Oeuvres* and have included them in footnotes, signalled thus: '[1701 adds:]'. I have also amended, on the basis partly of the 1701 edition and partly of common sense, the numbering of sections which is often very erratic in the 1610 edition.

Apart from the supplementation already indicated, the footnotes are limited mainly to recording and, as necessary, amending and expanding the references which Loyseau built into his text. My own editorial corrections and amplifications of the information which he provides are shown between square brackets. That information is quite often misleading or incomplete: quotations may be naked of attribution, references may amount to no more than a writer's name. In a number of instances Loyseau's unacknowledged quotations are evidently maxims well known in his day, and I have left these unattributed. Where his references are inaccurate I have substituted correct details without re-stating his errors. Otherwise, I hope to have supplied sufficient guidance for his 'proofs' to be traced to their sources. Indeed, by far the most laborious and time-consuming part of preparing this edition has been the task of verifying Loyseau's many hundreds of citations. In the event I can claim to have tracked down almost all of them. A few have defeated me, and in respect of these I have either in one or two instances offered suggestions for further inquiry, or simply left them unattributed, confident in the expectation that more learned readers will readily supply the lack and that others will not be unduly inconvenienced by it.

I have modernised all Loyseau's references to civil and canon law which, in accordance with the conventions of his day, he gives by *titulus*, *lex* and *incipit*. Standard numerical references are given to the works of classical authors. Where Loyseau's sometimes cryptic methods of referring to other works have enabled me to locate relevant passages without excessive difficulty once the works themselves were identified, I have silently substituted page references to specified editions for the chapter-headings and other conventions which he employs. For material on French history he provides relatively few references in detail, and is evidently drawing upon the well-known chroniclers, annalists and historians whom he occasionally names. In this connection, as throughout, I have confined myself to verifying and stating the sources which he himself notes, and by and large I have refrained from cluttering the pages with comment upon fact and opinion as they appear in his own treatise.

A selection of biographical notes is included, mainly for the benefit of readers unfamiliar with Loyseau's intellectual world and the types of source upon which he chiefly draws. All persons whom he mentions in his text are identified in the index.

Abbreviations

Annales	Nicole Gilles, *Les chroniques et annales de France . . . revues, corrigees et augmentees par François de Belleforest* (Paris, 1573).
Bacquet	Jean Bacquet, *Les oeuvres de Maistre Jean Bacquet* (5 vols., Paris, 1664).
Choppin	René Choppin, *Commentaires sur la coustume d'Aniou* (5 vols., Paris, 1662): in fact, Choppin's collected works – the *Commentaires* in vol. I, other treatises in subsequent vols.
Code J	*Corpus iuris civilis* (3 vols., Berlin, 1928–9), vol. II (*Codex Iustinianus*), ed. P. Krueger.
Code Theod.	*Codicis Theodosiani libri XVI*, ed. J. Cujas (Paris, 1607).
Comm. in Aeneidos	Maurus Servius Honoratus, *Servii grammatici qui feruntur in Vergilii carmina commentarii*, eds. G. Thilo and H. Hagen (3 vols., Leipzig and Berlin, 1923–7).
Conc. omn. gen.	*Concilium omnium generalium et provincialium* (37 vols., Paris, 1644).
Const. Sirm.	*Theodosiani libri XVI cum constitutiones Sirmondianis . . .* (2 vols., Berlin, 1954), vol. I, eds. T. Mommsen and P. M. Meyer.
De antiq. jur.	Carlo Sigonio, *De antiquo jure civium Romanorum* (Frankfurt, 1593).
Decretales	*Decretalium collectiones*, in *Corpus iuris canonici*, ed. E. Friedberg (2 vols., Leipzig, 1879–81), vol. II.

Decretum	*Decretum magistri Gratiani*, in *Corpus iuris canonici*, ed. E. Friedberg (2 vols., Leipzig, 1879–81), vol. I.
De iure prim.	Andreas Tiraqueau, *De iure primigeniorum*, in *Operum omnium*, vol. 1 (Frankfurt, 1616), pp. 278–478.
De nobil.	Andreas Tiraqueau, *De nobilitate*, in *Operum omnium*, vol. 1 (Frankfurt, 1616), pp. 1–276.
De Rep. Angl.	Sir Thomas Smith, *De Republica Anglorum*, ed. M. Dewar (Cambridge, 1982).
De verb. signif.	Sextus Pomponius Festus, *De verborum significatu quae supersunt, cum Pauli epitome*, ed. W. M. Lindsay (Leipzig, 1913).
Digest	*Corpus iuris civilis* (3 vols., Berlin, 1928–9), vol. I, pt. ii *(Digesta)*, eds. T. Mommsen and P. Krueger.
Fontanon	A. Fontanon, *Les edicts et ordonnances des rois de France* (4 vols., Paris, 1611).
gl. ord.	*glossa ordinaria.*
Hist.	Titus Livy, *Ad urbe condita [historiarum].*
Inst. J	*Institutes* of Justinian, in *Corpus iuris civilis* (3 vols., Berlin, 1928–9), vol. I, pt. i *(Institutiones)*, ed. P. Krueger.
Isambert	*Recueil général des anciennes lois françaises*, ed. F.-A. Isambert *et al.* (29 vols., Paris, 1821–33).
Le Bret	Cardin Le Bret, *Recueil d'aucuns plaidoyez faicts en la Cour des Aydes* (Paris, 1609).
Leg. Nov.	*Theodosiani libri XVI cum constitutionibus Sirmondianis . . .* (2 vols., Berlin, 1954), vol. II *(Leges novellae)*, eds. T. Mommsen and P. M. Meyer.
Mansi	*Sacrorum conciliorum nova et amplissima collectio*, ed. J. D. Mansi (51 vols., Paris, 1901–27).
Nat. hist.	Pliny the Elder, *Naturalis historiae.*
Noct. Attic.	Aulus Gellius, *Noctium Atticarum.*
Nov. J	*Novellae* of Justinian, in *Corpus iuris civilis* (3 vols., Berlin, 1928–9), vol. III, eds. R. Schoell and G. Kroll.

Opera B	Guillaume Budé, *Omnia opera* (4 vols., Basle, 1557).
Opera C	Jacques Cujas, *Opera omnia* (9 vols., Paris, 1658).
Operum C	Jacques Cujas, *Operum* (4 vols., Lyon, 1606).
Ord.	*Ordonnances des rois de France de la troisième race* (22 vols., Paris, 1723–1849).
Origines	Claude Fauchet, *Origines des dignités et magistrats de France* (Paris, 1606).
PG	*Patralogiae cursus completus . . . series graeca*, ed. J. P. Migne (161 vols., Paris, 1857–1903).
PL	*Patralogiae cursus completus . . . series latina*, ed. J. P. Migne (221 vols., Paris, 1845–1904).
Pithou	Pierre Pithou, *Les coustumes du bailliage de Troyes en Champaigne* (Paris, 1600).
Recueil	Jean du Tillet, *Recueil des roys de France, leurs couronne et maison* (Paris, 1580).
République	Jean Bodin, *Les six livres de la république* (Paris, 1583).
Rom. antiq.	Joannes Rosinus (Johann Rossfeld), *Romanorum antiquitatum libri decem* (Lyon, 1585).
Rom. hist.	Dio Cassius, *Roman histories.*
Sext	*Liber Sextus Decretalium*, in *Corpus iuris canonici*, ed. E. Friedberg (2 vols., Leipzig, 1879–81), vol. II, cols. 937–1124.
Semestrium	Petrus Faber (Pierre Favre), *Regii consiliari et libellorum ordinarii magistri semestrium liber primus* (Paris, 1570).
s.l./v.	*sub littera/verbo* (under a specified letter/word).

Biographical notes

ARISTOTLE (384–322 BC), Greek philosopher. Born at Stagirus in Chalcide, he was the son of a physician and a pupil of Plato at whose school in Athens he worked until his master's death in 347. After an interlude devoted mainly to natural scientific studies, Aristotle accepted an invitation from Philip II of Macedon to act as tutor to his son Alexander, an experience that no doubt stimulated his own interest in politics. In 335 he returned to Athens and founded a school in a grove dedicated to Apollo Lyceius, with a covered walk (περίπατος) where Aristotle taught. There he collected manuscripts and scientific specimens for use in his own and his associates' researches. In 323 he retired to Chalcis where he died in the following year. Most of his works on logic, which are collectively known as the 'Organon' or 'instrument' of reasoning, were translated into Latin early in the sixth century AD by the Roman senator Boethius. Yet few even of these became widely known in the West until after the twelfth century when the bulk of Aristotle's other writings were translated from various sources. Thereafter his teachings became – and long remained – the foundation of learning in the arts faculties of Europe's burgeoning universities, owing not least to demonstrations by thinkers of the stature of Thomas Aquinas that principles discovered by pagan philosophers were compatible with Christian truths and aided understanding of the latter.

BARTOLUS OF SASSOFERRATO (1313/14–57), jurisconsult and commentator on Roman law. Born at Sassoferrato, he studied law at Perugia under Cynus da Pistoia who was also a poet and a friend of Petrarch and Dante. Cynus taught him that in interpreting the texts of Roman law he need not be bound by the literal approach of the thirteenth-century glossators. In 1334 he took his doctor's degree at Bologna before serving as an assistant judge and then as a magistrate at Todi and Pisa. Appointed to a professorship at Pisa in 1339, he moved four years later to Perugia where he spent the rest of his career. In the course of it Bartolus produced commentaries on the whole of the *Digest*, the *Code*, and Justinian's later acts (the Novels), as well as other tracts and opinions on various legal questions. To him such questions were not confined to the strict concerns of law as such. The civil law was a repository of science and wisdom with which only theology could compare. Thus, his writings contain statements on the nature and scope of imperial power and on the juridical status of Italian city-republics that amount to a far-reaching political theory. In particular, he conceived of the city as a corporate entity with a legal personality functioning, through the consent of its citizens and so on the basis of popular sovereignty, as 'its own prince'. Such ideas, which were further explored by his greatest pupil Baldus de Ubaldis, paved the way for constitutionalist doctrines of the modern sovereign state; and, despite Renaissance jurists' disparagement of his scholastic methods, Bartolus has retained his claim to the description, 'prince of jurisconsults'.

BELLEFOREST, FRANÇOIS DE (1530–83), French historian. Born at Sarsan in Navarre, he was orphaned at the age of eight and was brought up at the court of Marguerite, queen of Navarre and sister of Francis I. Having studied law at Bordeaux and Toulouse, he abandoned that occupation first for poetry, and then for historical writing which he undertook for payment by Parisian booksellers. His *Histoire des neufs roys Charles de France* (1568) earned him the position of royal historiographer; but the work which established his reputation was *Les grandes annales et histoire générale de France dès la venue des Francs en Gaule jusques au règne du roy très chrétien Henri III* (1579) in which he ascribed to the Franks a Gaulish origin. Belleforest was a prolific writer with more than fifty publications to his credit, including verse, translations from Latin and Italian authors, polemical tracts against seditious rebels in the period of the civil wars, and an account of *L'Innocence de la trés illustre, trés chaste et débonnaire princesse Madame Marie, royne d'Escosse* (1572), the widow of Francis II.

BODIN, JEAN (1529/30–96), French philosopher. Born at Angers, the son of a prosperous master tailor, he joined the Carmelite order as a novice, but left before taking his vows and proceeded to Toulouse to study law, a discipline which in France had strong links with humanist scholarship and attracted some of the outstanding intellects of his time. Denied a permanent university post, he joined the Paris bar as an advocate, but continued meanwhile with his many-sided academic pursuits. Having already drafted an analysis of universal law (the *Juris universi distributio*), he published in 1566 an analysis of universal history (the *Methodus ad facilem historiarum cognitionem*) and, two years later, an explanation of price inflation in terms of the quantity theory of money (the *Response à M. Malestroit*). In 1571 he was appointed a master of requests in the household of the duke of Alençon, youngest son of the late Henry II; but his opposition to royal taxation proposals at the estates-general of Blois in 1576 seriously damaged his prospects of high office in the royal household. Yet in that same year Bodin published his most influential work: *Les six livres de la république* with its exposition of his theory of unitary legislative sovereignty in relation to the state, a treatise that became required reading for students of public law in an historical and philosophical context. Despite that work's distinction, his own public career had passed its zenith. He ended it as king's attorney at Laon and as a collaborator with the Catholic League until that organisation's leaders succumbed one by one to Henry IV in 1594.

BRISSON, BARNABÉ (1525/30–91), French jurisconsult. The son of a deputy to the presiding judge at Fontenay-le-Comte, he studied law at Poitiers where he joined the bar of advocates and also associated with humanist scholars. In 1559 he published his handbook of legal terminology, the *De verborum quae ad jus pertinent significatione*, following this in 1564 with a study of matrimonial law, *De ritu nuptiarum*. By then he had moved to Paris and its *parlement* where he purchased successively the offices of attorney-general (1573) and senior judge (1580). At the 1583 assembly of notables at Saint-Germain, convened by Henry III to reform the kingdom, he played a prominent role, and subsequently produced the *Code du roy Henri III* (1587), a mediocre attempt at unifying the customs of the realm which none the less cast him as France's leading jurisconsult. Having forewarned the king of the 1588 populist rising which drove Henry from his capital, Brisson remained in Paris; but his position grew steadily less tenable as he connived at moves to overthrow the monarch whilst seeking to preserve a measure of allegiance to the latter. On 15 November 1591 he and two other magistrates were arrested by the central committee of the Catholic League's populist wing in Paris (the Sixteen), and hanged six hours later after a semblance of a trial.

BUDE, GUILLAUME (1468–1540), French humanist. Born in Paris, he spend a dissolute youth ostensibly studying law at Orléans, but in due course developed a passion for learning and especially for classical literature. Having taught himself Greek after some rudimentary instruction by the Spartan refugee Hermonymos who had revived tuition in the language at Paris, Budé was employed initially as a notary in the royal chancery. Through his linguistic skills he attracted royal patronage and more remunerative administrative posts, and so was enabled to pursue – at considerable cost to his health – studies which were marked by unusual philological expertise coupled with a critical and comparative approach aimed at discerning both the 'wisdom' inherent in ancient institutions and their distinctive historical character. Profoundly learned though often ill-organised, those studies included commentaries on the *Digest* of Roman law (the *Annotationes in XXIV libros Pandectarum*, 1508), a treatise on ancient coinage and measures (*De asse*, 1515), and a lexicographical account of the Greek language (*Commentarii linguae graecae*, 1529), as well as a handbook of instruction to Francis I (*L'Institution du prince*, 1518) in which he urged the merits of strong rulership. In Budé's view the monarch's role embraced responsibility for France's cultural mission. Accordingly, he encouraged Francis to found (1530) a college for the teaching of Greek and Hebrew, the precursor of the Collège de France; and, as Master of the King's Library from 1522, he promoted the collections of manuscripts and books which were to form the nucleus of the Bibliothèque Nationale.

CICERO, MARCUS TULLIUS (106–43 BC), Roman orator and statesman. Born near Arpino, the son of a prosperous knight, Cicero studied philosophy and rhetoric in Rome and in Greece, and rapidly proceeded to establish himself as a successful advocate at the Roman bar. Not content with a career in the law, he stood for public office and was elected quaestor and then praetor, on each occasion at the earliest admissible age. By 63 he had gained the consulship despite that office's virtual monopoly by families of consular rank to the exclusion of 'new men' such as he. But neither Cicero nor the Republican institutions which had facilitated his rise could withstand the consequences of the ambitions of Pompey the Great and Julius Caesar, and still less of the conflict which eventually developed between them. Relegated in due course to the tasks of provincial administration, Cicero refused to join Caesar after Pompey's defeat. He was permitted none the less to return to Rome, where he applied himself to literary activity and rejoiced at Caesar's assassination in 44. He promptly called for the condemnation of the dictator's would-be successor Antony, only to be out-manoeuvred and brought to his death by the latter in alliance with Caesar's great-nephew, Octavian. In the Middle Ages Cicero's writings on moral philosophy remained influential sources of information on Stoic ethical doctrines, whilst Renaissance humanists seized upon his rhetorical works as means to enrich if not to supplant the analytical methods of the scholastics as vehicles of argument and exposition.

CUJAS, JACQUES (1522–90), French jurisconsult. The son of a prosperous master cloth-worker of Toulouse, Cujas studied law at the local university, but despaired of the sterile instruction available there and so undertook a programme of self-tuition. Studies of a range of linguistic and philosophical subjects confirmed him in his view that laws must be interpreted in their historical and social context. From 1547 he offered his own course of instruction on Justinian's *Institutes*, and attracted numerous pupils including members of the powerful Du Faur family whose patronage he thereby gained. Seven years later, however, he failed in his candidature for a chair of civil law at Toulouse, and consequently embarked upon what became an itinerant career. This took him to Cahors, Paris, Grenoble, Turin, Valence, and four times to Bourges, with its distinguished law faculty, where he finally settled from 1576. Cujas's mobility sprang partly from the troubles of the era of civil wars, but also from his reputation as a teacher and juristic commentator which earned him insistent invitations from university communities and other patrons. Chief amongst these was Henry II's sister Marguerite, duchess of Berry and then of Savoy, the most learned Frenchwoman of her day. His pupils included the historians Etienne Pasquier and Jacques-Auguste de

Thou, the classicist Joseph-Juste Scaliger, and the defender of the liberties of the Gallican church, Pierre Pithou. His own principal works were devoted to Roman law and institutions, collected most notably in his *Observationes et emendationes* which began to appear in 1557.

DIONYSIUS THE AREOPAGITE. A Christian convert of this name figures in the New Testament account of St Paul's visit to Athens (Acts xvii.34). Four centuries later a collection of four treatises – *On the Heavenly Hierarchy, On the Ecclesiastical Hierarchy, On the Names of God* and *On Mystic Theology* – as well as several others was attributed to Dionysius as their author. These treatises in fact constitute an attempt of unknown authorship to marry Christian dogma with neo-platonism as expounded by the Greek philosopher Proclus (AD 411–85). Initially designed to synthesise the wisdom of the ancient world, neoplatonism acquired religious, mystical and magical overtones, purporting to demonstrate how the soul could ascend to unity with the One, the source of all energy and illumination. Among the pseudo-Dionysian themes is a hierarchic conception of the universe with orders of beings descending from the One to the material world where the earthly hierarchy corresponds to that of the heavens. Translated from Greek into Latin in the ninth century at the court of Charles the Bald, the treatises in question exercised a profound influence upon medieval and Renaissance thought, and not least in France where their supposed author was identified, falsely, with the kingdom's patron saint.

DU TILLET, JEAN (d. 1570), French archivist and antiquarian. Born at the very beginning of the sixteenth century and appointed at an early age a secretary to Francis I, he became a recorder in the Paris *parlement* upon his elder brother Séraphin's resigning the post in 1521. Twelve years later he married the daughter of a master of accounts and so acquired a landed estate at La Bussière in the Orléanais. His taste for antiquarian researches prompted him to extract from the registers of the *parlement* the texts of numerous treatises and royal acts, a task undertaken with the encouragement of the king for whom the ready availability of such materials was politically useful. His services were certainly useful to the leaders of the house of Guise, advisers to the young king Francis II in 1560, when Du Tillet published two treatises to show that, *pace* the arguments of the princes of the blood of the house of Bourbon, French kings reached their majority at the age of fourteen, and that Francis was therefore competent to choose his own councillors. His opposition to the Huguenots earned him denunciation by the Calvinist theologian and propagandist Théodore de Bèze, and led to the sacking of La Bussière by protestant rebels. Following his death in 1570 several of his works were edited and published by his son, Elie. They included a *Recueil des guerres et traictez d'entre les rois de France et d'Angleterre* (1588), a *Mémoire et advis ... sur les libertez de l'Eglise gallicane* (1594), and above all the *Recueil des roys de France* (1580); the chronicle bound with the last of these was in fact the work of Du Tillet's brother, bishop of Meaux and, confusingly, also named Jean. Du Tillet's works were based in part upon documents which he and his associates discovered and sometimes filched from the Trésor des Chartes and other royal archives, repositories reduced through their rummagings to much disorder.

GELLIUS, AULUS (*c.* AD 130–*c.* 180), Roman compiler. A student of literature at Rome in his youth, he pursued further studies at Athens: hence the title (*Noctes Atticae*) of his collection, in twenty books, of chapters on legal, philosophical, historical, linguistic and various other matters. According to its author, his object in compiling it was to teach and entertain his children. The chapters are strewn with quotations from earlier writers, many of whose works would otherwise have been altogether lost. Widely used in the Middle Ages, his compilation and the squirrel-like approach to learning which it exemplifies stimulated numerous Renaissance imitators to put together their own miscellanea. Apart from indications which he provides in his preface and elsewhere, little is known of Aulus Gellius's life, though he served as a judge in private lawsuits after his return from Athens to Rome.

GRATIAN (*fl.* 1140), compiler of canon laws. A member of the Camaldolite order, he worked in Bologna where the study of Roman law had recently revived and was developing apace at the university, thanks principally to the rediscovery of Justinian's *Digest*. At Bologna civilian glossators were setting themselves to interpret and harmonise the often conflicting statements by Roman jurists of which the fifty books of the *Digest* were composed. The condition of the law of the church, consisting of canons and directives culled from multifarious sources, apostolic and liturgical, papal and conciliar, was still more problematical. The task of Gratian and his associates was to compile a 'concord of discordant canons' (*Concordia discordantium canonum*), the work that became known as the *Decretum*. In the form which it eventually took, the *Decretum* is divided into three parts, beginning with the nature and sources of law, continuing with sections on clerical conduct, procedure, religious orders and other matters, and ending with the sacraments and doctrine. Providing a coherent means for canonists known as decretists to embark upon a systematic elucidation of canon law, it was followed a century later by a compilation of subsequent papal decretals – the *Liber extra-vagantium decretalium* – upon which decretalists could likewise work. Further compilations ensued, until in the sixteenth century Gratian's contribution was finally subsumed within the official collection of the church's laws known as the *Corpus iuris canonici*. Yet the significance of that contribution is such as to warrant the status of the otherwise obscure monk whose name it bears as the father of the study of canon law.

HISTORIAE AUGUSTAE SCRIPTORES. The authorship of this collection of biographies of Roman emperors and usurpers from AD 117 to 284 has excited much debate amongst modern scholars. On the face of it, the biographies were composed, severally, by six individuals writing in the late third and early fourth centuries: Iulius Capitolinus, Vulcacius Gallicanus, Aelius Lampridius, Trebellius Pollio, Aelius Spartianus and Flavius Vopiscus. These alleged authors claim to have drawn upon a range of literary and documentary source materials which, though unevenly cited, lend their work an appearance of authenticity. Amongst such sources are the writings of Marius Maximus, possibly prefect of Rome in AD 217. However, the citations and quotations which the *Scriptores* provide are now regarded as at best questionable, at worst complete fabrications. Yet, while nineteenth-century and subsequent scholarship has shown that the *Historia Augusta* is in fundamental respects a forgery and very possibly the work of a single author, it exerted a considerable influence upon Renaissance historiography. Modelled upon Suetonius's lives of the twelve Caesars which were much in vogue, it furnished the only continuous account of the emperors of the second and third centuries and therefore had a powerful appeal for readers intrigued by the events of that critical era.

JEROME, ST, alias EUSEBIUS HIERONYMUS (AD *c.* 347–419/20), Latin Father of the Christian church. Born of prosperous Christian parents at Stridon in Dalmatia, he was educated and baptised in Rome. He then visited a number of European religious centres before arriving in 374 at Antioch, where he experienced a dream warning him against the evils of pagan literature. From 375 he lived for two years as a hermit in the desert of Chalcis, fighting temptation with fasting and prayer, and meanwhile learning Greek and Hebrew as well as corresponding with his friends. Upon his return to Antioch he was ordained a priest and proceeded to apply himself to scriptural studies. In 382 he returned to Rome as secretary to Pope Damasus I, where he intensified his work on Biblical texts whilst propagating views to which he was deeply committed on such questions as the merits of the ascetic life and the importance of virginity as exemplified in the case of the mother of Jesus. Following Damasus's death he left the 'Babylon' of Rome for Bethlehem, and there founded a monastery where he lived for most of the remainder of his life. Yet monastic seclusion proved no bar to his engaging vigorously in contemporary ecclesiastical and theological controversies. Most notably, in his *Adversus Jovinianum* (393) he attacked the monk Jovinian who had held marriage and virginity to be equally meritorious; and in his *Dialogi contra Pelagianos* (415) he assailed the negative stance of the British monk Pelagius on original sin, predestination and divine grace as the necessary and sufficient source of human salvation. Coupled with his Latin translation of the Bible (the Vulgate) and his numerous exegetical writings, the positions which Jerome espoused with dogmatic certainty on such issues as these were formative upon the medieval church and, indeed, upon Western society.

PLINIUS SECUNDUS, GAIUS, alias PLINY THE ELDER (AD 23/4–79), Roman historian and natural philosopher. Born at Comum (Como), he was probably educated at Rome before embarking on a military career. One product of that career was his handbook on the use of javelins on horseback, written in the course of his service with the armies of the Rhine in which he commanded a squadron of cavalry. During those same years he began a history of Rome's campaigns against the Germans, which Tacitus was later to use as a source. Having completed his military service, Pliny returned in 57/8 to Rome where he was active as a lawyer whilst also engaging in studies of grammar and rhetoric. His civilian career prospered following the accession of Vespasian (69–79) with whose son and successor, Titus, he had served in the German wars. He held a series of commissions as administrator of imperial revenues, and in due course became a counsellor of the emperors themselves. In 77 he dedicated to Titus his *Naturalis historia*, an encyclopaedic work which deals in thirty-seven books with the universe, geography, man, other animals, botany, zoology, metals and stones, art and architecture, as well as a host of incidental topics. Widely used in the Middle Ages, the work was treated in the Renaissance as a standard source of scientific data and attracted multitudinous editors and commentators, many of them bent upon exposing Pliny's errors whilst exploiting the information which he had provided. Its author's enthusiasm for scientific observation led to his own death when, in August 79, he sailed to witness the eruption of Vesuvius and was overcome by the fumes.

POLYBIUS (*c.* 200–after 118 BC), Greek historian of Rome. The son of a statesman, he was born at Megalopolis in the Peloponnese. After a liberal education, he followed a political career and rose to prominence in the Achaean League, a confederation of cities originally formed to defend their liberties from external domination, particularly by the Macedonians. Following Rome's defeat of Macedon at Pydna in 167, Polybius and other Achaeans were deported to Italy. There he became a protégé of Scipio Aemilianus, member of the leading noble family of the Cornelii and a patron of Greek learning. Having travelled in Spain and Africa, Polybius witnessed Scipio's destruction of Carthage (146) and, after the sack of Corinth in the same year, assisted in the settlement of Greece. These events provided the *terminus ad quem* of his *Histories*, a work written to demonstrate how and why Rome had risen to dominate the world from the time of her first war with Carthage for control of Sicily (264–41). Adopting a universal historical approach (which involved him in numerous digressions) and disparaging the sensationalism of other historians, Polybius found his explanation of Rome's rise ultimately in the inexorable influence of Fortune, and more immediately in the merits of her army and her constitution. He analysed the latter with reference to a cyclical conception of political change – from monarchy to aristocracy to democracy – which much impressed Renaissance readers. Of the *Histories*' forty books the first five survive, with excerpts from the rest. Polybius himself died after a fall from a horse.

SIGONIO, CARLO (1523–84), Italian philologist and historian. The son of a wool-worker, he was born at Modena where, as a boy, he learned Latin and Greek from the celebrated Hellenist Franciscus Portus of Crete, before proceeding to study logic and medicine at Bologna and Pavia. Having succeeded Portus at Modena, he moved to Venice in 1551 as professor of classical literature, and then to Padua before returning to a well-paid post at Bologna where he spent the remainder of his life. A shrewd investor of his earnings, he acquired considerable wealth, and throughout his career cultivated leading figures in Italian academic and ecclesiastical circles. Even so, he richly deserved his scholarly reputation which rested upon his exhaustive documentary researches and his refusal to sacrifice accuracy on the altar of literary effect when presenting his findings. In addition to various philological studies and the *De antiquo jure* (1560) in which he examined the rights of citizens in ancient Rome and the administration of Italy and the provinces beyond, he published accounts of the acts of Roman rulers (*Regum, consulum, dictatorum ac censorum Romanorum Fasti*, 1550) and of the Athenian constitution (*De repubblica Atheniensium*, 1564), a history of his adopted city of Bologna to 1257, and, above all, a history of medieval Italy: the *De regno Italia* (1574), which took its place as a masterpiece of Renaissance historiography.

TIRAQUEAU, ANDRE (*c.* 1480–1558), French jurisconsult. He was born at Fontenay-le-Comte where for many years he held the office of *sénéchal*, in his case effectively that of chief justice as distinct from the military figurehead which the position had become elsewhere. It was in this capacity that he secured the release of the renegade friar François Rabelais whom the latter's fellow Franciscans had imprisoned in the town. In 1541 Francis I appointed him counsellor in the Paris *parlement*, waiving the usual requirements of payment for the office and preliminary service in the *chambre des enquêtes*. Thereafter Tiraqueau discharged a number of commissions for the king and his successor. Widely celebrated for his learning, he was sometimes described as the Varro of his century, after the Roman antiquarian and polymath Marcus Terentius Varro of the first century BC. His familiarity with French customary laws was especially extensive, as was evident in his study of matrimonial matters (*De legibus connubialibus*, 1513) and in treatises on other aspects of the law of persons. His best-known publication, however, was his *De nobilitate* in conjunction with his *De jure primogenitorum* (1549). Dedicated to Henry II, the work examined the question of the source of true nobility and found that it consisted not in wealth, nor in ancient blood, nor even in royal conferment so much as in virtue publicly and judicially acknowledged. On this basis he condemned the pretensions of petty lords and their abuses of power, and could claim for the magistracy a status comparable with that of the high nobility.

ULPIANUS, DOMITIUS (d. AD 223), Roman jurist. Born into an ancient family of Tyre, he held office in Rome at the culmination of the most creative period of the law's development from the second to the early third century. With his contemporary Paulus he served as assessor to the great jurist and praetorian prefect, Papinian. Apparently banished for a time by the emperor Elagabalus, he became a member of the council of Severus Alexander to whom he was related, but whose succession to the imperial dignity he did not long survive. Praetorian prefect in his turn, he sought to introduce reforms prejudicial to the privileges of the praetorian guard, who mutinied and killed him. Ulpian's chief contributions to the formulating of the law lay less in his originality than in his synthesising approach and the clarity with which he summarised the positions of his contemporaries and predecessors. For this reason his statements proved extremely useful to the commission appointed by Justinian to compile the *Digest* or *Pandects* which appeared in 533. Almost a third of the *Digest* consists of extracts from his works, and he and Paulus together occupy almost a half of it. Indeed, to jurists of the Middle Ages the name of Ulpian seems almost to have been synonymous with Roman law; and by and large his reputation survived Renaissance scholars' adoption of more critical attitudes towards the *Digest* and their development of fresh legal approaches.

CHARLES LOYSEAU
A Treatise of Orders
and Plain Dignities

Dedicatory epistle

To My Lord, the Honourable Jean Forget, Knight, Counsellor of the King in his Council of State and Privy Council, and President in his Court of *Parlement*:

My Lord:
If it is the same with writings given to the public as with painted pictures, the excellence and grace of which are not well perceived unless they are placed in the light of those qualities: where better than in your hands could I place this treatise *Of Orders and Plain Dignities*, so as to reveal it to France under the lustre of your merit? Indeed, my Lord, the subject of this my discourse has disclosed to me that it ought to be addressed to you as the one who has the most perfect knowledge of the matter. For your virtue has passed before our eyes via the principal places and degrees of honour, to ascend and arrive at the illustrious dignity which you use so worthily. And, moreover, when the question is mooted of bringing some order and good regulation to the confusion and disorder which today pervert the eutaxy and good arrangement of this state, it is immediately upon you that eyes are cast as the one recognised amongst the most capable of dealing with it, under the august designs of our great King. That is why, having used the few enough hours of respite remaining to me from the ordinary duties of my post to continue the studies which I have reserved and devoted to my country, I enclose herewith this little discourse which is emboldened to take its flight under the auspices of your favour. Thus may my compatriots see that, if I lack the skill to bring the work to perfection, at least I sketch the matter for those

3

more expert who may wish to display and employ for the public the talent of their art. So, my Lord, I do not expect the commendation and honour which a perfect work might merit. It suffices for me that my attempt and project, full of honest desire, should be agreeable to you, and that it serves as testimony to posterity that I am and shall be throughout my life,

my Lord, your most humble and obedient servant,

C. Loyseau.

Preface

1. In all things there must be order, for the sake of decorum and for their control. The Latin name of the world itself evokes the adornment and the grace that proceed from its admirable disposition; and in Greek it is called κόσμος because of its beautiful order and arrangement. For the perfect Workman, says Plato,[1] 'brought it from disorder to order', which Cicero renders thus:[2] 'he constituted order out of disorder'.

2. Inanimate creatures are all set in their places there, according to their high or low degrees of perfection; their times and seasons are certain, their properties regulated, their effects assured. As for animate creatures, the celestial intelligences have their hierarchical orders which are immutable. In the case of men, who are ordained by God to command other animate creatures in this sublunary world, their order may be changeable and subject to vicissitude. This is because of the freedom and peculiar liberty which God has given them for good and evil. Nevertheless, they too cannot subsist without order.

3. For we cannot live together in a condition of equality, but of necessity it must be that some command and others obey. Those who command have several orders or degrees: sovereign lords command all those in their state, addressing their commandment to the great, the great to the intermediate, the intermediate to the minor, and the minor to the people. And the people, who obey all of these, are again divided into several orders and ranks, so that over each of them there may be superiors who account for their entire order to the magistrates, and the magistrates to the sovereign lords.

---

[1] *Timaeus* [30A].
[2] [*Timaeus* ix. 11.]

5

4. And so, by means of these multiple divisions and subdivisions, one general order is formed out of many orders, and of many estates a well-ordered state where there are good harmony and consonance and a correspondence and interrelationship from the highest to the lowest: so that, through order, an infinite number results in unity. As the canon puts it:[3]

> With this purpose the foresight of the highest steward established various ranks and orders to be distinct so that, as long as the lesser showed respect towards the greater and the greater bestowed affection upon the lesser, true harmony was made and union from diversity. For the whole community could not subsist by noble reason unless the great order of difference should preserve it: for every creature cannot be governed by one and the same quality. The model of the heavenly hosts teaches us this: there are angels and archangels, and so it is clear that they are not equal, but they differ the one from the other in power and order.

5. How could the general of an army be instantaneously obeyed by all its soldiers if the army were not divided into regiments, the regiments into companies, the companies into squadrons? This being so, the general's commandment is conveyed at once to the colonels, then by them to the captains, by the captains to the corporals, and by them to the plain soldiers, so that the lowest soldier in the army is very soon told of it.

6. But the effect of order is still more admirable in a state than in an army. For while the army is crowded together in a small space, the state ordinarily embraces extensive territory; and while the army as a whole does not last very long, the state endures almost for ever. All this happens by virtue of order. For the sovereign lord has his general officers near him, and they send his directives to the provincial magistrates, they to the municipal magistrates, and these last see to it that the people carry them out.

7. So much for those who command. As for the people who obey, because it is a many-headed body it is divided by orders, estates or particular occupations. Some are particularly dedicated to the service of God, others to conserve the state by arms, others to nourish and maintain it by the exercises of peace. These are our three orders or

---

[3] *Decretum* D.89 c. 7.

estates-general of France: the clergy, the nobility and the third estate.
8. But each of these three orders is further subdivided into subordinate degrees or subaltern orders, in accordance with the model of the celestial hierarchy. On this St Denys the Areopagite says elegantly:[4]

> Among those of the same rank the principle that orders everything whilst itself being beyond everything has established this decree: that, as far as each function is concerned, the orders and powers be first, and intermediate, and last; and that the more divine initiate and guide those less so in their approach to God, their illumination by Him and their fellowship with Him.

9. The subaltern degrees or orders of the clergy are well enough known. Beyond the four minor orders and that of the tonsure, there are the holy orders of subdeacon, deacon, priest and bishop; to them that of cardinal has been added, and there are also the various orders of monks. Those of the nobility are the plain nobility, the high nobility and the princes. Finally, in the third estate, which is the most numerous, there are several orders – to wit, men of letters, of finance, of commerce, of craft, of tillage and of toil; though most of these are simply trades rather than fully fledged orders.

10. I have already dealt[5] with those who have command or public power, whether as officers who exercise it themselves and by function, or as lords who have it as property for exercise by someone else. It now remains to explain the orders and various ranks of those who obey. This is the third species of dignity, which had to be discussed after the other two – that is, offices and lordships – so that all three species might be explained. And amid the orders I shall also deal with plain dignities which are, strictly, neither offices nor lordships nor orders. In respect of these I shall likewise postulate three species, to wit, honorary offices, lordships and orders, epithets, and forenames: a subject which is no less useful and agreeable than the former.

---

[4] [*PG* III, col. 181. For 'St Denys' (Dionysius) see above, p. xlii]
[5] [I.e., in *Offices* and *Seigneuries*.]

CHAPTER ONE

Of order in general

1. Two modern jurisconsults have engaged in a great debate as to whether the Roman senate was an order or else a company of officers. Budé says[1] that it was an order, on the grounds that in law and in other fine books it is always termed 'the most honourable order' and the senators are never called officers or magistrates. Cagnolus[2] takes him up on this, supporting Accursius and the ancient doctors who share his own opinion. These, misled by the usage of their time, have agreed that the Roman senate was a body of officers.

2. Much the same difficulty occurs with the dignity of decurions, that is, the town councillors of the Roman Empire. In law this is sometimes called an 'order' and sometimes an 'honour', meaning an office of a town or commonwealth: 'For an honour is an administrative position in a commonwealth with the rank of dignity', says Callistratus.[3]

3. Now it is only order that I have left to consider, the nature of office having been sufficiently explained in my *Offices*. Order, then, to which this book is devoted, is a species of dignity, or honourable quality, which appertains in the same way and by the same name to several persons. It does not of itself ascribe to them any particular public power; but, beyond the rank which it gives them, it brings them a particular aptitude and capacity to attain either offices or lordships. It is called 'order' either because its effect is only to attrib-

---

[1] [*Opera B.*, III, pp. 74, 93.]
[2] [Gerolamo Cagnolo, *In constitutiones & leges ... Pandectarum ... Reportorio copiosissimo*, I (Venice, 1554), p. 47.]
[3] *Digest* 50. 4. 14.

ute the rank of honour to the person, or because it places those who have it in order and in rank such that they may attain public power.

4. In Greek it is called τάξις, which amounts to signifying a certain class and condition of persons.

5. In France it is particularly termed 'estate', signifying the most stable and inseparable dignity of a man: as will be proved in due place. And as for its definition, order can be defined thus: *dignity with aptitude for public power*.

6. For, as I said at the beginning of the first book of *Offices*,[4] there are three species of dignity – office, lordship and order. These have not only their common genus, which is dignity, but also much congruity in their differentia, which is public power. In this, each of the three species participates differently. Office has the function and exercise thereof, and accordingly I have defined it as 'dignity with public function'. Lordship has the property of it, and so I have defined it as 'dignity with power in property'. Finally, order has only the aptitude for it, which is why I have stated as its definition that it is 'dignity with aptitude for public power'.

7. For example, the clergy are an order which, while it confers of itself no public power, none the less renders a man who is thus honoured capable of ecclesiastical benefices and offices. Likewise, nobility is an order which of itself is in no way a public office, but which gives to him who is noble an aptitude for many fine offices and lordships assigned to nobles. Similarly, being a doctor or licentiate in laws is no office, but it is an order necessary to attain offices of judicature. Hence it follows that office follows order and is conferred on him who is of the order to which it is assigned. If there are some orders which do have some public function, yet their members have it only as a public collectivity and not privately and in several; and thus it can be said that such orders participate in the nature of offices.

8. So it is easy to resolve the difficulty which has just been propounded about the decurions. For the truth is that they participated both in order and in office. The decurionate was an order in that it was an honourable rank of persons separated from the rest of the people, and a required quality for attaining municipal offices where administration chiefly resided. It was also an office, in so far as the decurions had a hand in some way in that administration, even to the

---

[4] *Offices*, I [i. 6–7].

point where the assets of all of them were liable for municipal affairs. As they thus participated in the one and in the other, it ought not to be found strange that the decurionate should be termed sometimes an 'honour' and commonly an 'order'.

9. Likewise the Roman senate from its first institution was a pure order, the senators having no command nor administration, at least severally. But when – as will be discussed in the next chapter – it was reduced under the emperors to a kind of ordinary jurisdiction, it thereafter participated in the nature of office.

10. There is yet another well-known difference between order and office. This is that office is something which has an actual, or positive, existence; it can subsist separately, with no one appointed to it; and it passes from one person to another without disappearing and being altogether nullified. In short, office seems to be in the category of substance. On the other hand, there is nothing positive about order, and it is not a substance which could subsist of itself; but it is a simple accident, and is in the category of quality. As a simple accident inseparable from the person, it perishes with that person. It is not transmissible to another, at least in undivided fashion and to the very same extent; what may appear to be transmitted is only a similar quality.

11. For example, the office of bailiff, lieutenant or king's attorney subsists even though no one is appointed to it. It does not perish when the officer dies nor when he resigns, but only changes its possessor. But the quality of priest, of knight or of licentiate in laws originates and dies with the person, just as it is the property of an accident to perish with its subject. And although after the death of a knight another may be put in his place, what is given him is not the same quality in its entirety, but another very like it.

12. To conclude, there is a fine passage in Cassiodorus which sets out very well the qualities of order. Speaking of the patriciate (which was a species of order), he says:[5]

> Honour itself is a girdle and yet is empty, having nothing of jurisdiction and not displacing the girdle of judicial authority. In it perpetual happiness is begotten, while the ambition of a successor is not feared. For as soon as it should be given, it is made coeval with the man, an undivided ornament, a trusty belt,

[5] *PL*, LXIX, col. 681.

incapable of being removed until the man should happen to leave the world.

13. So, in order to examine here the nature of order in general, this must first be considered: that, as it is more inherent to and inseparable from the person than office, because it forms his condition and imprints upon him a perpetual character, more solemnity is usually needed in conferring it and more ceremony in removing it than is the case with office. For an office is conferred by the simple will and word either of the patron or of the electors: 'a mark of grace and favour is bestowed by word alone', say the canonists. And as proof of this 'grace' one receives letters of provision to collative offices, but not to elective ones, at least when the election is well known and public. Be that as it may, from the time of that collation or election one becomes lord of the office, and one then becomes officer upon taking the oath. For there is no need to consider the ceremonies currently used in the reception of officers, which were introduced only after offices began to be conferred upon the highest bidder, without bringing selection or judgement into play.

14. But at all times examination has taken place or proof been otherwise obtained of the capacity of those who would be admitted to orders. This was the case among the Romans when the censors, and afterwards the emperors themselves, saw to it. 'The order [*sic*] of the senate compels punctiliousness in examining those admitted to the senate', says Theodoric, according to Cassiodorus;[6] and Lampridius tells us[7] about the exact inquiry which the wise Emperor Alexander Severus made into the reception of senators. It was also the case in the ancient church,[8] as was proved in my first book.[9] And beyond that we find that certain very numerous ceremonies are still involved in the very act of conferring all sorts of orders, whether ecclesiastical, holy or otherwise – and even in conferring religious orders such as the novitiate and the profession. In making knights there are quite different ones; and the reason why there are none in the making of princes and gentlemen is that these orders are unusual in as much as they are obtained by lineage and not by particular concession. For

---

[6] *PL*, LXIX, [col.536].
[7] *Alexander Severus*, [xix. 2–4].
[8] *Decretales* I. 12.
[9] [*Offices*, I.iii. 70.]

the rest, certain solemnities manifestly take place in the making of licentiates and doctors, advocates and attorneys, and so on, as far as master craftsmen.

15. Furthermore, each order usually has its particular badge, sign or visible ornament with which one is solemnly decorated upon admission to it. So, for example, Roman senators had the tunic with the broad purple stripe, and crescent-shaped shoes; Roman knights had the narrow-striped tunic and gold ring; plain citizens had the appropriate or unstriped tunic, and the general badge of the Roman citizen was the overgarment called 'toga', as will be explained in the next chapter.

16. Finally, the mark of the soldier was the sword-belt passing over the shoulder, called in one word the *balteus* which we have termed the 'baldric'.

17. And just as ancient Roman citizens had the toga, so nowadays the clergy indiscriminately all wear the long robe with which, in accordance with the ceremonial of the Roman church,[10] whoever receives the tonsure, being the mark of entry to ecclesiastical orders, should be publicly invested. This badge is common to ecclesiastics and to men of learning; and so ecclesiastics (at least, those who are admitted to holy orders) wear the tonsure, otherwise called the 'crown', upon their heads as a particular badge.

18. In former times this was the common badge of the clergy in general who were all tonsured clerics. It was even worn by those who had only the plain order of the tonsure, as can still be seen nowadays when boy choristers wear it. Even at the time when married clergy enjoyed the privileges of clericality, it was necessary for them to be 'in proper attire and tonsure', as I said in my *Seigneuries*.[11]

19. In addition to this general badge, acolytes and other clerics of the four minor orders wear the surplice or the alb – the white robe which, formerly in Rome, was a token of dignity, as the red robe is with us; this would be worth a separate discourse. Subdeacons have the maniple as the mark of their order; deacons, the stole; priests, the chasuble. Bishops have the mitre, the cross, the gloves and the ring; and cardinals have the hat or bonnet, and the scarlet robe.[12] To deal briefly with members of the regular religious orders, these have

[10] *Sext* 5. 9. 2.
[11] *Seigneuries*, xv. [71].
[12] *Decretum* 11 q.3 c.65.

a larger crown or tonsure than the secular clergy. Even the Jesuits, who are half-regular and half-secular, have a crown which in size is mid-way between that of the seculars and of the regulars. Otherwise, every religious order has its distinct habit: I say 'distinct' not only from one order to another, but also from the novice to the professed members of the same order of religion.

20. Among the nobles, plain gentlemen have their timbred or crested coats of arms. Knights have their spurs and gilt harness (at least that was of old their particular badge, but nowadays he has it who will buy it). Knights of a chivalric order have the collar or other badge of their order; and, in short, princes have the prince's cloak – and it would be seemly for them to wear it always.

21. Amongst commoners, doctors, licentiates and bachelors have various kinds of hood according to the various faculties, over and above the long robe which they have in common with ecclesiastics. Advocates have the cornet. Attorneys have only the long robe to differentiate them from plain legal practitioners who do not swear an oath to justice; and they inopportunely usurped the unlined hood and bonnet of the sovereign courts when scholars wore it lined. But it warrants no surprise that at all times advocates have worn similar hoods to those of high court presidents and counsellors, as the hood is the insignia not of office, but of the order of licentiates in laws which is common to them all.

22. So much for the badges and insignia of each order. There is a very fine passage on this in Lampridius:[13]

> He had it in mind to give every office-holder and to every rank a particular kind of clothing so that they might be distinguished by their garments. But this was displeasing to Ulpian and Paulus who said that it would cause much strife, men being so ready to quarrel. So it was resolved to be enough that Roman knights should be distinguished from senators by the width of the stripe on the tunic.

23. But, beyond this external decoration, two other prerogatives of honour proceed from orders, namely title and rank. In respect of title, it is well known that everyone may qualify himself with the title of his order and join it to his name, even more so than with that of his office: for order is still more inherent to the person than office.

---

[13] *Alexander Severus*, [xxvii. 1–3].

This is why the title of the order remains after resignation, as will shortly be said; while the title of the office does not remain after resignation. Also, the title of the order ought always to be placed immediately after the name and before the title of the office, because the office is most often conferred in consequence of the order to which it is assigned, as has just been said.

24. Like office, order yields certain epithets or titles of honour, used both in Rome and in France. Roman examples are the titles 'honourable', 'notable', 'most renowned', 'most excellent', 'distinguished'; French ones, those of knight, king's counsellor, esquire, and many more. Such titles are not directly attributed to the persons, as are those of orders and offices, but immediately concern orders and offices, 'and are epithets or attributes of certain orders and offices'. Nevertheless, because of the resemblance which they bear to true orders they are counted as honorary and imaginary orders. This is why they are added immediately after the name, as with true orders, while some of them are even placed before the name.

25. Order also yields, like office, another quality which is peculiar to us in France. I call it the forename. It is one of the three titles which I term 'plain dignities' in the inscription of this book, the others being honorary orders and offices, and epithets; and I will deal with them in my last two chapters.

26. As for rank, which is precedence in sitting or in walking, it is certain that this springs principally from orders rather than from offices; for the very name 'order' denotes and signifies as much. It is also well known that in Rome the senators ranked before the knights, and the knights before the humbler sort of people. The prime instance of this was at the theatre or public games where the Roman people assembled daily.

27. For there were several laws made expressly to regulate places at the theatre. These reserved for senators the most honourable places, which were the ones below 'on the lowest benches or orchestra at the bottom of the theatre', close to the players. Places fourteen degrees lower [*sic*] were reserved for knights; and the other or higher rows or degrees, being consequently more distant and inconvenient, were left to the humbler sort, as Sigonius has shown very learnedly.[14]

28. Likewise in France, the three estates have their order and rank, the one after the other. Thus, the ecclesiastical order is first of all,

---

[14] *De antiq. jur.*, fo. 110.

that of the nobility after, and the third estate last. There is, however, no ordinance to this purpose: considerations of law scarcely arise, because honour alone is involved. Ranks of honour are observed voluntarily by honour; and certainly they are more honourable when they spring from voluntary respect.

29. So Valerius says[15] that the first Roman law to distinguish places in the theatre was only made 656 years after the building of Rome and that, even so, before then no one was seen to take a place in advance of the senators. But Livy tells[16] how, when this law was made, the people were offended by it, denouncing

> all such distinctions, by which the orders are set apart and the harmonies and equities of freedom reduced, as a novel and arrogant caprice, neither desired nor established by anyone, especially the people.

And after Roscius had made the law which gave separate rank to the knights in the theatre, a great revolt occurred there. This was during the consulate of Cicero who quickly pacified it with his eloquence, for which Plutarch praises him highly.[17]

30. I say this in order to show that rank ought to be maintained gently and courteously rather than with arrogance and assertiveness. For honour and love are two such prime and sublime things that they cannot be commanded nor readily obtained by force; nor is there any action called for in order to obtain them. If one thinks to have them by force, this is not love, but fear and subjection: it is not honour, but fear and oppression, as I have already said in *Of Offices*.[18] Yet, just as love is necessary in the world, so too are honour and rank – otherwise there would be only confusion amongst us. But both the one and the other must be gained by merit and maintained by gentleness.

31. Now, since the ecclesiastical order is the first among us, it seems that the least among the priests, even the lowest of tonsured clerics, ought to take precedence over the greatest of the plain gentlemen of the court (I mean among private persons, for it is otherwise with officers upon whom office confers a particular rank). Such a cleric

---

[15] [Cf.] Valerius [Maximus, *Factorum*, II. iv. 3].
[16] *Hist.* [xxxiv. liv.5].
[17] *Cicero* [xiii.2–4].
[18] *Offices*, I. [vii. 1–21].

enjoys precedence not through his own particular merit, but because of his order and, to be still more exact, because of God whose minister he is: 'not to him, but to reverence for God'. And in former times, when our ancestors were more devout, this was how he was treated. A lord would make his parish priest or any other churchman sit at the head of his table; and there is no doubt whatsoever that such honour was agreeable to God who is jealous of it with good reason, as the One in whom true honour perfectly resides 'and to Whom alone be honour and glory for ever and ever'.

32. But in the temporal body politic the ecclesiastical order is considered to be an abnormal and extraordinary order. Our Redeemer himself said that His kingdom was not of this world, and His last commandment to His apostles was to make themselves the least in the midst of the world. This is why it is commonly observed at present that those who are in some secular dignity do not wish to give way to priests unless they have some ecclesiastical dignity.

33. Likewise I say that the least of gentlemen ought to take precedence over the richest and most honourable of the third estate, though here again I mean among private persons and when the question concerns only the rank of orders. Yet the dignity of office is greater, just as it enhances that of order, in so far as it is ordinarily necessary to have order before being an officer. Thus, great difficulty arises when a commoner invested with an office disputes a place with a gentleman who is not an officer.

34. To settle the matter, care must be taken over the point made earlier, that there are two, even three, degrees of nobility: to wit, plain nobility, high nobility and the princes. As the members of the high nobility – that is, the knights, and even more so the princes – have an enhancement of dignity above their nobility as such, they do not give way to any officers. An exception is that knights may give way to certain officers who are also knights, because of their offices; for the latter have the same order as the former, and the office as well. But as for princes, they do not yield precedence to any officers whatsoever, except when the latter are actually exercising their main official function. Even so, when they themselves are officers they hold the rank of prince as the greater and not that of officer which is the lesser; and they give way only to kings and sovereign princes.

35. Yet, while plain noblemen sometimes give way to officers who are of commoner extraction, this does not apply to all kinds of officers, but only to magistrates in the district and compass of their

power. For it is only magistrates (that is, the principal officers of government and of justice) who have established rank, and not officers of finance, nor the lesser officers of war and of justice.

36. Such is the rank which the three orders or general estates ought to have, the one over the other. In considering what rank their respective members keep amongst themselves, it must be borne in mind that in each of these three general orders there are particular degrees, some more worthy than others.

37. Amongst the clergy there are the tonsure, the minor orders, and the orders of subdeacon, priest, bishop and cardinal. Amongst the nobility there are the esquire, the knight and the prince. In these two estates there is no difficulty at all about the rank of these particular orders, because no one has the higher who does not also have all the lower ones.

38. Similarly, a third set of orders or subaltern degrees is to be observed among these particular orders. Thus, among the members of the episcopal order there are plain bishops, archbishops, primates and patriarchs. These walk together according to the rank which I have just mentioned, except that, in as much as bishopdom is an order and an ecclesiastical office all together, a bishop who is in his own territory or in a place where he has superiority ought in that case to precede all others of the episcopal order, even though he may have less dignity than they. For example, in Paris the archbishop of Paris ought to precede all archbishops, primates and patriarchs except the archbishop of Sens, whose suffragan he is, and the primate of Lyon, under whose primateship he is, as are others. Likewise, among princes there are foreign princes, French princes and crown princes: subordinate degrees, the ranks of which will be explained later in the appropriate place.[19]

39. But the third estate embraces so many divers sorts of particular orders and also so many lesser offices that it is very difficult to particularise the rank of each of them. The difficulty is greater still with the rank of orders among the officers, for confusion here is so extreme. And although President Chasseneuz, one of the great personages of his time, wrote on the subject an immense volume entitled *Catalogue of the glory of the world*,[20] he nevertheless omitted even more than he said about it.

---

[19] [Below, ch. 7, especially sections 93 *et seq.*]
[20] [Barthélemy de] Chasseneuz, *Catalogus gloriae mundi* [(Lyon, 1528)].

40. As for the power of orders, their members taken severally do not have any as a rule; that they have no public administration is what makes them different from offices. Even so, orders do exist which have definite corporate and collegiate standing. This sometimes gives rise to the privilege of being able to make statutes and to elect superior officers with disciplinary powers over the whole body, as in the case of gilds.[21]

41. Again unlike offices, orders receive no regular pay, nor even casual salaries or emoluments, at least in the form of a fixed rate due for public administration. But some do have legitimate earnings for private work, 'for instance, the practice of a skill for which expenses accrue'. Priests, however, owing to the sublimity and excellence of their function, have available no action in law for direct redress against a defaulter, and cannot even strike an open bargain for payment for celebrating divine service. They can pursue the matter only by petition, entreating a judge to intervene to maintain the praiseworthy custom, which is the usual term in legal practice.

42. But advocates, doctors and masters of arts can licitly demand their honorarium. In this connection a procedure applied whereby the judge could determine the claim by administrative as distinct from strictly judicial action: thus, 'the praetor himself, not a petty judge appointed by the praetor, took cognisance of these cases, by "extra-ordinary" procedure, summarily, and not in his judicial capacity as such'.[22] And as for artisans, 'the ordinary action accommodated them, doubtless one of the various actions relating to hire, purchase, or loan on agreed terms', depending upon the type of bargain struck with them.

43. However, the law[23] mentions the presents or gratuities of the decurions, saying that, 'when minors of under twenty-five years were made decurions, they might receive the presents of decurions, even though they might not be able in the meantime to deliver judicial opinions'. This seems to contradict what I have just said, that orders have no salary for public administration. But it must be noted that these presents were the entry fee which, by the ancient custom, new decurions paid in cash to established ones, instead of the feast which

---

[21] *Seigneuries*, xvi. [21].
[22] [Cf.] *Digest* 50. 13.
[23] *Digest* 50. 2. 6. 1.

18

was made voluntarily in honour of the company, as Cujas observes.[24]

44. Further, it is commonly found in law that upon entering certain orders (as has been said before on offices and militia) one paid some small sum of money to those of the order for right of entry. This happened even in the ecclesiastical orders, though by comparison with benefices the sale of these was still more strictly prohibited as an act of the most unmitigated and arrant simony.

45. For the offence of Simon Magus, from whom simony took its name and origin, was that he wished to buy not a benefice, but the ecclesiastical order itself. It is true that, because order and benefice were conjoined at that time, simony was understood with good reason to relate to the sale of benefices. Nevertheless, it is evident[25] that even bishops were charged some small sum at the time of their consecration, a sum which is called 'inauguration fee'; and what simple priests paid upon reception into their order is called 'admission fee'.[26]

46. It remains to consider loss or deprivation of order. This cannot properly be called 'vacating', because, unlike an office or a benefice, an order – at least the individual quality of the one who is deprived – is altogether lost and does not remain vacant to be transferred indivisibly to someone else. That is also why order is more difficult to lose than office, whether by resignation or by forfeiture: for the occurrence of death itself, which settles everything, makes no difference to it

47. In respect of resignation, it is well known that as a rule an order cannot be resigned; and in fact a priest does not resign his order to another – nor does a knight, nor a licentiate in laws, nor an advocate.

48. True, there are certain orders whose number is limited, as are offices. In such cases, someone who wishes to give way to another does abdicate his order and leaves it, or, to put it more precisely, his place in the limited number. He may do so in order to remove the obstacle preventing the admission of the one whom he wishes to bring into the order. This is properly called 'demission', and not resignation. It is the practice with attorneys in places where the king does not sell their positions, and where the ordinance is observed that their number be limited, as that of advocates is in law.[27]

---

[24] [*Opera C*, II, pt. i, pp. 77–8.]
[25] *Nov. J* 123. 3.
[26] *Nov. J* 56. 1.
[27] *Code J* 2. 7. 8, 13, etc.

Decurions are another instance of it, and here the law in question[28] informs us that the order and the ordinary place are separable: which is very well worth noting.

49. That is why I hold that demission applies only to the leaving of the place and the function thereof, and not to the order as such which, in itself, is so appropriated to the person that it cannot be resigned nor lost otherwise than by forfeit. There are legal rulings relevant to this,[29] and notably on 'from what civil duties those persons are exempt who, after completing military service or the responsibilities of counsellor in the provinces, are free to spend time on their own affairs'.[30] So my view is that an attorney keeps the title and rank of attorney after his demission and should even retain the privileges, if there were any, although he cannot any longer plead. For, as shall be shown later in its place, there are actual orders and offices which have immediate powers and involve functions, and others which are simply honorary and without such attributes.

50. A manifest example of how order is not lost by demission or resignation is the bishop who, after resigning his bishopric, none the less retains his episcopal order which he can in no way resign nor separate from his person. Lest this should seem a peculiarity of sacred orders, I have already proved in my first book[31] that those who have been received into ennobling offices remain noble after resigning their offices.

51. I have also drawn attention there to the well-known practice in France that even the epithets attributed to each office remain with the person after resignation from his office, although such epithets may not be true orders, but are only like honorary orders. In Rome, where offices were not perpetual, it is quite certain that after their period had elapsed those who had them retained the relevant epithet and quality of honour: a quality which in law is specifically termed 'dignity', as will be seen in innumerable passages of the last three books of the *Code*.

52. Deprivation through forfeiture is, again, neither as ordinary nor as easy in the case of order as it is of office or of benefice. I say 'ordinary' in respect both of the cause and of the kind of order. The

---

[28] *Digest* 50. 2.
[29] *Code J* 2. 7.
[30] *Code J* 10. [56].
[31] *Offices*, I. ix. [35–7].

causes which induce deprivation of office or benefice do not induce deprivation of order, even though the order may be united to the benefice. When a bishop is deprived of his bishopric or a priest of his benefices, they are not thereby deprived of their order. When a gentleman is deprived of his office he does not therefore lose his nobility. When a judge forfeits his office he none the less remains an advocate and licentiate in laws, even though he cannot practise as an advocate in the sovereign courts owing to the infamy which he has incurred.

53. However, in this connection I consider there to be a very notable exception. It concerns the order which has occurred only because of office. Take the case of an officer who is non-noble by ancestry and has been deprived of his ennobling office. There appear to be grounds for holding that he ought to lose his nobility, for it is not reasonable that, having forfeited the office for his crime, he should retain dignities and privileges which he had only because of the office; and on even stronger grounds he should lose the epithets and honorary orders which he had because of it. The point seems decided by this law,[32] that

> judges convicted of being defiled by dishonesty and other criminal acts shall be deprived of their commissions and dignities and degraded to the lowest rank of plebeians, nor shall they afterwards enjoy those honours of which they have shown themselves unworthy.

And in this further law[33] it is said that 'they were deprived of the honour which they would have bequeathed'.

54 Deprivation does not arise in all species of orders because of infamy. I said in my first book[34] that infamy does induce deprivation of all kinds of office. But it is true that the only orders which are lost through infamy are those which have some of the characteristics of office, such as the order of senator or that of decurion.[35] In France the order of chivalry is lost by infamy because every stain is formally contrary to it. Some also hold that the order of advocate in the *parlements* is lost through infamy. I do not agree with this, though it is

---

[32] *Code J* 12. 1. 12.
[33] [*Code J* 10. 32. 47.]
[34] *Offices*, 1 [xiii.38–40].
[35] *Code J* 12. 1. 12; *Digest* 50. 2. 5. 12.

certainly true that the function is lost because the infamous cannot plead there.

55. But as for other orders, whether the ecclesiastical, the nobility or the third estate, so far at least as I remember at present they are not lost through infamy alone, nor even in consequence of some other punishment. One has to be deprived of these expressly, by sentence. In the case of the sacred orders of the church an actual degradation is requisite, over and above the express deprivation.

56. This is not necessary with other orders; in these cases the verbal deposition is enough. So much may be gathered from the ignominious deprivation of a Roman soldier, which was done in two ways. One was by solemn removal of arms or of military insignia; the other, by the general's simple verbal declaration when dismissing him by cause of ignominy. So says the law,[36] and President Faber states it very well.[37]

57. It sometimes happens that after the sentence containing the deprivation of order the person's decorations are publicly removed. This is done at the time either to inflict greater ignominy or, rather, so as not to injure the order when, after such a dishonourable discharge, the death penalty is then executed upon the condemned man. Thus, when a knight of the order is judicially executed his collar is first removed, so that he should not be reputed to have been executed in the quality of a knight. This practice was observed in the execution of Marshal Biron. I will examine it comprehensively in chapter 10 which I have reserved for consideration of the form of degradation.

[36] *Digest* 3. 2.
[37] *Semestrium*, p. 169.

CHAPTER TWO

Of the Roman orders

1. In Rome, as in France, there were three orders, or estates, which included all the people. But they were different from ours: for whereas we have the clergy, the nobility and the third estate, they had the senate, the knights and the common people. 'Rome, city of Mars, has three orders: knights, plebeians, senators', says Ausonius.[1] The senate was for counsel, the knights for the exercise of force, and the common people for supplying the needs of the commonwealth.

2. Some ascribe this differentiation of the people to Romulus. As [Servius][2] and Dionysius of Halicarnassus[3] say, he chose a hundred elders from among the most noble of his people for his council, and called them priests. He also chose three hundred young men for his guard, and called them 'the swift' either because of their speediness or after the name of their first captain who, indeed, was the second person in the kingdom, just as afterwards in the Republic the master of the horse was the second person after the dictator, and in the Empire the praetorian prefect after the emperor.

3. But [the elder] Pliny[4] tells us that the Roman knights never constituted a distinct order until the time of the Gracchi and when they had acquired the authority and duty of judging cases at law. They then began to form an order by the name of judges, separate from the common people:

---

[1] [*PL*, XIX, col. 898.]
[2] [*Comm. in Aeneidos* XI. 603.]
[3] [*Roman antiquities* II. xiii.]
[4] *Nat. hist.* XXXIII. [34].

The Gracchi were the first to institute the title of judges to distinguish that order, aiming to affront the senate by fomenting popular discontent; but subsequently, in the wake of those troubles and through other disturbances, the authority of the title was transferred to the farmers of public revenues, and for some time these farmers were the third part [of the body politic]. At length Marcus Cicero during his consulship settled the title of knight, meanwhile winning over the senate, boasting that he himself sprang from that order and seeking to gain power by popular favour. From that time onwards the equestrian order definitely became the third element in the body politic and began to be added to the Senate and the People of Rome. That is the reason why it is now written after 'People', because it was the latest to be added.

4. According again to Pliny,[5] the arrangement instituted by Romulus was initially that considerations of virtue and capability should determine conferment of these dignities of senator and knight, the former to the most prudent and most upright, and the latter to the most valiant. In fact, however, they were conferred on the basis of wealth. And indeed, if in a republic the people were distinguished from one another by virtue, everyone would think himself virtuous or at least would wish to be thought so; and therefore everyone would desire to be in the first order, and would account it a great injury to be placed in the last. That is why, as far as the general orders are concerned, another form of distinction has to be established. Hence the principal offices. As far as possible these must be conferred on the most virtuous. Yet it is always expedient that they be given to persons who are not necessitous;[6] for poverty diminishes authority and puts men's integrity to the test.

5. Thus in Isaiah it is said:[7] 'In my house is neither bread nor clothing: make me not a ruler of the people'. And Aristotle reproves the Spartans for allowing their ephors to be taken from amongst the poor.[8] In short, public responsibilities should be given if possible to those who have virtue and means together – 'those worthy by merit and resources', as the law puts it.[9]

---

[5] [*Ibid.* 29–35.]
[6] *Digest* 50. 4. 6.
[7] iii.[7].
[8] *Politics* 1270[b]10.
[9] *Code J* 10. 32. 46.

6. So it is not without reason that the property of senators and of knights was rated at a certain sum, that they had to have such and such an amount of disposable wealth in order to be either a senator or a knight, 'lest it be seen that the lustre of the orders was corrupted by paucity of appropriate possessions', observes Seneca.[10] He also says:[11]

> It is property that raises to the rank of senators, property that distinguishes the Roman knight from the common people, property that wins promotion in the camp, by property that the judge is chosen in the forum.

7. Suetonius says[12] that 'before Augustus's time the registered property of senators was eight hundred thousand sesterces, which Augustus doubled'; and that 'a knight's was four hundred thousand sesterces, or half a senator's'. So much is clear from what Suetonius reports of Julius Caesar.[13] After crossing the Rubicon he exhorted his army and, suddenly raising and touching the finger on which he wore his ring, he declared that he would rather sell it than not reassure all those who had helped him. The soldiers who had seen this action and heard these words at a distance thought that he was promising to make them all knights and to have them wear the gold ring, and so to furnish each of them with four hundred thousand sesterces. It also appears from the passage in Horace:[14]

> If there are six or seven thousand short of the four hundred
> You shall be a plebeian.

I take this to mean (for the Latin words are confused and therefore hard to understand) that if, out of a capital of four hundred and six thousand, you lack seven thousand and so have only three hundred and ninety nine thousand, you shall be ranked with the common people and shall not be made a knight. Thus it clearly follows that the capital of Roman knights was rated at four hundred thousand sesterces.

8. Not only were these rates required in order to become a senator or a knight, but anyone who had been raised to one or other of these

---

[10] 'In his *Declamations*'.
[11] Seneca [the elder, *Controversiae* II.i. 17].
[12] [Cf. *Divus Augustus* xli. 1.]
[13] *Divus Iulius* [xxxiii].
[14] [*Epistularum.* I. i. 58–9.]

orders and happened afterwards to decrease his wealth so that he no longer had the requisite property qualification was removed from his order. So it seems from what Cicero says of Curtius that, having lost his small farm, he could not retain the order of senator.[15] Dio, too, says [16] that after Augustus had doubled the capital necessary for senators some of them, knowing that they did not have it, left the order voluntarily. This is how Cicero's remark[17] should be understood: 'He keeps the name of the equestrian order, but has squandered the trappings'. Likewise Suetonius:[18] 'Since many knights whose property had been diminished during the civil wars did not dare to watch the games from the fourteen rows', which was the most evident mark of Roman knights, 'Augustus allowed them to do so if they themselves or their parents had ever possessed a knight's property'.

9. Even plain decurions or town councillors ought in some instances to have a certain amount of property, as this passage from [the younger] Pliny informs us:[19]

> It appears from your being a councillor in our town that you have enough capital of one hundred thousand sesterces. So, in order that you should enjoy Roman knighthood as well as decurionship, I offer you three hundred thousand in money to make up a knight's resources.

This provides still further proof of the rating of Roman knights. And the position of decurion figures again in Paulus's statement:[20]

> In an enduring marriage the dowry forms part of the husband's goods; however, if persons are called upon for municipal duties above a certain property level, the dowry ought not to be counted.

10. The same practice is observed today in England where one must have a certain revenue in order to be made noble. If the revenue should be significantly reduced, nobility is lost – though when this happens through misfortune the neighbouring nobles club together to make it up. And no other ceremony is needed there in order to

---

[15] *Epistulae ad familiares* [XIII. v. 2].
[16] [*Rom. hist.* LIV. xxvi. 3–4.]
[17] *Pro Sestio* [li. 110].
[18] *Divus Augustus* [xl].
[19] *Epistularum* I. xix. [2].
[20] *Digest* 50. 1. 21. 4.

be ennobled than to make an affidavit of one's revenue before the King of Arms or Herald of England and to take from him a device or blason of arms, as we gather from Thomas Smith.[21]

11. Likewise in Rome, whoever was found to have the requisite capital at the time of the censors' review of the property of the Roman citizens was enrolled among the senators or among the knights, and nothing else had to be done for this purpose. So great was the power of the censors over the orders of Rome that, just as senators and knights were made by their enrolment, so too was deletion or omission from the roll enough to deprive them of the order. The ancient authors give many examples and proofs of this; and the deprivation, although made without full knowledge of the facts, was ignominious provided only that it was done on grounds of ignominy,[22] as I will discuss later. The ignominy lasted until the persons concerned were rehabilitated either by the people or by the other censors, as I proved in my *Offices*.[23]

12. To revert then to enrolment of senators, this was done normally by the censors, but sometimes by the consuls or dictators also. According to Varro[24] it was a rule that without enrolment no one was a true senator, whatever great offices or magistracies he may have had. Yet, from the time that a person was chosen and placed among the senators, he instantly became a senator without any need either of examination or of installation – nor even, as I believe, of taking an oath, though this was needed to join the military order. It is said in Cassiodorus that 'the honour of the senate compels punctiliousness in examining persons admitted into the senate'.[25] This means that new senators were chosen by whoever elected them, as may be inferred from the rest of the passage; but not that after being elected and enrolled they were examined on their learning.

13. Now they were ordinarily chosen from among the knights, which is why Livy calls the knights 'the seminary of the senate';[26] or else, from among those who had been principal magistrates, which is why Cicero holds it 'necessary for the senate to be drawn from the

---

[21] *De Rep. Angl.* [pp. 67, 72].
[22] *Digest* I. 9. 2.
[23] *Offices* I. [xiii. 67–8].
[24] [*Noct. Attic.* III. xviii. 6.]
[25] [*PL*, LXIX, col. 536.]
[26] *Hist.* [xlii. lxi.5].

magistrates'.[27] At first the magistrates were taken from the ranks of the senators, and in Tacitus the senate is in fact called 'the nursery of all dignities'.[28] But, conversely, after the great offices had been opened up to the common people, the senators were chosen from among those who had been magistrates.

14. In fact, those who had held the principal offices of Rome, which were anciently assigned to senators, thereafter wore the senatorial robe and had entry and deliberative voice in the senate. According to Varro:[29]

> Those whom the censors had not yet enrolled in the senate were not senators as such; but, because they held offices from the Roman people, they came into the senate and had the right of voting. Yet, as they were among the last, they were not asked for their opinions, but they acquiesced in those things which the leading members had said, and so they were called footmen (*pedarii*).

Festus states as much:[30] 'Those who have held magistracies vote in the Senate, but are not called senators before their property is assessed'. Hence, says he, in the writs of summons which were issued to convene the senate 'it was customary to give notice that senators should attend and to those permitted to vote in the senate'. Fenestella says this too.[31]

15. Again, the sons of senators had the senatorial garment and entry to the senate after the age of seventeen years. At that time they laid aside the outer garment bordered with purple which higher magistrates and free-born children wore (*praetexta*), and put on the toga of manhood. This was permitted them by Augustus: Suetonius observes that [32]

> he allowed the sons of senators to assume the broad purple stripe immediately after the gown of manhood and to attend the senate

---

[27] *De legibus* III. [ix, xii].
[28] [Cf. *Leg. Nov.*, Nov. Valentinian 2.2.: 'in seminarium dignitatum', referring to the body of advocates.]
[29] *Noct. Attic.* III.xviii. [5–6].
[30] [*De verb. signif.*, p. 454.]
[31] [Lucius] Fenestella [= Andrea Domenico Fioccol], *De magistratibus sacerdotiisque Romanorum* [(Cologne, 1607), pp. 35 *et seq.*].
[32] [*Divus Augustus* xxxviii.2.]

in order that they might quickly familiarise themselves with public affairs.

It is true that they formerly entered there from their youth, but that was prohibited at the time of Praetextatus's case, as Macrobius records,[33] saying that 'it was formerly the custom for senators to enter the senate-house accompanied by sons who were wearing the *praetexta*'.

16. It also appears that formerly in France all those who had the dignity of bishop could enter and speak in the *parlement*. Nowadays they still have the right to enter the court when it is in session, but not to speak, unless they are peers of France or unless they are counsellors of the *parlement*. The only exception is the bishop of Paris who always has entry and voice there.

17. In Rome this right of entering the senate appertained to the priests of Jupiter, called the flamens of Jove. As these had let it be lost through long disuse, it was renewed by Gaius Flaccus. Livy recounts how,[34]

> when Galus Flaccus had entered the senate-house and the prae-
> tor Licinius had conducted him out, he appealed to the tribunes
> of the people. He claimed the ancient right of the priesthood:
> this had been given long since, with the toga and the *praetexta*,
> to the flamen. The tribunes took the view that, while the indol-
> ence of the flamens caused their right to be forgotten, that of the
> priesthood was not thereby lost. And so, against the inclination of
> the praetor but with the general assent of the senators and the
> people, they led the flamen into the senate.

But the other priests, and even the pontiffs, did not have this right by virtue of their quality. So much appears from these passages in Cicero:[35] 'There was a full meeting of the senate and all the high priests who were senators were summoned'; and, 'On the following day, a crowded senate with all [the pontiffs] who were members of this order attending'. The passages indicate that even in the pagan era the senate was honoured by the presence of the high priests.

---

[33] [*Saturnalia*] I.vi. [18–26. The surname 'Praetextatus' was conferred upon a youthful ancestor of Vettius Agorius Praetextatus, one of the twelve chief characters in Macrobius's *Saturnalia*, for showing exceptional discretion in respect of senate business.]

[34] [*Hist.* XXVII. viii.10.]

[35] *Epistularum ad Atticum* IV.ii; *De harispicum responsis* [vii.13].

18. Now, the fact that our bishops who were formerly counsellors of the *parlement* still have deliberative voice there is a residual effect or mark of order rather than of office. The honours and privileges of offices are entirely lost through resignation, but not those of orders by demission. I do not want to argue that our present *parlements* are orders, like the Roman senate. We are credibly told that Roman senators were almost like the councillors of state of today. They were appointed governors of provinces and towns who in this connection were commonly called counts, 'sent as if from the ruler's own retinue'; and the officers of the crown still hold the rank of count by virtue of their offices, and have the right to wear the cloak of a count, as some modern writer has observed.

19. In the same way, the consistory of the cardinals of Rome, which undoubtedly constitutes the first degree of the ecclesiastical order, bears much resemblance to the Roman senate. Just as the senate was the council of the emperor, even of the world which was governed under the Roman Empire, so too is this august consistory the council of the pope, even of the universal church.

20. For it must be carefully noted that the Roman senate at its first institution did not have jurisdiction over disputes between parties, as Bodin has well shown.[36] It served only to deliberate upon public affairs, like the consistory of the cardinals. Polybius's point[37] that it was the senate's responsibility to punish crimes committed in Italy should be understood thus: that complaints about these things were made to the senate which then entrusted judges with their adjudication.

21. For while the general commissioners, chosen annually to adjudicate legal cases and called judges, were usually taken from the body and order of senators, sometimes they were taken from among the knights. On other occasions they were chosen from the senate and the knights, and still other variations might occur, called 'transfers of judges': Hotman distinguishes very neatly between them.[38] At any rate, the senate did not adjudicate as a body, and neither did particular senators simply on the strength of their senatorial status. If they did adjudicate, they did so as chosen judges – that is, as delegated commissaries. This is how Polybius should be interpreted in the

---

[36] [*République*, p. 357.]
[37] [*Histories*] VI. [xiii.4].
[38] *Lexicon iuridicum* [(Paris, 1615), *s.v.* 'transferre', 'translatio' (p. 1169)].

passage which suggests that senators adjudicated crimes; for he wrote of the time when judgements were the senators' concern.

22. Cicero has made it clear that the Roman senate had no corporate jurisdiction on the basis of its own authority. On the question where the accusation against Verres should be brought, he says:[39]

> Where do his associates take refuge? Upon whom shall they call for aid, who should inflict punishment upon Verres? They will come to the senate; but it is not customary, it is not for the senators [to do these things].

As Budé comments,[40] when in the time of the Republic the senate was in its glory, it did not stoop as a body to adjudicate legal cases. Its duties at that time were to direct who should command armies and who should be sent to govern the provinces, to receive and license ambassadors – in short, to arrange and determine almost all aspects of the Republic's affairs.

23. The senate began to adjudicate actions at law, and notably criminal cases, only under the emperors. Standing aside of their own accord, they referred judgement to the senate to condemn or to acquit whoever they chose. The senate normally, by the emperor's permission, deputed judges to deal with the less important cases. Cases of greater consequence they adjudicated as a body, and mostly in the emperor's presence. By Dio's account,[41] Tiberius himself ordered that when cases were adjudicated in his absence the condemned could not be executed for a further ten days, so that he might have time to be informed of it. This recalls Augustus's earlier directive about senate resolutions made in his absence, that they should have no effect until he had authorised them; such is still the present practice in England. From this great body of the senate the same Augustus recruited to attend upon him a privy council, composed of fifteen senators drawn by lot every six months, with whom he himself ordinarily rendered justice. At length, being old and no longer able to go to the senate, he himself chose twenty annual councillors, instead of those fifteen half-yearly ones, says Dio.[42]

24. But Tiberius, his successor, was the first who, with a view to making the senate abandon cognisance of affairs of state, took it into

---

[39] [Cf.] *In Verrem, divinatio* [6–9].
[40] [*Opera B*, III, pp. 83, 86–7.]
[41] [*Rom. hist.* LVII.xx.4.]
[42] [*Rom. hist.* LIII.xxi.4–5; LVI.xxviii.2–3.]

his head to divert it with adjudicating important cases more as a matter of course. Even so, it was not as yet to have cognisance of them by way of ordinary jurisdiction, but only by way of commission and by means of referral from the emperor himself.

25. Subsequently, says Suetonius,[43] Nero gave the senate ordinary cognisance of appeals which formerly were adjudicated by the emperor himself. Tacitus adds[44] that he wanted the penalty for false appeal judged by the senate to be as great as if he himself had adjudicated the matter, though Vopiscus indicates[45] that it was Probus who ascribed cognisance of appeals to the senate. However, this did not last very long, no trace of it being found in our law, except in one instance.[46]

26. In France, in just the same way, Philip the Fair aimed to remove the *parlement* from his retinue. It was at the time the kings' ordinary council and even opposed them quite often. In order delicately to remove cognisance of affairs of state from it, he erected it into an ordinary court and gave it a fixed location in Paris. Still retaining a remnant of its ancient institution, it verifies and confirms royal edicts. The emperor Probus ascribed such a role to the Roman senate, 'that it should hallow by its own decrees the laws which he enacted', as Vopiscus again says.[47] Likewise, the *grand conseil*, which thereafter succeeded the *parlement* as the king's ordinary council, has been reduced to a court, that is, to an ordinary judicial body.

27. Even now, the council of state spends so much of its time on legal proceedings which masquerade as affairs between parties that it is in danger of being made some day into another court and company of judges. It is already divided into three chambers or sessions; one for affairs of state, when it is specifically called the council of state; another for the king's finances, called the council of finance; and the third for cases at law, called the *conseil des parties*.

28. Is it not apparent that each session has its clerks or secretaries to take down its decrees or pronouncements? There are even three kinds of secretaries, to sign the dispatches of each council: the secretaries of commands, for dispatches concerning the state; the financial

---

[43] *Nero* xvii.
[44] *Annales* [XIV.xxviii].
[45] *Probus* [xiii.1].
[46] *Nov. J* 62. [1–2].
[47] [*Probus* xiii. 1.]

secretaries, for those of finance; and plain secretaries, for communications in affairs between parties.

29. Let us return to the power of the Roman senate. So great was it that, in Dionysius of Halicarnassus's summary statement,[48] the entire Republic was in the senate's power, apart only from the power of choosing magistrates, making laws, and absolutely determining peace and war.

30. Polybius discusses at length[49] how it had the conduct and administration of war, the charge of receiving and despatching embassies, the care and general management of public finance. Neither the consuls nor even the ancient kings of Rome were permitted to undertake any business of consequence without the senate's advice. Some have written that because Romulus tried to do this he was torn in pieces by the senators, and this was also the reason why Tarquin the Proud was driven out.

31. As to the number of Roman senators, the diligent Rosinus is probably our best guide.[50] Romulus first created a hundred of them; then he himself added a hundred more, after receiving the Sabines into the city – though some say that this was Tullius Hostilius, after bringing in the Albans. Be that as it may, these first two hundred were called 'fathers of greater lineages' in order to distinguish them from the third hundred, added by Tarquinius Priscus, who were called 'fathers of lesser lineages'. This number of three hundred lasted for a very long time. Whatever some may say, after the kings had been driven out Brutus and Publicola did not add any more, but only replenished and kept up that same number which had been much reduced during this upheaval.

32. The fact remains that Brutus did advance some in place of the old ones who were called 'conscript fathers' – a title which in due course applied to all the senators indiscriminately, after the memory of the first three hundred had been suppressed. A long time later Gracchus, as tribune of the people, doubled the number of senators, placing three hundred knights with them. Sulla added some more, at his whim.

33. Then Caesar added up to nine hundred in all; and after his death the duumvirate appointed to re-establish the Republic added

---

[48] [*Roman antiquities*] VI.lxvi.3.
[49] *Histories* VI. [xiii. 1–6].
[50] [*Rom. antiq.*, pp. 278–9.]

still more, placing in the senate persons of the common sort who were called 'senators *Orcini*', says Tacitus.[51] As there were then a good thousand or twelve hundred, Augustus reduced them to the old number of six hundred.

34. So, if it should have been necessary for all the senators to give their opinions one after the other, business could never have been completed (especially as each one gave his views at any length that pleased him and could meanwhile make new proposals). Decrees of the senate had therefore to be made 'by division', says Capito.[52] After the principals had given their opinion, those who were of their mind went to join them, or at least withdrew themselves apart. This was called 'going on foot to judgement'; and some think that the minor senators who never came forward to give an opinion aloud should be called 'footmen senators'. This is how Varro's remark should be understood, that 'decrees of the senate were made by the carefully considered judgements of individuals, or by division';[53] and when the law says that they were made 'by silence or by assembly', this means that 'the assembly was in silence', as Cujas has interpreted it.[54]

35. As to the number of senators required to make a decree, Sigonius proves[55] that before Sulla's time at least a hundred were needed; before Caesar's, two hundred; and at the beginning of Augustus's empire, four hundred. This always amounts to a third. If this number of senators did not find themselves in favour of the decree, each one of the contrary view could say to the consul or to whoever else presided, 'Count the senate'. But, as Dio reports,[56] Augustus no longer wanted there to be a fixed number to make a decree, but only that it should be made by the majority of those present. By consequence of his ordinance the point was finally reached that fifty senators would suffice. So much may be gathered from this passage of Lampridius:[57]

> He issued no inviolable statute without involving twenty expert jurists and at least fifty other wise men, so that there should be

---

[51] [I.e., 'senators by Caesar's last will and testament': see Suetonius, *Divus Augustus* xxv.1.]
[52] [Gaius Ateius] Capito, in *Noct. Attic.* xiv.vii.[13].
[53] [*Noct. Attic.* xiv. vii.9.]
[54] [*Opera C*, ii, pt. ii, col. 515] on *Nov. J* 62.
[55] *De antiq. jur.*, [pp. 74–8].
[56] [*Rom. hist.* liv.xxxv.1.]
[57] *Alexander Severus* [xvi.1].

no fewer judgements in his council than were needed for a decree of the senate.

Even so, Rosinus shows[58] that the number of all those present at the senate had to be written into the senatorial decree, and the proposer on whose advice it had been issued was specifically noted there.

36. Now the senate had its ordinary days, to wit, the calends, the ides and the nones, from which Augustus removed the ides. On these days the senate was said to be 'appointed by law'; on extraordinary days it was said to be 'announced', and only the principal magistrates could convoke it. The entire senate had to be held in the hours of daylight, not before sunrise nor after sunset; and after ten o'clock nothing more could be proposed.

37. The senate could be assembled only in a temple, and after sacrifice; and proposals about sacred matters had to be made before profane things, says Varro.[59] This shows how religious the Romans were.

38. At first the tribunes of the people, who in a way were examiners of the senate, did not enter it, but held their office at the entrance to it where they examined the decrees and marked those which they approved with the letter 'T'. But at length the senators found it expedient to give the tribunes room amongst them. Nevertheless they did not refrain from obstructing the finalising of decrees, whether by demanding postponement for further deliberation or by intervening and creating opposition.

39. Yet, even when some other impediment occurred to determining decrees – as when there was not a sufficient number of senators, or else when daylight failed before the decision, or when the assembly was held not to be legitimate for some other reason – the outcome reached by those present was still written up. Such a record was called not a 'decree of the senate', but a 'decision with demurrer', and it always served as authority and evidence of the senate's intention. But when the result was decided with no impediment or contradiction it was a decree of the senate and kept thereafter in the public treasury, say Suetonius[60] and Tacitus.[61]

---

[58] [*Rom. antiq.*, pp. 281–[2].]
[59] *Noct. Attic.* xiv.vii.7–9.
[60] [Cf.] *Divus Augustus* [xxxvi; *Divus Iulius* xx.1].
[61] *Annales* iii. [li.3].

40. On the age of senators our books do not agree. Coras says[62] that it was twenty-four years; Fenestella,[63] Sigonius[64] and Manutius[65] say thirty years. The latter opinion seems correct, as the curious reader may see from Langlé's learned proof.[66] True, those who held the great magistracies could attain the degree of senator at an earlier age.

41. Now the senators constituted an order distinct from the rest of the people, and so they had a costume which distinguished them from those others. This was the tunic or undergarment, ornamented and enriched with many little pieces of purple cut in the form of broad studs and called for that reason the 'broad stripe' or 'broad-striped tunic'.

42. The broad stripe itself often signifies the order and dignity of a senator. Suetonius records how Tiberius 'deprived a senator of his broad stripe when he learned that the man had moved to his gardens just before the first of January in order that he might lease a cheaper house in the city';[67] and how Claudius 'even gave the broad stripe to the son of a freedman, though on condition that he should first be adopted by a Roman knight'.[68] That the broad stripe was the mark of a senator also appears from another passage in Suetonius, this time on Augustus:[69]

> When he was assuming the gown of manhood his broad-striped tunic fell at his feet, and there were some who interpreted this as signifying that some day the order of which it was the badge would be subjected to him.

43. That is why this tunic with broad studs is called by the Greeks 'broad-bordered garment', as Herodian says.[70]

44. Just as the broad stripe was the mark of the senator, so was the narrow one the mark of the knight. 'For this reason Paterculus, Maecenas, Agrippa no less, were esteemed by Caesar, but less distin-

---

[62] [Jean de] Coras [*Operae quae haberi possunt omnia*, I (Wittenberg, 1603), p. 47].
[63] [*De magistratibus sacerdotiisque Romanorum* (Cologne, 1607) p. 39.]
[64] [*De antiq. jur.*, p. 76.]
[65] [Paolo Manuzio] *Antiquitatum* [*Romanorum libri duo*, II: *De senatu* (Cologne, 1582), p. 113].
[66] [Jean de] Langlé [*Semestria, senatusconsultis et observationibus* (Paris, 1611), pp. 383–93].
[67] *Tiberius* [xxxv.2].
[68] *Divus Claudius* [xxiv.1].
[69] *Divus Augustus* [xciv.10].
[70] [Cf. *History*] III. [ii.2].

guished; for each of them lived content with the narrow stripe, that is, with the equestrian dignity'.

45. Lampridius notes[71] how 'it was resolved to be enough that senators should be distinguished from knights by the nature of the stripe'. So the tunic distinguished the three orders of the Roman people: to wit, the senators by the broad stripes, the knights by the narrow stripes, [46] and the ordinary people by that which had no stripe and was called 'the sheer or unmarked tunic', the 'tunic of the people'.

47. This is how Juvenal's shaft should be understood:[72]

White tunics are enough for the highest municipal officers

that is, unstriped, for normally the magistrates of Italian towns were neither senators nor Roman knights. Besides, it is certain that Roman citizens ordinarily wore white tunics. Vopiscus observes[73] that Aurelian 'gave to the Roman people white tunics with long sleeves'. And Cicero objects to Verres 'because he used to sit in his workshop wearing a Greek mantle and a grey tunic'[74] – that is, all disguised, because the common dress of the Romans was the toga and the white tunic, on which Lipsius should be consulted.[75]

48. However, Turnebus[76] and Manutius[77] say that the children of senators and of knights used the broad stripe indiscriminately from the time when they took men's robes, specifically from the age of twenty-five years until the age of becoming senators; and if they did not then become senators they took the narrow stripe.

49. But the knights had another mark or insignia: the gold or signet ring. 'Rings', says [the elder] Pliny,[78] 'distinguished the second order from the common people, just as the tunic distinguished the senate from the wearers of rings'. What he has in mind is that the gold ring was common to senators and knights (while the common people wore rings of other metals). So much may be gathered from the fact that

---

[71] *Alexander Severus* [xxvii.3].

[72] [*Saturae* III.179.]

[73] *Divus Aurelianus* [xlviii.5].

[74] *In Verrem* [II.iv.24].

[75] Justus Lipsius, *Electorum* [*liber* I (Antwerp, 1580), pp. 88–93].

[76] [Adrien Turnèbe] *Adversariorum* [*libri triginta*, I (Paris, 1580), pp. 390–1].

[77] [Aldo Manuzio the Younger] *De quaesitis per epistolam* [*libri* III (Venice, 1576)], II, [pp. 40–3].

[78] [*Nat. hist.*] XXXIII. [vii.29].

after the defeat at Cannes Hannibal collected three bushels of rings, which could not have happened if they had been worn only by senators and knights. Livy does report[79] that the person who presented these three bushels of rings to the people told him that only the principal Roman knights wore them; but, he adds, this was said only to gain more admiration for Hannibal's victory. In fact, by Dio's[80] account only senators and knights were permitted to wear gold rings.

50. Pliny also says[81] that at first only senators wore gold rings – and not even all of them, but only those who had been sent on an embassy. The public gave them the ring to serve as a seal, its main usage. Afterwards they wore them for the rest of their lives, for honour's sake, yet only on days and in places of solemn ceremony. Otherwise they usually wore only iron ones, not as ornaments, but to make use of them to seal their letters, their coffers and their doors, as I have discussed in my *Offices*.[82]

51. Pliny, once more, comments[83] on the account in the ancient annals of Rome that after Gnaeus Flavius, son of a freedman and clerk to Appius Claudius, had been made a tribune and Roman magistrate responsible for shows, the Roman nobility gave up gold rings out of spite. His comment is that according to the annals it was the nobility, not the senate, who gave up the rings, and that the former were only the principal members of the senate, as will be explained shortly. He also comments on the remark of another annalist telling the same story, that the senate and the knights gave up their rings and their ornamental horse-armour. The rings, says Pliny, related only to the senate, and the horse-armour to the knights.

52. This tells us in passing that ornamental horse-armour was the ancient mark of the knights, like gilt harness in the France of old. Pliny's conclusion is that in Rome the gold ring was worn at first by the principal senators, and not by the knights.

53. But when the Gracchi had transferred judgements to the knights – that is, when they had ordained that the judges should be taken from the equestrian order – it was then, in Pliny's view, that

[79] [*Hist.* XXIII.xii. 1–2. The reference is to the battle of Cannae, 216 BC.]
[80] [*Rom. hist.* XLVIII.xlv.8.]
[81] [*Nat. hist.* XXXIII.iv.11, vi.21.]
[82] *Offices*, II.iv.[4].
[83] [*Nat. hist.* XXXIII.vi. 17–18.]

they began to use gold rings and seals more habitually and with more justification. It was then too that their order (which until that time was still not clearly distinguished) became quite established, to make a third order in the Republic with those of the senate and the common people, as I said at the beginning of this chapter. Before then it was not an established order, for all those who had the means of making war on horseback were called knights.

54. True, the censors gave a horse at the public expense as a mark of honour to the most distinguished of them who had accomplished some great service or noble act, and even gave such horses to senators.

55. But, having so increased their authority by the transfer of judgements, Gracchus made of the knights a separate order. Now the senate complained that all the power had been taken from it and that only honour pure and simple had been left to it, says Livy.[84] Thereupon, great strife arose between the horsemen and the knights, 'between the military and the city equestrians'. The former were contrasted with the infantry or foot-soldiers, the latter with the senate and the common people of Rome; the former served abroad and in war, while the latter kept their station in the town and in peace. Our modern Frenchmen distinguish them from each other at present, calling the ones *cavaliers* (an Italianised word), and the others *chevaliers*. Therefore these knights of the town wanted to have an emblem other than the horse which was more appropriate to knights of war: the gold ring or seal, assigned to them as judges.

56. Finally, Pliny records,[85] Tiberius ordained that no one should wear gold rings unless he was the son of a free-born father and grandfather, and had four hundred thousand in capital and the right to sit in the fourteen levels of the theatre, these being the other marks of Roman knights. So from then on the order of knighthood was called the right of gold rings. At first that right was given to few people, as may be gathered from the fact that under Augustus there were not enough Roman knights to supply the four divisions of judges. Then the emperors' freedmen, who were usually their favourites and anxious to conceal their own condition, obtained in common

---

[84] [Cf. *Hist.: Pariochae* LX, LXX.]
[85] *Nat. hist.* XXXIII. [viii.32].

this right of wearing gold rings, and even got them for other freed-men. Thus, Dio observes,[86] it became a sort of particular right of freedmen, conceded them by the emperor alone.

57. This is what Pliny means when he says,[87] in his discourse on gold rings, 'that an order intended to be distinct from other men of free birth is being shared with slaves'. In fact, the laws 'on the right of gold rings'[88] tell us that in later times only freedmen asked for it – just as it is said in France that the way to become noble without confessing oneself to be a commoner is to be made a knight.

58. Further, through this right of gold rings freedmen were made tantamount to the free-born and even, it seems, more than free-born, because they constituted a dignity above the free-born pure and simple. However, the truth is that they were not quite free-born, inasmuch as the prince's favour could not prejudice the patron's right over the freedman. So should the laws be interpreted, that by this right 'honour is certainly increased, but native condition is not reduced'; and that 'they lived as freemen, but died as freedmen'.[89]

59. Even so, free-born status was absolutely acquired 'by restitution of birth', though this too was authorised only with the patron's con-sent[90] – a very notable difference 'between the right of gold rings, and restitution of birth'. Finally, Justinian ascribed 'the right both of gold rings and of restitution of birth' indiscriminately to all freedmen whose masters had declared in the relevant acts of enfranchisement an intention that they should be Roman citizens.[91]

60. Yet the fact remains that, before the freedmen had defiled the right of wearing gold rings, Justinian gave status as knights to those who had procured that right, and even gave them leave to sit in the fourteen levels of the theatre reserved for knights. However, they were not true knights and did not have the exercise and functions of judges until they had been entered in the roll of knights. Thus the right was obtained by those who did not have this authority, or who did not have the monetary means and other qualities requisite to be fully-fledged knights – for example, when the dictator Sulla gave it

---

[86] [*Rom. hist.* LIII. xxx.3.]
[87] [*Nat. hist.* XXXIII. viii. 33.]
[88] *Digest* 40. 10; *Code J* 6.8.
[89] *Digest* 38.2.3.
[90] [*Digest* 40.11.]
[91] [Cf.] *Nov. J* [78.1].

to Quintus Roscius, an actor; Verres, to a clerk of his; Julius Caesar, to Labienus, a man of inferior metal. So, just as some who were not senators wore the senatorial tunic and had entry to the senate, likewise some were not true knights even though they wore the ornaments of knights and had the right to sit amongst them in the theatre. At length, as under the emperors there were no longer censors to keep up the roll of knights, only those remained who had obtained this right from the emperor. Eventually the free-born took no heed of it when they saw that it was conferred upon freedmen as a matter of course; and so the order of Roman knights was abolished.

61. The common people who in Rome, as with us, constituted the third estate was again a true order – that is to say, a species of dignity, which is not the case with us. To be a Roman citizen was a quality of no small importance, for it was actually to participate in the state.

62. Furthermore, the Roman citizen had great rights and advantages over persons who were not citizens: to wit, 'rights of civil freedom, kindred, religion, intermarriage, paternal power, ownership, testamentation, guardianship, registered property, military service, taxpaying, suffrage, appointment to public offices'. I will not spend time on explaining them here, as Sigonius explains them very learnedly in his book[92] from which I freely admit to having taken almost all the rest of this chapter.

63. Roman citizens were divided in four ways: 'by tribes, or by registered property, or by families, or by orders' – that is, by districts, or by fortunes, or by lineages, or by orders and occupations. I omit yet another, fifth division which existed in the Republic – to wit, by party or faction, into the 'aristocratic party' (the great) and the 'popular party' (the lesser fry). However, we must note once and for all that, just as the quality of Roman citizen appertained to all three orders of the Roman people, so did these five divisions comprise all the Roman people in general – senators and knights as well as the common people.

64. The districts (called 'tribes' in Rome because originally they were only three) were at first distinguished from each other by differences between races, and then by the cantons and distinct places of the town and territory of Rome. Romulus, who first ordained them, had three sorts of people in his town: local people, who were called

---

[92] *De antiq. jur.* [pp. 21–67].

Albans; the Sabines, whom he overcame and mingled with the rest; and finally, the mixture of other races who had come to take shelter there as refugees.

65. Out of these three sorts of people he made three several tribes, assigning to each one its separate canton to live in. But Servius Tullius, recognising how this distinction of three peoples could cause parties to form and seditions to break out, wanted Rome to be divided only by cantons and regions. He distributed it into four districts, desiring everyone to be identified with the district where he lived regardless of his race of origin.

66. Yet many notable citizens, being addicted to the rustic life, lived in the countryside around Rome and therefore had no district. So Servius Tullius made a further twenty-six districts out of the rural territory, and these were called 'rural tribes'. Consequently, there were then thirty Roman tribes in all, and the number afterwards rose to thirty-five.

67. Finally, the rural tribes came in time to be deemed more honourable than those of the town which were mostly made up of freedmen or artisans. So such notable inhabitants as were left in the former had themselves enrolled by the censors in the rural tribes whilst continuing to live in the town. At length, in making the rolls and distinguishing between tribes attention ceased to be paid to the places where Roman citizens lived. The censors composed the rolls as they willed, very often placing town dwellers in rural tribes in order to honour them, and country dwellers in town tribes in order to single them out and penalise them. It was even a kind of disgrace and punishment to be transferred from a rural to a town tribe, as I will indicate shortly.

68. Each of the four town tribes was made up of ten sub-districts, called *curiae*. These were formed as a means of uniting and assembling the people, solely for religious purposes; hence, no doubt, the derivation of our 'cures', or parishes. I will not spend time on them here: my subject in this work is not religion, but only the temporal body politic.

69. The second division of the Roman people was 'by registered property' – that is, by reference to the means of each and every one, in relation only to finance and tax-gathering. The same Servius Tullius devised it because in his time the tribute levied on the people for the

purpose of wars was paid in equal shares and by poll. Considering this most unfair, he instituted the census, a solemn listing of each citizen's property.

70. This listing being done, he divided all the people into five classes. The first contained those found to have a hundred thousand sesterces clear; the second, seventy-five thousand; the third, fifty thousand; the fourth, twenty-five thousand; and the fifth, eleven thousand. Only the members of these five classes contributed to the tribute. There was also a sixth class, of the poorer sort, and they were called 'proletarians' because they did not contribute to the state otherwise than by multiplying and producing children. They were also called 'those counted by the poll' as they were enrolled only because of their persons and not of their means – though Aulus Gellius draws some distinction 'between proletarians and those counted by poll'.[93]

71. Even so, this second division of the people 'by registered property' was mixed up with the first, 'by tribe'. The six classes occurred under every tribe, and each class was divided again into centuries or hundreds of inhabitants. Thus, in the committees or assemblies of the people which were held for electing magistrates, voting was ordinarily by centuries, for it would have been impossible to gather the votes of all the citizens without this distinction.

72. To turn to the third division of the Roman citizens, which was done by lineages, this was of four kinds: the patricians, the nobles, the new men and the commoners. The patricians were those who issued in the male line from the first two hundred senators instituted by Romulus. These were called 'fathers', though the patriciate was something else entirely under the last emperors: to wit, a title of dignity which I will explain in my penultimate chapter.

73. The nobles were those whose fathers and grandfathers had been successively among Rome's principal magistrates. For this reason they had the right of images, as Sigonius shows very clearly.[94]

74. The new men were those who were beginning to enjoy noble status and who themselves or whose fathers had been among the principal magistrates. I have noted this in my first book *Of Offices*,[95] and will explain it fully later.

---

[93] *Noct. Attic.* XVI.x.[10].
[94] [*De antiq. jur.*, p. 111.]
[95] *Offices*, I.ix.[13–14].

75. Lastly, commoners were of two kinds. The free-born were those 'who could cite a father and a grandfather', as Livy puts it;[96] in other words, they were born of free fathers and grandfathers.

76. Freedmen too, or enfranchised persons, were Roman citizens and enrolled among the tribes. Yet they were not quite citizens. They were called 'citizens by the most favourable law', being by ancient law not capable of voting nor of honours – nor, equally, of military service, for they were not enrolled in the Roman legions except at times of extreme necessity. And as for suffrage and honours, from the first they were not capable of these and could only be beadles for the magistrates and not scribes or clerks.

77. The sons of freedmen had voting rights only among the town tribes and were not capable of enrolment among the rural tribes. But the free-born who were children of freedmen in the sense that they were grandsons of enfranchised persons had every right of suffrage, even among the rural tribes, though they could not be senators or knights nor, consequently, attain the great Roman offices. Their children in turn, however, were capable of all orders and magistracies.

78. All this was the case under the ancient law, as Sigonius demonstrates.[97] But from the time of Appius Caecus the difference between emancipated persons and their children was removed. Thereafter, the terms *libertus* and *libertinus* both signified freedmen, though the difference was preserved that they were called the former in respect of their fathers and the latter in respect of their own status. The effect of this was to place freedmen on the same footing as their children under the old dispensation, and their children on that of the free-born. So at length the term *ingenuus* was applied to all who were born free, and this is how the word is understood in our law.

79. The fourth distinction of the Roman people, by each one's order or occupation, is the most relevant to this discourse. We must note that the common people had several orders and degrees of occupation, some more honourable than others.

80. Here are the main ones, according to their rank: 'paymasters, scribes, merchants, artificers, servants of civil officers, and the mob of the market-place'.

81. Paymasters or quaestors were generally those whom we call financiers, though more particularly those 'who collected money by

---

[96] [*Hist.*] x. [viii.11].
[97] [*De antiq. jur.*, pp. 21–31.]

district and paid out their procurements to the military'. But, as Sigonius shows,[98] Rome's financiers constituted an order which comprised all those who managed public finance or monies, apart from the principal quaestors who alone were magistrates. The financiers of Rome were not officers, as they mostly are with us. Out of all forms of activity, we have made them into offices in order to get money from them.

82. These financiers were also different from tax-farmers or contractors who 'were called publicans' and made an offer for the public revenues, that is, took them in farm wholesale. The former were men of quality and much more highly esteemed than the latter: witness the fact that they were ordinarily of the equestrian order. The same author proves as much, and it also appears from the passage in Pliny noted at the beginning of this chapter.[99]

83. Scribes were those whom we call legal practitioners wearing the long robe, such as our attorneys, clerks and notaries. Although in Rome they were amongst the servants of magistrates, they nevertheless constituted an order separate from that of the other servants, called beadles. They were also much more honourable, as Cicero says of Verres, 'for surely the public accounts and magistrates' writs of judgement are entrusted to those men'.[100] As Roman magistrates were men rather of war than of letters, and as their term of office was short, they had to learn the difficulties of office from the scribes whom they had in their retinues. Consequently, scribes acted so excessively on their own authority that when Cato was public prosecutor he had to rouse himself against them. Plutarch observes[101] how they put themselves on the same footing as magistrates on the pretext that they taught the latter their duties. There were almost as many kinds, even companies, of scribes as of magistrates: to wit, scribes to the quaestor, to the aedile, to the praetor, and so on.

84. Merchants (I take these to signify only persons who sell wholesale and not retail, the latter of whom are hawkers or hucksters, rather than merchants) were of three kinds. Ordinary merchants engaged in Rome in all sorts of wholesale merchandise. They had of old their gild or company, as may be seen in Livy.[102]

---

[98] [*Ibid.*, pp. 83–6.]
[99] [Above, section 3.]
[100] *In Verrem* [II.iii.79].
[101] *Cato the Younger* [xvi. 2–3].
[102] [*Hist.*] II.[xxvii.5].

85. Bankers were called 'money-changers'. Money was their particular merchandise, but meanwhile they conducted all sorts of business involving monetary receipts and outlays. This was very necessary because Roman money was not easily portable, and so business had to be conducted rather by bills of exchange through these bankers than with ready cash. They therefore enjoyed a good many privileges, for they brought great relief to the people; yet it must be noted that 'bankers as such were different from money-changers', again as Sigonius shows very well.[103]

86. Finally, there were those called middle-men, and they were provincial merchants, so called as if they had merely been simple business intermediaries of the merchants of Rome to whom for honour's sake they left the title of merchant.

87. In Rome magistrates' servants, such as 'attendants, translators, public criers, lictors, summoners, etc.', were not fully-fledged offices as they are with us, but a low and base condition of men: so much so that a town (the name of which I do not remember) which had several times rebelled against the Romans was required to supply servants to the magistrates as a perpetual mark of ignominy. These functions, moreover, were performed only by freedmen. At length, however, when under the emperors the freedmen had gained more credit they were placed among the militia.

88. I will defer consideration of the artisans and tradesmen of Rome until later, when I deal with our own. Lastly, as to those whom they called 'the mob of the market-place', these came from the dregs of the people, with no occupation. We used to call them 'the rabble', and the English, imitating our example, use the term 'rascals'; but nowadays our vulgar term for them is 'workmen'. These creatures served at Rome only to generate plots and popular seditions.

89. To conclude this discourse, I must observe that in the Roman Republic the censors were all powerful over the other orders. They made senators and knights by enrolling them, and also unmade them by removing them from the roll. In respect of taxes, it was they again who prepared the rolls as they willed; and so, able as they were to remove senators and knights from those orders, they could likewise remove the common people from the tribe. They could in fact chastise the latter in three ways. One was to transfer them to a [less]

---

[103] [*De antiq. jur.*, pp. 92–5.]

honourable tribe, such as from a rural to an urban district, or from a more highly to a less highly esteemed tribe.

90. Another was to deprive them of voting rights. This was called 'returning to the voting lists of the Caerites' because, while the inhabitants of Caere in Italy had the right to be Roman citizens, they had no right of suffrage, as Aulus Gellius notes.[104]

91. Finally, there was 'reduction to citizenship of the lowest class'. Such persons were stripped of all the privileges of Roman citizens. They were still left in the tribe, but only so that they might contribute to payment of dues, as Sigonius explains fully and learnedly.[105]

---

[104] *Noct. Attic.* XVI.xiii.[7].
[105] [*De antiq. jur.*, p. 106.]

CHAPTER THREE

Of the order of the clergy

1. The three estates of France are very different from those of the Romans. In the first place we have no senatorial order. Budé's comment[1] is very true, that our *parlements* scarcely resemble the Roman senate. The senate was not a body of officers, but an order from which public functionaries of war, justice or finance were ordinarily taken. In France, however, military officers ought to be taken from the order of the nobility; judicial officers are taken indiscriminately from the three estates, apart from the fact that ecclesiastics cannot hold offices of criminal justice; and financial officers are taken from the third estate, because the clergy and the nobility for the most part disdain them.

2. But in this most Christian kingdom we have reserved the first rank of honour for the ministers of God, making the clergy, or the ecclesiastical order, the first of the three estates of France, with good reason.

3. On the other hand, the Romans, being more interested in the state than in religion, did not make of their priests a separate order, but commingled them with the three estates, just as justice is with us. This is how matters are arranged in almost all the states of Christendom. Scarcely anywhere else are the clergy a separate order as is the case in France which has always been more Christian and has honoured the church more highly than has any other nation in the world.

---

[1] [*Opera B*, III, p. 83.]

48

4. In this matter we have followed in the wake of the ancient Gauls, our predecessors. They assigned the first order to the druids, who were their priests, and even made the druids their judges and magistrates. So the entire company of the druids was in Gaul what the senate was in Rome and the clergy is in France. For in France, as in almost all of Christendom, religion has been quite separated from the state.

5. In the order of the clergy, as in each of the three orders or estates general of France, there are several degrees, or subaltern and particular orders, depending subordinately from one another. Further, because the general division of the clergy or ecclesiastical persons is that they are secular or regular, there are several secular orders and several regular ones. At this point it must be noted that the secular orders relate to regular as well as to secular persons; but the regular orders relate only to regular persons because they concern the particular rule and institution of life to which they are dedicated.

6. Here, then, in the first place are the secular orders. First, the tonsure, which is the way into all the ecclesiastical orders. This is what makes the cleric and distinguishes the clergy from the people: shaving the hair, formerly in the way which we nowadays observe amongst altar-boys.

7. This constitutes a public testimony of giving oneself to God by renouncing and cutting off bodily superfluities, notably the hair, which is on the uppermost part of the human body, with which those of the world are apt to bedeck and adorn themselves. By means of this tonsure one becomes a cleric, or, in Greek, 'heir', which is understood in the highest sense of the celestial heritage, acquired through renouncing the terrestrial and worldly heritage.

8. Then come the four orders which we call minor, to wit porters, lectors, exorcists and acolytes; and then the three sacred orders of subdeacons, deacons and priests. Above all those there are, again, the bishops, distributed into bishops, archbishops and primates or patriarchs. Finally, the order of cardinals has been added, though no particular consecration applies to them as it does to all the others, and yet they are rather an order than an office, as shall be shown later.

9. My view of the ecclesiastical orders is not that of the theologians who take orders to signify only those who are appointed and

ordained directly for the precious body of Our Lord. In this sense, order is one of the seven sacraments of the church. Some theologians take only the three sacred orders of subdeacon, deacon and priest to be orders; some of them add the four minor orders; but in general they do not take either the tonsure or the episcopal order to be true orders, even though St Denis indicates otherwise.[2] They draw this distinction, that 'in respect of the real body of Christ there is no order above the priesthood; but in respect of the mystical body of Christ, which is the church, the episcopal is an ecclesiastical order'.

10. But we who consider these things in political terms say, in reviewing all these orders, that the tonsure is undoubtedly an order, or at least the mark and even the form of the ecclesiastical order in general. Those who hold otherwise argue that, as unity is not a number but the beginning of numbers, so the tonsure is not an order but the beginning of orders. The argument is not good, for this reason. Unity is not a number inasmuch as the word 'number' necessarily presupposes several unities which are accumulated and numbered together, whereas a simple unity cannot be numbered. This reason is inapplicable to the tonsure, which can be an order of itself.

11. As for the other orders, they were at first not true orders, but certain functions and ministers of the ecclesiastical order, as their name testifies. The porters kept the door of the church in order to prevent pagans, catechumens and excommunicates from entering. The lectors were those who read the holy books in church so as to keep the people who had come from afar at their devotions in the church until the office or ordinary service began. The exorcists had to do with demoniacs who were very common among the pagans at the time of the early church. The acolytes had the duty of following the bishop and the priests. The subdeacons were those whom the deacons sent hither and thither on church business. The deacons had the principal administration of the church's temporalities. The priests had charge of spiritualities. Finally, the bishops were the heads and superintendents of the church in their dioceses.

12. These, then, were not simple orders with no particular duty nor administration, but functions which were consigned to the usual

----

[2] *PG*, III [col. 505].

clergy in every church. In ancient times the wealth of the church was possessed in common, as I have said elsewhere. Accordingly, each church maintained as many clerics as its revenue could bear; and ecclesiastical duties and functions were distributed amongst them in so regular a fashion that it was necessary to pass step by step via all the lesser ones in order to attain the highest, as had to be done in military bands or companies. Thus all these charges which we call orders related to the degrees by all of which one passed in order, before arriving at that of priesthood. Yet they were still not true orders, because they had public functions annexed to them.

13. For it must be recognised (and this seems to me very noteworthy) that in the early church no one was made priest, deacon or sub-deacon, and not even acolyte, exorcist, lector or porter, unless he had the place of an officiator in some church. I do not call it a benefice, as benefices were not yet in use and the revenue of the church at that time was in common. So when a man received these orders he was not made priest, deacon, subdeacon, acolyte, etc., absolutely and without qualification, but was expressly appointed priest, deacon, subdeacon, acolyte, of such and such a church, to wit, the one in which he was placed and officiated.

14. This was called the title of those promoted to the ecclesiastical orders. A promotion made without title – that is, without specifying a certain church where the promoted person was to officiate – was called 'absolute ordination, that is, unqualified and without title given'. At the Council of Chalcedon [AD 451] (one of the four ancient general councils of which Justinian said that their canons ought to be observed like the four gospels) and then at the Council of Piacenza [AD 1132], it was decided that persons promoted in such a way 'received an empty laying on of hands', and that 'their ordination was utterly invalid'.[3]

15. The priest, then, being ordained particularly to a certain church, seemed to have been ordained only for that one and not for others, and so he was of the lesser orders. Since the character of sacred orders is ineffaceable, this title taken at ordination could not be changed or lost.[4] Hence the origin of what is still said, that ordination is a spiritual marriage contracted between the cleric and his church;

---

[3] *Decretum* D. 70, cc. 1, 2.
[4] *Decretum* D. 66 c. *ult.*: *gl. ord.* [*s.v.* 'ordinatus'].

and from that time it was held that for a priest to leave and change his church was no more licit than for a layman to leave or change his wife.[5]

16. Here, truly, was a fine arrangement! By these means, only as many clerics were made as there were places in the churches to employ them and means to support them. Consequently, there were neither ecclesiastics without churches nor churches without ecclesiastics. No ecclesiastic could suffer poverty nor enjoy excessive wealth; nor could he change his church, nor have several churches.

17. But this fine order has disappeared little by little since positions in churches were converted into benefices through division of ecclesiastical assets and their ascription to each particular place and function. True, only persons in sacred orders had their several shares in this division and constitution of benefices. In various churches some little substance was left in common for the lesser clerics in minor orders who, unlike the others, could not have their distinct shares as they were not yet pledged to a church. But so small were the shares of these younger ones that they were not enough to maintain as many clerics as were needed successively to fill and supply the sacred orders. So (in order to maintain at least a semblance of the ancient rule about progressing via all the minor orders in order to be promoted to the sacred ones) all the minor orders had to be conferred at the same time.

18. The functions of the minor orders were thus abolished, and no trace of them remains except in the case of altar-boys of cathedral and collegiate churches. Nevertheless, the Council of Trent has tried hard to re-establish them, ordaining:[6]

> That the functions of orders from deacon to porter, which were laudably admitted in the church from the time of the apostles, should be restored in accordance with the sacred canons, lest heretics disparage them as useless. Filled with zeal to refurbish the former custom in this matter, the holy synod determines that these functions of the said orders shall not in future be exercised except in accordance with the established laws.

19. Even so, the four minor orders no longer needed to be conferred in terms of the title of some church, as they no longer had any

---

[5] *Decretum* 7 q. 1 c. 11.
[6] *Conc. omn. gen.*, XXXV, p. 566.

function. However, care was always taken to confer holy orders in this way, until the Lateran Council held under Alexander III about the year 1160.[7] This Council found the rigour of the ancient councils reported above, in declaring null and void ordinations made without title, to have been too great, as it could result in dangerous scruples and cast doubt and uncertainty upon the characters of many priests. So the Council ordained that thereafter promotions without title to the orders should not be null, but that the bishop should be bound to maintain those whom he had thus promoted until they were assigned to a benefice capable of providing them with the means of livelihood. Yet it added the amendment which has caused the subsequent disarray in these orders: 'unless such an ordinand could support himself from his own paternal inheritance'.[8]

20. By this pretext, candidates for ordination as priests no longer had to furnish proof of appointment in and support from a particular church, provided they had some patrimony of their own. This property was then called the 'clerical title' because it became customary to say, in appointing to the order, that the specified patrimony should serve as title, again following the same Council's ruling.[9]

21. This is the reason why there are at present so many unbeneficed priests, many of whom beg for their living to the dishonour of the clergy. Our ordinance of Orléans[10] has aimed to remedy this, rating the patrimonial title at fifty *livres* of annual revenue, directing that it should be certified and guaranteed by four bourgeois notables before the ordinary judge of the place, and that it should be inalienable.

22. The Council of Trent has yet again prohibited ordination without title of benefice. It lays down that no one may be promoted 'on title of patrimony', and so renews the penalties of the ancient canons.[11] But the decree is poorly observed in France.

---

[7] [Rightly, 1179.]

[8] *Decretales* 3.5.4,16.

[9] *Decretales* 3.5.23. [1701 adds: Some blame this upon Gratian who, when reporting the canon of the Council of Chalcedon which prohibited absolute ordination [above, section 14], translated the Greek phrase 'in the church of a city or village' into 'in ecclesia civitatis, aut possessionis' instead of saying 'aut pagi'. Thus the ambiguity of this word 'possessio' made the canonists believe that the ancient council approved title by goods or possessions. The fact remains that the invention of this patrimonial title [continues as section 21, omitting 'This'].]

[10] [1561 (art. 12): Isambert, XIV, p. 68.]

[11] *Conc. omn. gen.*, XXXV. pp. 536, 566.

23. The fact is that the custom has been established of maintaining the ecclesiastical orders absolutely and without reference to title, even in respect of those who had no benefice at all. Thereby the ecclesiastical orders have become separated from all benefices and charges of the church. So they have become true and pure orders: that is, dignities without administration nor function other than to serve at the altar.[12]

24. Yet ordinations without title have hitherto been tolerated and authorised only in respect of priests. Hence it has followed that in respect of bishops care is taken not to ordain nor to consecrate them unless they have a bishopric by title of which they can be consecrated and made bishops. In them, therefore, the order and the benefice are conjoined and are virtually one. Even so, owing to the example of other benefices separation of the one from the other is sometimes allowed by special permission of the pope, as when a bishop is licensed to resign his bishopric. This could not be done in ancient times,[13] and afterwards it was permitted only in certain cases.[14]

25. In as much as order is an ineffaceable characteristic, a bishop who resigns his bishopric still remains a bishop as far as order is concerned, though not in respect of benefice as he no longer has a bishopric. The one is thus separated from the other, and bishops are found without bishoprics. This cannot happen with benefices of other kinds which are not orders and benefices together. Nor can it occur with offices: he who has resigned his benefice or his office is simply no longer its beneficiary or office-holder.

26. Now it must be noted that there is only one kind of episcopal order, even though the functions of bishops may be of many different kinds or degrees. In the celestial hierarchy there are many degrees and species of angels who have various names and prerogatives and are, none the less, all angels. Likewise in the terrestrial hierarchy there are several sorts of bishops with various names and different powers. Some are plain bishops with jurisdiction only in their diocese. Others are archbishops who, beyond the primary jurisdiction of their dioceses, also have an appellate jurisdiction in the dioceses of the bishops of their several provinces. Some, furthermore, are primates or patriarchs (in my view there is no difference between these two,

[12] [1701 adds: and to produce an aptitude for possessing benefices.]
[13] Above, note 5.
[14] *Decretales* 1.9.10.

54

other than the name) who have superior appellate jurisdiction over a number of provinces and archbishoprics.

27. Finally, over all primates and patriarchs and consequently over all ecclesiastics, even over all true Christians, there is a sovereign hierarch: the bishop of Rome, whom we call pre-eminently 'pope'. He is the vicar and lieutenant of God in the universal church.

28. As for the cardinals, this – as I have just said – is an order added after the others. Nevertheless, and whatever Baldus may say,[15] it is rather an order than an office. This is partly because through appointment to the cardinalate one gains aptitude for several offices in the court of Rome, and notably for the supreme dignity of the pope. It is also because in the church the holy consistory of the cardinals represents the Roman senate which was an order and not a body of officers.

29. Further, the cardinals *qua* cardinals have no jurisdiction nor any other public function apart from giving their opinions in the consistory, like senators in the senate. And while most of them have titles – that is to say, certain Roman parishes or churches in which they have full jurisdiction, like bishops in their dioceses, as I shall show very shortly – some of them have none. Those who do have it can be said to have benefice and order together, as I have just observed of bishops. In fact, all the properties and marks of orders cited in this book's first chapter apply directly to them.

30. I have said that they represent the Roman senate, and everyone agrees with that. Some trace the origins of cardinals to an ordinance of Constantine the Great,[16] the authenticity of which is much debated by our modern writers. Among them, Alciato holds that it is not authentic,[17] and Génébrard that it is.[18] By this ordinance Constantine, newly converted to the faith and motivated by devotion, ceded the town of Rome to St Sylvester, the pope, declared him to be head of the ecclesiastics, and in that capacity resigned to the latter his imperial ornaments. Then this is what he adds:

> We ordain that men belonging to the distinct order of the most reverend clergy of the holy Roman church shall enjoy that

---

[15] *Commentaria . . . super decretalibus* [(Lyon, 1523)], fo. 56ʳᵒ, col. 1.
[16] *Decretum* D.96 c. 14 [Donation of Constantine].
[17] *Opera*, IV (*Tractates & orationes*) [(Frankfurt, 1617), cols. 403–4].
[18] [Gilbert] Génébrard, *Chronographiae* [*libri quatuor* (Lyon, 1609), pp. 410–11].

supreme power and excellence with the glory of which our senate
is most amply endowed, that is, to rank as consuls and patricians,
and we also pronounce them to be adorned with the other imperial dignities.

In sum, this devout Emperor, declaring that he is transferring his
empire to Constantinople, gives a fine reason for his measures:

> For when the pre-eminence and headship of the Church are
> constituted by the celestial Emperor, it is not right that a terrest-
> rial emperor should have power over it.

31. Now the truth is that for several centuries afterwards the order
of cardinals was not established, at least in the authority which it has
at present. In my view, a good many authors who have written about
this have not explained it well. I will therefore state in a nutshell my
modest conception of the matter, with apologies for stumbling after
so many authorities on so obscure an issue.

32. From the book of Acts[19] we see how the apostles, in order not
to be distracted from spiritual affairs, elected seven deacons to
administer the church's temporal affairs. Hence the origins of our
deacons whose number was limited by the first Council of Rome,
held shortly after that of Nice. Its sixth canon reads:[20]

> That there shall be not fewer than two deacons per parish, and
> seven cardinals of the city of Rome; and that they shall wear an
> undergarment of Dalmatian wool, and an overgarment of wool
> and linen.

The management of the property of the church, amongst other
powers, appertained to these deacons. So their authority grew in
accordance with the clergy's wealth and avarice.

33. The deacons of Rome in particular continually encroached upon
more authority than the others, as they were ministers of the supreme
church, and they gained the right of commonly preceding the priests
of the same church. There is a canon to this effect, from St Jerome.[21]
Being himself a priest of the Roman church, he is at pains to prove
that the deacon is inferior to the priest. He agrees that the custom

---

[19] [vi.1–7.]
[20] *Conc. omn. gen.*, II, p. 155. [The Council of Rome was in fact held immediately before
that of Nice, AD 325.]
[21] *Decretum* D.93 c.23.

of the Roman church is to the contrary, but he says that this is not important 'as the world is greater than the city'.

34. He himself proves on a number of grounds that in several respects the deacon is to be preferred to the priest, and even, says he, to the bishop. In sum, this argument over precedence between priests and deacons is discussed throughout the canon in question, and we gather from the Council of Angers[22] and that of Meaux[23] that it took place in France as elsewhere.[24]

35. In due course, however, the debate proved easy enough to resolve. The custom emerged of making honorary deacons, without office or function other than to assist the priest at the altar. The observance grew exact that one must have this simple order of deacon before becoming capable of being made a priest. By these means, then, the order of deacon was separated from the ancient office and function which had given it precedence over priests. Plain deacons no longer made any difficulty about giving way to priests who, over and above that same order of the diaconate, had also that of priesthood.

36. But those first and principal deacons who, beyond the order, had retained the ancient office and function of managing the property of the church, easily retained precedence over the priests to whom they supplied pensions and maintenance. The sixth synod '*in Trullo*'[25] ruled sharply enough on this debate, 'lest a deacon, however much he may be in dignity, should sit before a priest, unless he had occupied the place of a bishop'.[26] Yet, in order to harmonise the position with this exception, it was held that 'in all things they were the vicars of the bishop'.[27]

37. Once this difference was established between plain deacons 'in order' and those who were in dignity and ecclesiastical office, the latter wished to have a separate name and called themselves

---

[22] [AD 453: Mansi, VII, col. 901 (c. 2).]
[23] [AD 845: Mansi, XIV, cols. 811–42 (the Council's eighty canons contain none explicitly to this effect).]
[24] [1701 adds: Although it was decided clearly enough in favour of the priests, by the general and well-known ruling of the Council of Nice, it still lasted for a long time after that.]
[25] [I.e., the *Concilium 'Quintisextum'* held at Constantinople in a domed hall (*trullus*) of the imperial palace, in AD 692.]
[26] [Mansi, XI, col. 943 (c. 7).]
[27] *Decretales* 1.23.1.7.

archdeacons, or cardinal deacons. This may be seen in St Gregory:[28] 'If a freedman is not yet made a cardinal deacon, he ought not to take precedence over those ordained by you'; and, a little later, 'but if his request should find favour with you, you shall be able to make him a cardinal'. Elsewhere St Gregory is reported[29] to have allowed Fortunatus, bishop of Naples, to make a deacon called Gratian a cardinal of the church in Naples.

38. Yet the deacons in office in the Roman church had always wanted to be greater than the rest. Having been of old tantamount to directors and superintendents of the universal church, they were not content with the title of archdeacon which those of simple bishoprics had. At length they alone called themselves cardinals, meaning the principal archdeacons. This is the term used by the ancient Council of Rome,[30] the oldest authority that I have read on the matter.

39. Hence it follows that the first cardinals of Rome were the deacons of the Roman church. But as time went by the officiating priests of that place wanted a share of this magnificent title and to be called cardinal priests. They held that the name of cardinal, which is taken to mean principal or universal (because the Roman church was the principal and universal), ought to appertain to priests as well as to deacons: just as in cathedral churches there were archpriests as well as archdeacons.

40. In certain archiepiscopal churches, too, the officiating priests, whom at present we call canons, began to call themselves cardinals; this happened at Ravenna, at Compostella, and elsewhere. In due course it became ridiculous, like the 'king of Yvetot';[31] yet there are authorities[32] where the canons of cathedral churches are indiscriminately called cardinals.

41. Finally, the ordinary suffragan bishops of the pope, who are those of the province and particular territory around Rome, wishing not to yield precedence to the priests of the Roman church, wanted also to be called cardinals. It is true enough that in the same St Gregory and other ancient ecclesiastical authors of his time 'cardinal's priest'

---

[28] Gregory the Great, *Operum*, IV [(Paris, 1605)], col. 42 (*Epistola* LXXXI).

[29] [*Decretum* D.71 c.5.]

[30] [AD 324, c.6: 'diaconi cardinales urbis Romae' (*Conc. omn. gen.*, II, p. 155).]

[31] *Decretum* 32 q.2 c.1: *gl. ord.* [*s.v.* 'principem mundi'. The phrase which Loyseau renders 'ainsi que le Roy d'Ivetot' is the untranslatable ' sicut rex scacorum'.]

[32] [François] Duaren, *De sacris ministeriis ac beneficiis libri* VIII [(Paris, 1551), p. 70].

signified someone who was standing in for a bishop – in a phrase, a commendatory bishop;[33] this would be worth a longer discussion.

42. But in the end deacons in the church of Rome were made without title, just as they were in other churches and dioceses. So the number of cardinals, deacons and priests is not at present certain, but depends on the will of the pope. Yet some consider that all the cardinals together ought not to exceed seventy, which was the number of our Lord's disciples; and, again, that there might be a certain number of titles of these cardinals – to wit, six of bishops, twenty-eight of priests, and twenty of deacons, which are listed by Petrus à Monte[34] and variously by Onufrius.[35]

43. Even so, as popes were desirous of gratifying their favourites with this high dignity when there was no vacant title, they hit upon the device of making them cardinals 'in expectation of title', as Jean André tells us.[36] He also says that in his time Pietro Colonna was cardinal without title, and that the latter called himself 'cardinal of the holy Roman church until he should recover the title of St Angelus'.

44. Likewise, before the Council of Trent the pope made canons in cathedral or collegiate churches in countries obedient to Rome 'in expectation of a prebend, for the purpose of obtaining a dignity', or else to be assured of the first vacant prebend.[37]

45. But in as much as the fashion of making bishops without title has not yet arrived in the church, the number of cardinal bishops has remained, as of old, six: to wit, of Ostia (who is always doyen of the cardinals), of Sabine, of Porto, of Frascati, of Palestrina, and of Albano.

46. So the cardinals who have title – meaning, some church or benefice to serve – are bound to reside in it unless they are dispensed from that requirement. Thus the canon[38] of Leo IV which records that 'Anastasius, cardinal's priest of the title of St Marcellus, is deposed by the canonical synod for five years' absence from his parish, contrary to the canonical statutes'.

---

[33] *Decretum* 7 q. 1 c.42.

[34] [*De primatu Papae et maiestate Imperatoris*, in *Tractatus universi juris*, XIII, pt. i (Venice, 1584), fo. 151ʳᵒ.]

[35] [Onofrio Panvinio, *De episcopatibus, titulis & diaconiis cardinalium* (Paris, 1609), pp. 8–36.]

[36] *Speculum clarissimi viri Gulielmi Durandi* (Basle, 1563), II, p. 67, col. 1 (*additio* f).

[37] *Decretales* 3.5.9; 3.8.3 [cf. 3.8.8].

[38] *Decretales* 3.4.2.

47. For their benefice is reputed a benefice-cure. This is the root cause why in France promotion of a bishop to the cardinalate provides an opening for the right of regale, as M. Le Maistre proves.[39] By common law, and regardless of papal dispensation (of which no account is taken in matters of regale), the bishopric is vacated through such a promotion. However, at present the relevance of the regale in this connection is otherwise explained: to wit, that the cardinals are papal councillors, that the pope is a temporal prince, and that such a role is prohibited to bishops of France because of their oath of loyalty to the king.

48. In fact, the cardinals have so much power in their titles or churches that they can use episcopal ornaments there even though they may not be bishops, and may even confer minor orders. In short, they have all the honourable rights of bishops.[40]

49. I will not spend time on reviewing their other privileges and prerogatives. The main one is this. Just as the election of plain bishops, which in the early church was done by the clergy and the people together, has in the end been left entirely to the clergy of the cathedral church, so has the election of the pope been at last left peacefully to the cardinals, by the common consent of the whole church and, notably, of the German emperors, the kings of France and the people of Rome, who respectively pretended to this right.

50. This was decreed[41] in the time of Nicolas II in the year 1059, ordaining, moreover, that the pope should be elected from among the cardinals. And afterwards, in about 1245 Innocent IV gave them the red hat, and Paul II the scarlet robe as an adornment and sign of their order, whether instead of the Roman senators' purple or of the priests' *dibaphus* which Cicero mentions;[42] or so that this garment should continually remind them to be always ready to shed their blood for the faith.

51. It therefore follows that our painters avail themselves of the privilege common to them and to poets when they paint St Jerome with the scarlet cap and robe, given that he lived under and wrote several epistles to Damasus, more than nine hundred years before Innocent

[39] [Gilles] Le Maistre [*Decisions notables* (Paris, 1566), fos. 31vo–35ro].

[40] Hostiensis [*In tertium Decretalium: De praebendis & dignitatibus* (Venice, 1581), XIX. 2, 3]; Jean André, *Speculum clarissimi viri*, II, p. 92, col. 1.

[41] [*Decretum* D.23 c.1.]

[42] *Epistularum ad Atticum* [II. ix.2]; *Epistulae ad familiares* [II. xvi.*fin.*].

IV. Although he was a priest of the Roman church, nevertheless in his time those priests did not yet call themselves cardinals. St Augustine says in his epistle to St Jerome that 'although according to the accustomed terminology a bishop is greater than a priest, yet Augustine is less than Jerome'. So the canon records;[43] but this must be construed as a piece of self-deprecation or civility in respect of the particular merit of persons, not a comment on the rank of their dignities. Gratian too understands it in this way, saying, 'This should be interpreted as relating not to ecclesiastical office and dignity, but to purity of life and sanctity of conversation'.[44]

52. In fact, the gloss on this same canon[45] indicates that the dignity of bishop is greater than that of cardinal. Certainly it was more highly esteemed in ancient times.[46] But with the passage of time two things have raised the cardinals above the bishops. First, almost all the cardinals are bishops, and there are hardly any others. Secondly, not only do the cardinals elect the popes, but also the supreme dignity of the pope is particularly associated with them. So it is true to say that they participate by aptitude and by expectation in both the spiritual and the temporal sovereignty of the Holy See, as do the princes of the blood in the temporal sovereignty of their country.

53. This is why they are regarded as princes of the church and now walk everywhere in the rank of princes. Further, the papal formulary in creating cardinals is to say of them, 'Be thou my brothers and princes of the world', as in the case of Antoninus, archbishop of Florence.

54. So much for the secular orders of the clergy. As for the regulars, these are not arranged one above the other like the degrees of the seculars, but are quite different and separate orders. In my view, they consist of five different kinds: the hermits, the religious, the regular canons, the mendicants, and the knights' fraternities.

55. I have placed the hermits first as they are the most ancient. The Greek name for 'monk', signifying 'solitary', appertains properly to them. They are the ones who, in emulation of Helie[47] or of St John

---

[43] *Decretum* 2 q.7 c.34.
[44] [*Decreti divi Gratiani* (Lyon, 1572), col. 693.]
[45] *gl. ord.*[see under 'Augustinus'].
[46] *Decretum* 2 q.4 c.2.
[47] [Possibly Elias, fourth-century hermit of near Antinous, capital of the Thebaid (*PL*, LXXIII, col. 1154, and XXI, col. 432).]

the Baptist, retired into the deserts to apply themselves more freely
to contemplation. They are also called 'anchorites', or 'those retired
from the world', and 'hesychasts', or 'the quiet ones'. The first of
these were St Paul in the district of Thebes and St Hilarion in
Palestine. Some would place St Jerome in this order because he
retired into the deserts of Egypt. These hermits have never been
bound by the three vows. They are still, I believe, not bound in this
way, few genuine ones as there are nowadays (for I do not reckon
amongst them those wanderers and supplicants who take their name
and garb in order to beg). Further, they have no certain rule of life,
but they form it, add to it and depart from it as the spirit moves
them. They even abandon it altogether when they choose, and without censure, though not without some mark of inconstancy. In Justinian's time such conduct was general amongst all monks.[48]

56. I call 'religious' those who have a certain rule of living in a
community. In our books they are termed 'coenobites' and 'companions'. The order seems to have been introduced into Christianity in
imitation of the Essenes who were a very devout Jewish sect. Their
mode of life, which Philo recounts at length,[49] was very similar to
that of our religious. It was first practised by St Antony in the district
of Thebes, by St Benedict in Italy and by St Basil in Greece.

57. St Basil was the first to bind them by the three vows which we
say are essential to religion: to wit, obedience, chastity and poverty.
In a word, the vows constitute a resignation and abandonment, in
honour of God, of the three kinds of wealth with which man is
endowed in this world: obedience in respect of the soul; chastity, of
the body; and poverty, of the goods of fortune. There are so many
of these orders, or such a variety of rules, that to review them all
would be a lengthy and inconvenient business. Polydore Vergil relates
most of them,[50] as does the Italian book entitled *Piazza universale*.[51]

58. In ancient times these religious were not promoted to the ecclesiastical orders: 'a cleric's motive was one thing, a monk's another',
says St Jerome.[52] So when they were promoted they had to quit the

---

[48] *Nov. J* 5.4.
[49] In Eusebius, *Evangelicae praeparationis* [ed. E. Gifford (Oxford, 1903), I, pp. 482–9, and II, pp. 409–15].
[50] [*De rerum inventioribus, libri octo* (Basle, 1554), pp. 477–501.]
[51] [Tommaseo Garzoni] *La piazza universale* [*di tutte le professioni del mondo* (Venice, 1605), pp. 63–9. I am grateful to Dr Judith Bryce for help in identifying this work.]
[52] [*PL*, XXII, col. 352.]

monastery,[53] even though they were incapable of performing ecclesiastical functions outside the monastery. When St Augustine appointed to the religious life the officiating priests of his church of Hippo who were charged with administering the sacraments and other ecclesiastical functions, he called them not monks, nor religious, but canons. This meant that they were subjected to a certain rule of life, a mixture of the clerical and the purely monastic. It was called the apostolic life because the Apostles lived in common, observed poverty, obedience and chastity, and furthermore administered the sacraments. This is why St Thomas traces the origin of the regular canons to the Apostles, and says that St Augustine only renewed and re-erected the order.[54]

59. At all events, this order was found to be so useful and so honourable that in due course there was no cathedral church which did not have its canons. From that first institution they all lived as religious. They were bound by the three vows and even kept to the cloister. Our proofs of this are their cloisters, the name of brother by which they called each other, their winter cope equipped with a cowl, their chapter bread, their canonical hours and their nocturnal matins, which still remain in some churches: in a word, they used their income in common. But little by little, as their affluence induced them to relax this austerity, they were dispensed from poverty when ecclesiastical wealth came to be shared out, and consequently from the obedience in which the cloister plays its part. Thus they have converted their order into a benefice.

60. Therefore, those who adhered to the arrangements of their first institution and to observance of the rule of St Augustine were called regular canons. They were distinguished from the others who no longer observed their rule and were called seculars. Strictly, however, 'canon' and 'regular' signify the same thing, the one in Greek and the other in Latin: so that, in truth, it is a superfluous duplication, 'and a tautology'.

61. Subsequently the mendicant orders appeared. Beyond the vow of poverty (which binds the religious only in several, for they can hold in common as many possessions as they can find), these have vowed mendicity – that is, to live only by alms. The difference

---

[53] *Decretum* 16 q. 1 cc. 2, 8, 10, 11.

[54] [*Contra impugnantes Dei cultum et religionem*. 17, in *Opuscula theologica*, II, ed. R. M. Spiazzi (Rome, 1954), p. 10.]

between 'poor and beggar', between the indigent and the mendicant, is common knowledge. Accordingly, these orders avowed mendicity in several as well as in common, and are incapable of possessing any property at all.

62. Finally among the regular orders come those of the knights' fraternities: those of St John of Jerusalem whom we call Hospitallers or Knights of Malta; the Teutonic Knights; the Knights of the Sword; the Knights of Jesus Christ; the Commanders of St Antony; those of St Lazarus; and others like them.[55] The Templars, whom Clement V condemned wholesale,[56] are no longer to be mentioned. I call all of these knights fraternal or knights religious in order to distinguish them from the lay knights of the nobility with whom I will deal in the next chapter.

63. These are at one and the same time monks, in as much as they are bound by the three vows; and knights, in as much as they profess to fight for the defence of the Christian religion. Here is how St Bernard puts it:[57]

> So they live in a marvellous and singular manner, in order that they may be gentler than lambs and fiercer than lions. I therefore consider it doubtful whether to call them monks or soldiers. Perhaps a more appropriate name should be found, a name suggestive neither of the one thing nor the other, neither the mildness of a monk nor the bravery of a soldier.

64. This double nature of theirs has often induced changes in our French law. Formerly it was held that they could inherit absolutely, given that they obtained a dispensation or permission both from the pope and from the king. Then they were allowed to inherit only by usufruct.[58]

65. At present it is held that they do not inherit at all, as was adjudicated by the solemn decree of Christmas 1573. In this respect, then, they are reduced to the condition of monks who do not inherit in

---

[55] Polydore Vergil [*De rerum inventioribus, libri octo* (Basle, 1554), pp. 501–7; Garzoni] *Piazza universale* [pp. 70–3].

[56] [Strictly, suppressed rather than condemned, by the decree *Vox in ecclesio* (22 March 1312) read (3 April) in the second session of the Council of Vienne (Mansi, xxv, cols. 389 *et seq.* I owe this point to Professor J. A. Watt.]

[57] [*Opera*, iii, eds. J. Leclerq and H. M. Rochais (Rome, 1963), p. 221.]

[58] [Jean] Papon [*Recueil d'arrêts notables des cours souveraines de France* (Paris, 1584), p. 72 (vi)].

France, nor does the monastery inherit for them. They cannot even give it anything when they enter it: and yet, by Roman law, not only does the monastery inherit, but it even acquires all the wealth which they had when they entered it.[59] Conversely, relatives do not inherit from knights fraternal, no more than they do from monks, but the knights' savings belong to their religion after their death.

66. However, a religious who is made a bishop or a cardinal, and is thereby exempt from the jurisdiction of a monastery and the rigour of its rule, can inherit and be inherited from. So much was adjudged in 1585 by solemn decree concerning the deceitful Dominican, bishop of Châlons.[60]

67. I understand this to be so only in respect of professed religious. For novices are not true religious, as they are not yet bound by the three vows of religion. It must be observed that literal proof of their profession is necessary in order to exclude them from inheriting, following the express decision in the Edict of Moulins.[61]

68. This is very dangerous. In most religious cases, acts of profession are not made before notaries; the professed person is merely made to sign, either in the register of the monastery or on a separate paper. If the monastery should suppress this writing through avarice, or the professed one do so through malice, someone who has been a monk for ten or twelve years shall be admitted to sue for his relatives' inheritances. He may even apostasise, even throw his cowl into the nettles, as the saying is. So much for the religious who often take advantage of this pretext: let whoever has an interest in the matter take note.

[59] *Code J* 1.2.
[60] Following the express decision in *Decretum* 18 q.1 c.1.
[61] [1566] art.55 [Fontanon, I, fo. 617].

CHAPTER FOUR

Of the order of nobility in general

1. Nature herself has so distinguished between various plants and beasts that in one and the same species some are free and domestic, while others are rustic and wild. As they infallibly retain these qualities in propagating themselves, the wild never beget the domestic, nor vice versa. Further, it is naturally the case that plants and beasts retain the quality of their seed, because their vegetative or sensitive soul proceeds absolutely 'from the power of matter', say the philosophers. But the rational soul of men comes immediately from God, Who created it expressly when He sent it into the human body. So it has no natural participation in the qualities of the generative seed of the body where it is relegated.

2. That is why almost all the most admired philosophers and poets astonish me by not attending to this difference of souls. They have deluded themselves that there are certain principles of virtue which are transferred from fathers to children by the act of begetting. Witness the sorites or induction of Socrates[1] who concluded that, as the best-bred apple, wine or horse was the best, so is it with the man of most noble lineage. Aristotle, too, says[2] that all nations honour and esteem nobility because of the likelihood that whoever is excellent is born of excellent parents; and therefore he defines nobility as 'excellence of birth', virtue of lineage. As for the poets, Homer says[3] of Telemachus that the virtue of his father, Ulysses, was instilled in him, meaning that the substance of his father's virtues flowed into

---

[1] [Cf. Plato, *Republic*, v. 459–60.]
[2] *Politics* 1283ᵃ34–7.
[3] [*Odyssey* IV. 204–11.]

him with those few drops of the latter's seed. These are Plutarch's very words;[4] and it is also what Horace sings to us:[5]

> By the strong and the good are the strong begotten.
> The virtue of the sire is in young bullocks, is in horses,
> Nor do fierce eagles beget the timid dove.

3. The comparison is none the less false, and the similitude highly unlikely. As one sees often enough, the children of honest folk are hardly worth anything, and those of learned men are ignorant; witness the Greek proverb, 'The children of heroes are a bane'.[6] If their moral behaviour should sometimes be found to tally with their fathers', this proceeds not from procreation, which contributes nothing to souls, but only from education. On this count, indeed, the children of the well-off are much more likely to be virtuous. They are given careful instruction; their fathers provide them with a continual and pregnant example; they are under an obligation not to degenerate from nor to belie their lineage; and, finally, the memory of their ancestors secures standing and a good reputation for them.

4. Yet, whether they are presumed heirs to paternal virtue or because they continue to reap the rewards which that virtue merits, the fact remains that persons of good descent have at all times and among all the nations of the world been more highly esteemed than others. Thus they have constituted a certain order and degree of honour separate from the rest of the people. Dionysius of Halicarnassus tells us[7] that the people of Athens were divided into those he calls 'aristocrats' and those he calls 'populace'. He says that Romulus followed the same division in Rome; and it is certainly true that Romulus divided his subjects into senators (whom he called 'fathers') and the people.

5. But with the passage of time the descendants of these first fathers or senators (called patricians) whom Romulus chose wanted it established that only they might be made senators and consequently have senatorial dignities and charges – sacrifices, magistracies, virtually the entire administration of the state. In fact, they alone did enjoy

---

[4] In [John] Stobaeus [*Sententiae ex thesauris graecorum delectae* (Antwerp, 1551), fo. 372ʳᵒ].
[5] [*Carminum* IV.iv.29–33.]
[6] [Erasmus, *Adagiorum* I.v.32, in *Opera omnia*, II (Hildesheim, 1961), col. 235.]
[7] [*Roman antiquities* II.viii.]

these under the kings. During that time patricians and plebeians were so distinguished from each other that their descendants did not intermarry at all; and when the people were convoked the patricians were all called severally by name and by that of the founder of their lineage.

6. But, after the kings were expelled, the common people, being far more numerous than the patricians, gained much more authority, because everything was decided according to the number of voices in general assemblies. So, little by little, the people took from the patricians all their advantages. Roman history shows that they were admitted indiscriminately, first into the senate, then to the magistracies, after that to the consulate, even to the dictatorship, and finally to sacrificial responsibilities. Thus the patricians no longer retained any prerogative other than the glory of being descended from the first and most ancient families.

7. When contentions arose from time to time between the patricians and the common people, those of the popular party sought to disparage their opponents' dignity and proceeded to quibble, maladroitly enough, about the latter's name. They said that whoever could lay claim to a father and grandfather, meaning whoever was born of a free father and grandfather (for serfs were never heads of families), was a patrician. This is the pronouncement of Publius Decius Mus:[8] 'Have you ever heard how patricians were first made? They were not sent from heaven, but were those who could cite a father and grandfather: that is, nothing other than free-born persons'. Cincius, as reported by Festus,[9] puts it in the same way: 'Those who used to be called patricians are now called *ingenui* [free-born]'.

8. Indeed, the Latin word *ingenuus* – which is composed of *in*, meaning 'above', and *genus* – properly signifies a person who has something in particular above lineage. It refers directly to the Greek for 'well-born' which means someone who is of good ancestry: so that 'nobility of birth' properly means 'goodness of ancestry', 'excellence of race' according to Aristotle,[10] which we can translate as 'generosity'.

9. Now, two degrees of excellence of lineage are conceivable, and almost all nations recognise them. They are, ancestry free from

---

[8] In Livy, [*Hist.*] x [viii.10].
[9] [*De verb. signif.*, p. 277.]
[10] [Above, note 2.]

blemish, and ancestry adorned with dignity. As Horace said,[11] the first degree of wisdom was to be free from folly – and of virtue, to be free from vice. Some philosophers have observed that to be insensible or destitute of trouble was a kind of bliss. So 'well-born', which refers to both kinds of excellence of lineage, means someone born of parents who were, on the one hand, adorned with dignity and, on the other, exempt from servitude. So ambiguous an expression baffled Galen's translator, dealing with this passage in his book on maladies of the spirit:[12]

> It is not excellence, but chance that renders one the world's wealthiest man. Chance it is that makes even slaves and freedmen wealthier than those of us who are called high born.

Here the translator uses 'gentlemen and noblemen' instead of 'high born', whereas he ought to have used *ingenuos*.

10. The Romans employed the term 'nobility' to signify the second degree of excellence of lineage, which consists in dignity. So they scarcely used the term *ingenuus* except to signify that other degree which consists in exemption from servitude. Its opposite, *libertinus*, then included all those who were descended, however remotely, from a liberated or freed man, as Antonius Vacca shows.[13] This was mainly the case when these terms related to races or families, so that a 'free family' was one whose founding father was free, and a 'freed family' one where he was *libertinus*. But subsequently, and until the time of Appius Claudius, an *ingenuus* was someone born of a free father and grandfather, as in that passage from Livy already cited;[14] and a *libertinus* was a freedman's son.

11. Finally, in the time of our jurisconsults, *libertus* and *libertinus* signified the same person, called by the first of these terms in relation to his patron and by the second in relation to others. Similarly, *ingenuus* meant someone born strictly of a free father and thus born free, as the Institutes say.[15] This diversity of meanings is clearly expressed by Suetonius in his life of Claudius:[16]

---

[11] [*Epistolarum* I.i.41.]
[12] *Claudi Galeni Pergameni* [*Scripta minora*, ed. J. Marquarat (Leipzig, 1884), I, pp. 38 *et seq.*].
[13] [*Expositiones locorum obscuriorum et paratitulorum in Pandectas*, I (Lyon, 1554), p. 65.]
[14] [Above, at note 8.]
[15] *Inst. J* 1.5.
[16] *Divus Claudius* [xxiv.1].

Being fearful of criticism because he had given the broad stripe to the son of a freedman, he said that Appius Claudius, the censor and founder of his family, had appointed the sons of freedmen to the senate, but he did not know that in Appius's time and for some time afterwards the term *libertini* meant, not those who had been emancipated, but their free-born sons.

12. From then on the term *gentilis* was used to describe someone born of a family free time out of mind. Formerly that term had signified a distant relation of unimpeachably free ancestry. So much may be gathered from this fine extract from Quintus Mucius [Scaevola] which Cicero records:[17]

> *Gentiles* are those who have the same name in common and are sprung from free-born ancestors none of whom was ever in slavery nor ever suffered loss of civil capacity.

On this passage Boethius comments:[18]

> *Gentiles* are those who have the same name in common, such as Brutus, or Scipio. If they are slaves, there can be no gentility. If the grandsons of freedmen are called by the same name, there can be no gentility. For gentility is derived from free birth of ancient standing.

This is why Gaius says that ' *Gentilitas* cannot apply to freedmen or slaves'.[19]

13. It follows from this that there were three degrees of that first kind of excellence of lineage which consists in remoteness from servitude. They were *ingenui* who were born of free parents; *gentiles*, whose lineage was free time out of mind; and patricians, descended from the first two hundred senators instituted by Romulus and, as some hold, from the other hundred instituted by Tarquinus Priscus and called, they say, 'patricians of lesser lineages'.

14. So much for the free-born in Rome. As for nobility of dignity, which is what they called nobility proper and of which they took most account, it was gained only by means of the principal offices of their Republic. These they termed 'major magistracies', 'curule magistracies' or 'magistracies of the Roman people': to wit, the offices of

---

[17] *Topica* [vi.29].
[18] [*PL* LXIV, col. 1104.]
[19] [Cf. Gaius, *Institutes* III.17, I.164a.]

aedile, quaestor, censor and others, none of which could be conferred save by the general assembly of the people in which perfect sovereignty resided. The presumption was that, from among the thousands who might aspire to these prime charges of the state, no one could attain them unless he was avowed and recognised by all the people as being endowed with eminent virtue.

15. It is true that at first only patricians were capable of these great offices, and so by consequence only their descendants were capable of nobility. Thus, not even all senators were noble: so much is evident from this passage in [the elder] Pliny where he says that, although the freedman Gnaeus Flavius had been made curule aedile and therefore noble, 'rings were entrusted to the nobility, not to the entire senate, as is written in our ancient annals'.[20] But since the time when the common people were admitted to great offices, nobility was by consequence communicated to plebeians. This is what Livy says on the intrigue to admit plebeians to the consulship:[21]

> From then on the plebeians participated in all the things in which the patricians surpassed them: authority, honour, martial glory, birth, nobility – great things for them to enjoy, greater still to bequeath to their children.

In fact, Asconius remarks[22] that Cicero had three [sic] competitors for the consulship, two patricians and four plebeians, two of those four plebeians being nobles by lineage and the other two 'new men'. 16. It is Plutarch who tells us[23] that those who were the first of their line to attain these offices were called 'new men'; that is, newly ennobled and the first nobles of their lineage. Marcus Cato was one such, and Cicero another. Although Plutarch maintains[24] that Cicero was descended from the royal line, 'indisputably from King Tullius', nevertheless he always acknowledged himself to be a new man and never commended himself in terms of blood; yet he himself says[25] that, 'being elected aedile, I obtained the right of handing down my ancestral image to posterity'.

---

[20] *Nat. hist.* XXXIII.[vi.18].

[21] *Hist.* VI [xxxvii.11].

[22] [Quintus] Asconius [Pedianus, *In Ciceronis orationes commentarii* (Venice, 1498), sig. b.v^{ro}].

[23] *Marcus Cato* i.2.

[24] [Cf.] *Cicero* [i. 1; according to Plutarch, while Cicero's mother was well born nothing certain is known of his father's ancestry].

[25] *In Verrem* [II. v. 14].

17. For the visible mark of this nobility consisted in having the right of ancestral image: that is, to be able to place one's bust in the most conspicuous place in one's house. This was permitted only to those who had such great offices. Their posterity carefully preserved those images, decorated with the insignia of their magistracy and with their exploits inscribed around them: the whole thing enclosed in a wooden cupboard for conservation. These cupboards were opened on feast days; and at family funerals all the images were carried in great solemnity, as Polybius,[26] Pliny[27] and Juvenal[28] describe. So these images made the family egregious and remarkable and, consequently, noble. 'Certainly', says Varro, 'it is the well-known who are said to be noble'; the term's synonyms are 'manifest', 'distinguished', 'recognised', and its antonyms 'obscure', 'unknown', as Tiraqueau has amply shown.[29] And Cicero accordingly remarks[30] that 'nobility is nothing other than acknowledgement of virtue'.

18. The fact is that the nobility of Rome consisted in this right of images and arose only from great offices, as Sigonius has very learnedly demonstrated.[31] And this nobility appertained only to the Romans, as Cicero observes:[32] 'While noble quality formed of virtue is peculiar to philosophers, that which springs from images is peculiar to the Roman people', and no [other] nation has ever used it in this way.

19. It is true (as I have already said in my treatise on *Offices*)[33] that those who were descended from ancestors distinguished by military valour could be considered noble. Plutarch confirms this in his life of Cato[34] who, when he was called a new man, replied 'that he was indeed new in respect of offices of the Republic, but he claimed to be noble by lineage in respect of his ancestors' feats of arms'. Sallust, too, remarks on the nobility of the ancient Romans:[35]

---

[26] [*Histories*] VI. [liii. 1–5].

[27] *Nat. hist.* XXXV. [ii. 6].

[28] *Saturae* [VIII. 1 *et seq.*].

[29] *De nobil.*, pp. 16–21.

[30] [*Fragmenta epistolarum*, VII (in The *Correspondence of M. Tullius Cicero*, eds. R. Y. Tyrrell and L. C. Porter, VI (Dublin, 1899), p. 301).]

[31] *De antiq. jur.*, p. 111.

[32] 'in the same letter' [i.e., to Hirtius, much of whose correspondence with Cicero is now lost; cf. above, note 30].

[33] I. [ix. 14].

[34] *Marcus Cato* [i. 2].

[35] *Bellum Catilinae* [VII. 6].

So they deemed it high fame and great nobility to strike down the enemy, scale a wall, and be seen whilst performing such a deed.

And Pliny tells us[36] that, just as true nobility derived from offices had images and statues for its insignia or visible ornament, so this military nobility had its shields and escutcheons which were placed in temples and other public places.

20. It is also true enough that the Romans always took notice of those who were descended from ancient families, such as senators and knights: for instance, Cicero often glorifies himself for being descended 'from a knightly family'.[37] But in fact, neither the ones nor the others were actually called noble, and not even senators who had not held great offices, or their predecessors.

21. Now this nobility did not constitute a separate order or estate, as it does in France – nor even a title of honour attached to a person's name. Rather, it was an honourable and estimable quality which conferred only one advantage (though this was of no small importance): that it was highly serviceable to attaining great charges and principal magistracies of the Republic, upon which the great personages of Rome set such store. That is why Cicero speaks[38] of 'those who are of noble birth, upon whom all the favours of the Roman people are conferred while they themselves remain inactive'; and Sallust,[39] of how 'the nobles passed the consulate from hand to hand amongst themselves'. Cicero reproaches Piso[40] because 'he crept into public honours on the strength of his smoky family images'. 'Do not doubt', he adds, 'that you were made aedile by those who favour nobility in the shape of images'. 'As for me', he observes,[41] 'just as I had no ancestors to commend me when I was seeking support, so there are no images to intercede with you on my behalf when I shall have erred'. And Horace comments[42]

On the judge, the people, whom you know so well, who in folly
Often give offices to the unworthy and stupidly are slaves to fame,
Who are dazzled by titles of honour and by ancestral images.

[36] *Nat. hist.* XXXV. [iii. 12].
[37] [E.g., *Pro Cnaeus Plancio.* xvii; *De lege agraria* I. 27.]
[38] *In Verrem* [II. v. 70].
[39] *Bellum Iugurthinum* [LXIII. 6].
[40] *In Pisonem* [I. i].
[41] [Cf. *De lege agraria* II. i.]
[42] [*Satirae* I. vi. 15.]

22. However, the emperors suppressed most of those great offices from which nobility proceeded, and conferred the rest as they willed. So this practice of images degenerated little by little; Pliny, in the passage cited above,[43] complains that the decline began in his time. This type of nobility was at last abolished altogether, and I know of nowhere in all our law where it is mentioned. Instead, the emperors invented other dignities and titles of honour of which I shall speak in due place.

23. It is true that a title of honour and even of privilege still remained to the descendants of Roman senators and of urban decurions, for these particular charges – and these alone – ordinarily passed down to their children. The children of senators who had enjoyed the dignity of *illustres* were senators born, and had rights of entry and deliberative voice in the senate when they reached competent age. So much may be gathered from the law[44] that the sons of simple senators had full right to enter the senate, but not to speak, and therefore they were not true senators. Their dignity was only that of *clarissimi* which they retained, as did even the daughters of senators 'as far as great-grandsons and great-granddaughters lest they marry men of inferior degree';[45] that is why they could not marry freedmen.[46] In addition to the title of honour, this dignity brought them some privileges, notably that of being exempt from commoner status and from the penalties to which plebeians were liable: a privilege also enjoyed by the children of decurions and of war veterans.[47]

24. It follows from this that the Romans had the two sorts of ancestral excellence specified above, namely good birth or gentility, and nobility. Thus Cornelius Fronto says[48] that 'nobility proper we call noble, but gentility that which is called "well-born" in Greek; so the one is from the thing itself, the other from descent'. In the foregoing passage where Livy reckons[49] the advantages accruing to the common people through participating in the consulate, birth and nobility are counted separately. Yet there were two notable differences between

---

[43] [Note 27.]
[44] *Digest* 1.9.
[45] [Cf. *Code J* 12.1.13.]
[46] *Digest* 23.2.42.
[47] *Code J* 9.41.11; *Digest* 49.18.
[48] *De differentiis* [*vocabulorum*, in *Grammaticae latinae auctores antiqui*, ed. Helias Putschius (Hanover, 1605), p. 2199, col. 1].
[49] Above [note 21].

these two species. First, the more ancient the good birth or gentility, the more honourable it was. Nobility, on the contrary, steadily diminished with the passage of time. It even seems, from the aforementioned laws, to have been lost after the third generation, which was indeed the last that the fathers could have seen. The explanation of this difference is palpable: that the honour of good birth consisted in being farthest removed from servitude, while the honour of nobility proceeded from the brilliance remaining from the dignity of an ancestor which, accordingly, diminished in accordance with remoteness from him.

25. The other difference was that a father's infamy did not eradicate good birth or gentility from his child. So much may be gathered from Cicero's definition of *gentiles*, noted above,[50] where the requirement that 'no ancestor should have been in slavery' takes precedence over the requirement that 'no ancestor should have suffered loss of civil capacity'. But infamy does remove nobility originating in dignity: witness the implication of the law[51] that 'no stigma of violated honour attached to those of particular degree through whom this privilege was transmitted to their descendants', as will be explained more precisely in the next chapter.

26. The explanation of this second difference is twofold. First, each of the two species of ancestral excellence is lost only through its opposite: free-birth, which consists in exemption from servitude, through participation in the servile; and nobility, which consists in dignity, through infamy. Secondly, every individual who enjoys free-born status does so in his own right, for the child can claim descent more ancient than his father's by one degree. But nobility proceeds from the right of the ancestor who was adorned with high dignity. So it is in no way surprising that an obstacle which occurs in the course of descent should be prejudicial to those who come afterwards.

27. This, by and large, was the practice through time of Roman nobility. We in France have imitated it in some sort. For, when the matter is carefully considered, we have the nobility which proceeds from ancient birth, and that which proceeds from dignities. The former exists time out of mind; the latter has its beginning. The one is native, the other dative. And the one seems to be called *noblesse*,

---

[50] [Note 17; here Loyseau tends to distort Cicero's intended meaning.]
[51] *Code J* 9.41.11.

and the other *générosité*, or, rather, gentility – just as, amongst us, noble-men are commonly distinguished from gentle-men.

28. Let us, then, trace the origin of this gentle birth, or ancient and immemorial nobility. We must note that, in the same way that the Athenians and the Romans first divided their people into patricians and plebeians, from this monarchy's first establishment its people were divided into gentlemen and commoners. The former were destined to defend and maintain the state, whether by counsel or by force of arms; the latter, to nourish it by tillage, trade and exercise of crafts. This division has persisted down to the present time. It seems to tally with Julius Caesar's crediting the Gauls with being divided into nobility and common people.[52] The nobility comprised both the druids who were counsellors serving at sacrifices and affairs of state, and the knights who had control of force. For the rest, he says that little value was placed upon the common people, in as much as the nobility had almost enslaved them.

29. Alternatively, the nobility of France originated in an ancient mixture of two peoples who adapted themselves to each other. These were the Gauls and the Franks. The Franks conquered and subjugated the Gauls without wishing to drive out and exterminate them, and yet retaining over them the following prerogative. The Franks alone would have public charges, the handling of arms and the enjoyment of fiefs. They should not be required to contribute any money either to the lords of particular places or to the sovereign for necessities of state; instead of these, the only requirement upon them was to be at the wars.

30. But the conquered people were reduced, for the most part, into a condition of demi-servitude such as the later Romans devised for those whom they called 'persons assessed or enrolled according to their capacity to labour', or 'husbandmen, or persons bound to plots of land'. We call these 'persons in mortmain', or 'villeins', or 'mortgaged persons' – terms which I have interpreted elsewhere.[53] Beyond this condition of demi-servitude, such a person was incapable of bearing offices, arms or fiefs. He was required to pay his lord the quit-rent or tribute of his land, and was also required to furnish monies extraordinarily for the necessities of the state. Possibly this

---

[52] *De bello Gallico* VI. [xiii].
[53] [*Seigneuries* i. 56–7.]

was the same condition as that to which, by Caesar's account, the humble people of ancient Gaul had been reduced by the nobility.

31. As time passed these two nations grew hard to distinguish from each other. Those who either were descended from the ancient Franks or at least had found means of gaining their freedom (for it is unlikely that all the nobles of the country were reduced to this miserable condition) were called gentle-men. They may have applied the term to themselves, in imitation of the Roman *gentiles*; or the natives of the country, who were already Christian when the Franks came into Gaul, may have called them 'gentiles', that is to say 'pagans', by way of abuse.

32. As for rural dwellers, they were called *paysans*, meaning people of the country, or, as the Romans called them, 'civilians', meaning those who did not bear arms. They were also called *roturiers*, possibly because they had been put to rout, or else from *rus*, as in 'rustic'.

33. In time the two nations intermingled, and those early rigours of debarring commoners entirely from offices, armies and fiefs did not persist so exactly. Yet some vestiges of these restrictions have remained until now. Only gentlemen can hold principal offices such as those of the crown, of the royal household and of government. Commoners are not received into cavalry companies, and formerly were not admitted to the leading infantry commands. Finally, commoners still cannot hold the principal fiefs and lordships; and as for plain fiefs, they still pay today the tax of frank-fee for dispensation to hold these. But, whatever of that, gentlemen have carefully kept this franchise, of not being bound to pay any subsidies nor any dues other than assisting the king in wars.

34. From this account it clearly follows that our plain nobility, so called by us with a word scraped from the Latin, is nothing other than the gentility or *ingenuitas* of the Romans, and scarcely corresponds to their nobility proceeding from dignities. Our gentle-men are those whose blood has always been free from commonness. Perfect nobility, in our view, occurs when its commencement lies beyond reckoning, and not when the presence of common blood at any time can be proved.

35. In as much as such an eternity defies proof, we are constrained to observe the same thing that the Romans came to respect in *ingenuitas*, that those whose father and grandfather have continually sustained a noble lifestyle and enjoyed the privileges of nobility are

presumed noble time out of mind. Even so, our usage is that the more ancient one's proof of nobility, the more honourable it is. Furthermore, we take the view that a gentle-man who incurs infamy does not deprive his posterity of the order of nobility, for it resides in the blood and family and not simply in the father's person. In effect, therefore, we preserve the two differences noted above[54] which the Romans observed in respect of *ingenuitas* whilst they maintained the contrary in respect of nobility of dignity. So it is nowadays in all the other countries of Christendom, where, furthermore, nobility (as we call it) is more commonly termed 'generosity'. In fact, when foreigners speak of nobles in Latin they more often call them *generosos* than *nobiles*.

36. Now in the Roman Republic the citizens 'had rights of civil freedom and jurisdiction', meaning that they were free and exempt as much from public as from private lordship, and so had a hand in the state, as I have said in my book on *Seigneuries*.[55] There, as I showed earlier, *ingenuitas* signified only an ancient exemption from servitude and slavery, though it did endow the free-born with certain privileges and prerogatives which were not enjoyed by persons descended freely from freedmen.

37. But in the French monarchy those rights 'of civil freedom and jurisdiction' have no place. We hold that the humble people, though free in the sense of being exempt from slavery and private lordship, nevertheless are generally subject to public lordship, even by common law. They are regularly subject to certain base charges, such as paying taxes and other contributions for the necessities of the state, guarding towns and castles, lodging and billeting armed forces, and the like. Nobles are always free and exempt from these charges of the common people, because they are employed for a purpose more useful and important to the state – that is, to defend it from enemies. Thus, persons whose ancestors have at all times depended upon bearing arms and who have vindicated their exemption from popular charges can compare themselves to the free-born of Rome.

38. From this it follows that our 'gentility' or 'generosity', this ancient and immemorial nobility, nevertheless does not proceed from the

---

[54] [Sections 24 *et seq.*]
[55] *Seigneuries* [i. 36–43].

right of nature, as liberty does, but from the ancient law and disposition of the state.

39. The ancient philosophers have differed a good deal on this.
Their prince, Aristotle himself, has contradicted himself on it in the
same work. In the first book of his *Rhetoric* he reckons nobility among
the properties of nature, and in the second book among those of
fortune; in one place he even calls it fortune.[56]

40. However, nobility is not a simple privilege, peculiar to each case
and contrary to common law. Rather, it springs from a public and
general law, and proceeds from means anciently established to this
purpose in every country. It is therefore longer lasting and more
durable than are simple privileges. This is a fundamental proposition,
and it serves to resolve innumerable questions which occur on this
matter.

41. So much for gentility which exceeds the memory of men. As for
nobility of which the cause and commencement are known, it derives
in France from ennoblement by the prince, who is God's ordained
distributor of the secure honour of this world. We read in the book
of Esther,[57] 'He will be honoured whom the king will have wished
to honour'; and in [the younger] Pliny,[58] 'Caesar makes and preserves
nobles'. That is why Bartolus defines nobility thus:[59] 'Nobility is an
anointed quality preserved by the sovereignty and indicating whoever
is approved above respectable plebeians'. Now the prince can ennoble
in two ways: either by letters expressly to this purpose, or by collation
and investiture of ennobling offices and lordships. Nobility of dignity
properly consists in these. As the law says:[60] 'What, then, does it
matter whether the prince [*sic*] declares his will by words [*sic*] or by
the very substance of his acts?'

---

[56] *Rhetoric* 1360ᵇ30–9; cf. 1390ᵇ15–30. [1701 adds: For the state of nature is the liberty
of man: it is the true nature to which he is presumed to be born into the world, unless
the contrary appears to be the case. What is superior is called 'dignity'; what is inferior
is called 'condition'; and neither is presumed unless it so appears. That is why doctors
of law say of nobility, which is an order and thus a species of dignity, that 'it is an
accidental quality which does not belong by nature and, accordingly, is not presumed
unless proved'.]

[57] [vi. 9.]

[58] *Panegyricus dictus Traiano Imperatori* [lxix. 6].

[59] *Operae ... omnia* [(Basle, 1588–9), IV, pt. iii, p. 118, col. 2].

[60] *Digest* 1.3.32.1. [What in fact it says is: 'nam quid interest suffragio populus volunta-
tem suam declaret an rebus ipsis et factis'; see above, Introduction, p. xviii]

42. Such ennoblements purge the blood and posterity of the recipient of all commoner blemish, and bring it to the same quality and dignity as if his had always been a free-born lineage. Budé[61] is therefore quite right to term it 'restitution of birth' which, as I proved in the second chapter, was the fullest demonstration of *ingenuitas* that the emperors could bestow. It not only effaced and abolished all vestige of servitude, but also conferred the rights and prerogatives which perfectly free-born persons had – that is, those born of free ancestors time out of mind.

43. However, 'remission marks those whom it releases'; and, of course, this abolition of servitude or commonness is only an eraser whose mark remains. Indeed, it is rather a fiction than a truth, for the prince's action cannot reduce being to non-being. As the Poet[62] says:

> God Himself is unable, and denies Himself the ability,
> To undo what He does and what is done.

So men take the view that persons ennobled by letters or dignities are not as estimable as nobles by lineage, even though they enjoy in effect all the same privileges. In much the same way, the Romans did not esteem new men as highly as ancient nobles. This is why we in France are careful to conceal the commencement of our nobility in order to relate it to that first species of immemorial gentility. Even Budé says[63] that in some places only the grandson of someone who has been ennobled is truly noble.

44. But although antiquity made *ingenuitas* more worthy of commendation among the Romans, the fact is that in general they preferred nobility of dignity to gentility. In France, in much the same way, nobility proceeding from dignity – that is, from the greatest offices and lordships – is raised higher by one degree than plain gentility. Those who possess such dignities are ranked as knights or lords and style themselves by these titles, which are titles of nobility. Even sovereign lordships, which nowadays have been made hereditary almost throughout Christendom, have nevertheless established amongst us a third and supreme degree of nobility. This is the degree

---

[61] [*Opera B*, III, p. 76.]
[62] [Unidentified, but cf. Niccolo Perotti, *Cornucopiae* (Basle, 1526), col. 273.30.]
[63] Above [note 61].

of prince which we ascribe to those aspiring to such sovereignties by right of agnation or of kinship in the male line.

45. Therefore, we have three degrees of nobility: plain nobles, whom we call gentlemen and esquires; those of the high nobility, whom we call lords and knights; and those of the supreme degree, whom we call princes. Each of these degrees has its different effect. Plain nobility affects the blood and passes to posterity in such a way that the more ancient it is, the more honourable. High nobility does not pass at all to posterity, at least in its degree. It is personal: it is bestowed upon the person, either through his particular merit as in the case of knighthood (which is a perfect order, perishing with the person), or through his office or lordship, following the office and lordship in perpetuity. Finally, princedom can come only through lineage, but it resides there in a manner opposite to plain nobility, for it is ranked according to how recent it is and how near to its founder.

46. So much for a general and quasi-historical discourse, as much of the Roman nobility through time as of ours. It could not contain the great and numerous questions which arise on the three degrees of our nobility. To deal with these, each must have its separate chapter, beginning with plain nobility which is the foundation of the other two degrees.

CHAPTER FIVE

Of plain gentlemen

1. I have always been careful, in the few books which I have written, to choose quite new subjects, so that in dealing with them I have avoided running into matters already discussed. I have persuaded myself that there is not much honour in taking advantage of someone else's work, nor contentment of the spirit in showing oneself expert in ideas already devised – nor, finally, much use to the public in transcribing or embroidering what has already been written. But here I am engaged upon an extremely common matter. There is, perhaps, no subject in French law which has been treated by more authors than that of nobility. Moral and political philosophers, humanists, jurists, even modern legal practitioners have written about it, each in his own fashion. To particularise, what can one say anew after the copious Tiraqueau[1] who has won that honour in everything he has discussed, so that it is very difficult to add anything to it? However, I cannot avoid speaking of a matter so directly relevant to my subject. Yet it follows that I must try to deal with a common matter in an uncommon way. After all, the field is so great and so fertile that those who have harvested it hitherto have still left plenty to be gleaned by those who follow them. This is what I shall endeavour to do, without putting my scythe in their crops nor appropriating the sheaves which they have collected.

2. I will begin by explaining the terms 'gentleman' and 'esquire'. In respect of 'gentleman', I will not deviate from the two etymologies

---

[1] [De nobil.]

which I assigned to it in the last chapter: that is, deriving it from
gentilitas in its ancient meaning, 'the condition of a free-born man',
or from *gentilis*, meaning 'a person belonging to the same family', or
ethnicus.[2] But these must be examined a little more deeply. There is
no doubt that 'gentleman' is a term composed of two nominatives,
as the grammarians say, for it varies in the plural. Now 'gentle' comes
from *gent*, whether in the Latin or in the French; and, just as *gent*
signifies sometimes simply an ancestry and sometimes an entire
nation, so does its derivative 'gentle' have several meanings which
flow from it.

3. In as much as *gent* signifies an ancestry, the Romans called *gentiles*
those who were of the same ancestry and, consequently, of the same
name, termed by the Greeks 'eponymous', 'My *gentiles* are those who
are called by my name', says Cincius as recorded by Festus.[3] Hence
Cicero's calling King Tullius his *gentilem*.[4] Demosthenes calls the
judges 'eponymous with justice',[5] an expression which Budé renders
gentiles.[6] That is why the Twelve Tables often conjoin 'agnates' and
gentiles, meaning by the former the closest kin, and by the latter the
more distant who are recognisable as such only by the name.

4. Even so, gentility was in Rome a mark of honour, because those
of ancient stock were accounted more honourable. 'There is no gentility of freedmen nor, certainly, of slaves', says Gaius.[7] Cicero defines
gentiles after Quintus Mucius [Scaevola]:[8]

> Those who have the same name in common, who are sprung
> from free-born ancestors, none of whose ancestors has ever been
> in slavery, and who have never suffered loss of civil capacity.

This is the reason why several of our learned modern writers call
our gentlemen 'patricians who could indicate without doubt and by
name a father and a grandfather'.

5. In as much as *gent* signifies a 'nation', that which is in vogue and
deemed smart in the country is termed *gentil* in our language.

---

2 [Strictly, 'a heathen', but used here in the sense of the Greek ἔθνος.]
3 [*De verb. signif.*, p. 83.]
4 *Tusculanes disputationes* I. [xvi. 38].
5 *Against Aristogeiton* [i. 11].
6 *Opera B*, III, p. 7.
7 [See above, ch. 4, note 19.]
8 *Topica* [vi. 29].

Suetonius seems to have understood it in this way:[9] 'He wore his hair long at the back so that it even covered the nape of his neck, which seems to have been considered *gentile*'.

6. But the Romans commonly used this word in a quite different sense. They called *gentiles* those who did not obey their Empire, 'doubtless because they used their nations' law, not the civil law of the Romans'. So Cujas explains it,[10] and he confirms it from the *Theodosian Code* where *gentiles* are opposed to provincials[11] – that is, the inhabitants of provinces subject to the Romans.

7. Likewise in Holy Scripture and among Christian authors, idolatrous countries are called *gentiles* and ethnics, from the Greek name which also signifies a nation. According to Papius,[12]

> *Gentiles* are those who live without law and have not yet believed, because they are as they were at birth, that is sinful, servants of idols, and are called ethnics in Greek.

That is also why they are called 'pagans', *paganos*; however, some think this to be 'because they did not yet give the name of Christian to the soldiery'.

8. A modern writer's conjecture thus has some verisimilitude, that the name of our gentlemen comes from the ancient Franks. Pagans and gentiles, they had subjugated Gaul which was already Christian, and they alone retained arms and lordships with complete freedom and immunity. As I have just said, that is the reason why the Christians, natives of the country, called them, disdainfully or jealously, *gentiles* or gentlemen.

9. On the other hand, I find nothing plausible in the fantasy of another modern writer who would ascribe the origin of our gentlemen and esquires to the *gentiles* and *scutarii* who are often mentioned in certain texts.[13] These were the names of some bands or companies

---

[9] *Tiberius* [lxviii. 2. Suetonius's intended meaning seems closer to Loyseau's earlier point: 'quod gentile in eo videbatur (which appears to have been characteristic of his clan)'].

[10] [*Opera C*, x, col. 190.]

[11] *Code Theod.* 3.14.1.

[12] [Rightly, Papias, eleventh-century AD Latin grammarian; cf. Isidore, *Etymologiarum sive originum* (ed. W. M. Lindsay, Oxford, 1911), VIII. x. 11–15.]

[13] *Notitia* [*utraque dignitatum cum orientis tum occidentis, ultra Arcadii Honoriique tempora* (Venice, 1593), pp. 20, 22]; Ammianus Marcellinus, [*Rerum gestarum* XX. ii. 5, iv. 3, viii. 13, etc.].

of praetorian soldiers, charged with guarding and defending the Prae-
torium or imperial palace and, consequently, 'under the direction of
the master of ceremonies'.

10. We are now ready to consider esquires. As in the case of gentlemen, a double etymology can be assigned to them, derived equally
from the same Latin and French word, *scutum* and *escu*.

11. The *escu* is properly the buckler of cavalrymen. 'Oblong shields
(*scuta*) are for horsemen, round shields (*clypei*) for footsoldiers', says
Servius;[14] and *scuta* are shorter, *clypei* larger. By Livy's account,[15]
'This was the shape of the *scutum*: an upper part where it protected
the breast and shoulders, and a more tapering part below, for easier
handling'.

12. As for foot-soldiers' bucklers, we call the big ones 'targes'
because one protects oneself (*se targue*) behind [them], and the little
ones *rondelles* because they are round. That is the first etymology of
'esquire': someone who bore an *escu* or buckler on horseback. In
Latin these are undoubtedly called *scutarii* or *scutatores*, and Livy,
Vegetius[16] and Suetonius often mention them. It is certainly the case
that in all nations men of war have willingly taken the name of their
armour: in France we have our lancers, archers, crossbowmen, pike-
men, musketeers and arquebusiers.

13. But in so far as shields or escutcheons were the most common
arm amongst military men, they in particular were called arms. In
Greek ὁπλὸν signifies arms in general, but particularly the shield.
In Latin *arma* signify more properly defensive than offensive arms,
'doubtless because they would protect the arm or shoulder, or
because they would hang down from the arms', as Servius[17] and
Festus[18] say.

14. Our Frenchmen of old painted their devices on their arms, as
we gather from the old Romans and from ancient burial places. Vegetius tells us[19] that the Romans did so too. In due course these devices
came to be called *écus*, for as time passed everyone grew careful to
keep the device and shield of his ancestors who had been distin-

---

[14] *Comm. in Aeneidos* IX. [368].
[15] [*Hist.* IX. xl. 2.]
[16] [Flavius] Vegetius [Renatus: see below, note 19].
[17] [*Comm. in Aeneidos* IV. 495.]
[18] [*De verb. signif.*, p. 23.]
[19] [Flavius] Vegetius [Renatus, *De re militari libri quatuor* (Lyon, 1592)], pp. 38–9.

guished in military valour. The practice even continued of painting one's devices on the other arms, after the shields or bucklers were no longer in use. But they were usually painted in the shape of the old shield, and this is therefore called 'escutcheon'. The devices painted on it are called 'arms', not only in French, but also in Latin. Tiraqueau proves the point,[20] defending Bartolus against Lorenzo Valla who mistook it through confusing *arma* and *insignia*.

15. Consequently in France the right of having coats of arms applies only to nobles on grounds of descent from those ancient knights who painted their devices on their shields or bucklers. It appears from King Charles V's charter of 1371[21] that when he ennobled the Parisians he gave them the right to bear arms. The formulary of letters of ennoblement expressly contains this same right. And this is the second etymology of 'esquires': those who have *escus* or ancient coats of arms. These are the visible mark of our nobility, just as images were of Rome's. Pliny tells us[22] that it was likewise the custom of gallant warriors to paint their bucklers, and that 'their images were contained in their shields'. Hence Budé's observation[23] that the arms of our gentlemen have succeeded the images of the Roman nobility.

16. But because this privilege of bearing coats of arms was given to the Parisians, the most notable burgesses of the principal towns also ventured to bear them, so gentlemen bethought themselves to place above theirs a helm, or armour for the head, to distinguish themselves from those who do not in fact bear arms; and they called it 'timbre'.

17. In my view, this addition was at first made like a burgonet or iron cap which had the form of a *timbre*, of a bell. The latter ought rather to be called 'timbrel', as in 'tintinnabulation'.

18. Nobles of the towns, however, were anxious to ascribe their nobility to ancient military gentility, so they scarcely hesitated to adorn their coats of arms with crests, like gentlemen; even though subsequent ordinances[24] expressly forbade commoners to do this.

19. I will say in passing that it seems to me ridiculous to see the coat of arms of an officer of the long robe capped with a helm. It ought to be timbred with the quartered bonnet, as a bishop's is timbred

---

[20] *De nobil.*, p. 33.
[21] [*Ord.*, v, pp. 418–19.]
[22] [*Nat. hist.*] xxxv. iii.[13].
[23] *Opera B*, iii, p. 53.
[24] Orléans [(1561), art. 110]; Blois [(1579), art. 257. Fontanon, iii, pp. 57, 61].

with the mitre and a cardinal's with the hat. For, in sum, the crest is personal and refers specifically to the person and not to his family, like the coat of arms. So much may be gathered from the coats of arms of women which have no crest except the love-knot or girdle, as I will show again in the next chapter.

20. Now, as with coats of arms, so too with qualities and titles of honour: gentlemen professing arms have always tried to distinguish themselves from town nobles, and the latter have tried, conversely, to mix and merge themselves with the former. As the more honourable inhabitants of towns have long since formed the habit of calling themselves 'noble men', men of the sword have come to disdain this title and have wanted to call themselves 'esquire' even though a nobleman was, formerly, greater than an esquire. 'Noble man' was the title of nobility of dignity, and even of the high nobility. Du Tillet often notes[25] how the princes of the blood took the description 'noble men'; and Froissart frequently says[26] that in such and such an encounter there were killed so many nobles and so many esquires, always placing the esquires after the nobles.

21. Even today in England nobles or gentlemen are different from esquires and constitute a degree above them, as Thomas Smith expressly remarks.[27] It was anciently thus in France, as may be seen in the custom of Hainault where degrees of nobility are sharply distinguished: the prince, the knight, the nobleman and the esquire. And a heavier rate was levied for the pay of princes (a term which shall be explained in the next chapter) than for knights'; for knights' than for noblemen's; and for noblemen's than for esquires'.

22. It is also very likely that the true and original etymology of the name 'esquire' comes from bearing not one's own but one's master's *escu* – properly, those whom Plautus calls 'shield bearers'.[28] So the ancient Romans teach us, and learned men nowadays consider theirs to be the most sure testimony of our nation's minor antiquities. In fact, Fauchet cites[29] two or three ancient Latin charters where the *grand escuyer* of France is called *scutifer*.

[25] [*Recueil*, pp. 218 *et seq.*]

[26] [E.g.,*Oeuvres de*] *Froissart:* [*Chroniques*, ed. Kervyn de Lettenhove (29 vols., Brussels, 1867–77), VIII, p. 295].

[27] *De Rep. Angl.* [p. 70; in fact Smith's point is that esquires rank below peers and knights, but above ordinary gentlemen].

[28] *Cassina* [ii. 262].

[29] *Origines*, [fo. 32ʳᵒ].

23. For the ancient nobility of France were not as vainglorious as the nobility are now. A poor cadet of a gentleman may be almost dying of hunger in his thatched cottage, and yet consider it dishonourable to serve in the royal household. He even objects to giving way, in his parish, to a great lord, saying that he is as noble as the king. This phrase is so often on their tongues that it has become a proverb, which I will explain in the next chapter. But in times past all gentlemen without exception served greater persons than themselves as a matter of course: princes served kings, lords served princes, plain gentlemen lords. Indeed, for all kinds of persons, and especially for gentlemen, to submit oneself to a greater is a good way of prospering. Since a gentleman cannot do any work to support his family, he has no other means of maintaining his quality than to gain advancement to military command through the favour of the great. Moreover, in giving his children to princes and lords he has an honest means of providing for them. This is how the nobility, which has always wanted to form a clique separate from the people, formerly maintained itself by itself.

24. At first, young gentlemen were pages to lords, and young ladies were maids in waiting to ladies. As Ragueau explains,[30] pages 'are pedagogues to boys, or reared to serve at court'; though Pinet[31] derives them from 'rustics or civilians'.

25. There are two kinds of pages: pages of honour, and common ones. Pages of honour are found only in the houses of the king and sovereign princes, and are ordinarily sons of barons or knights. Their function, such as it is in France, is well described by Quintus Curtius [Rufus]:[32] 'This troupe was a kind of training school for generals and governors of provinces'.

26. Having risen from being pages, they become bachelors or squires, bachelor signifying a candidate for knighthood, squire (*damoiseau*) being the diminutive of *dam*, which signifies lord. Then, having become heads of households, they are fully qualified lords; or, having distinguished themselves by feats of arms, they are made knights by the king. These terms will be explained more fully later.

---

[30] [François] Ragueau [*Indice des droits roiaux et seigneuriaux, des plus notables dictions, termes et phrases de l'Estat* (Paris, 1609), p. 398].

[31] [*Ibid.*, p. 399, citing Antoine du] Pinet [sieur de Noroy, translator and editor of *Caius Plinius Secundus, L'Histoire du Monde* (Lyon, 1566)].

[32] [*Historiarum Alexandri Magni Macedonis*] VIII. [vi. 7].

27. Common pages are the issue of simple noblemen and serve knights or lords (for a plain gentleman ought not to have pages, but only lackeys, who are commoners). Having risen from being pages, they anciently became esquires because they had charge of bearing the *escu* or arms of the knight when he went to war. Thus at royal entries the *grand escuyer* of France bears the royal coat of arms and the royal sword, processing immediately in front of the king, mounted on a horse caparisoned with purple velvet sown with gold fleurs-de-lis.

28. And because the esquire had charge not only of the arms, but also of his master's horses – that is, the entire equipage – those in royal or princely households who had care of the horses were called esquires, and their stables *escuries*. This has prompted some modern writer to say that esquire is called 'from horse, as it were *equarius* (appertaining to horses)'. This strikes me as involving more rhyme or coincidence than reason; the term *escuyer* is undoubtedly from the French. In my view, Fauchet's contention[33] is scarcely better founded when he says that *escurie* is an old French word meaning 'stable'. He offers as proof an article in the Salic law: 'If anyone shall have burned a *scudem* with sows, a *scuriam* with animals or hay, etc.' I have never read this term anywhere else, and I consider it to be Latinised French rather than true Latin.

29. Anyway, the king's esquires were anciently called 'marshals', from the German term *marschall* which signifies an officer or servant of horses, according to Du Tillet.[34] The name persists for those who shoe horses or tend them when sick. But since the marshals of the royal household have been used to lead the men-at-arms – like the head of their office, the constable (so called from *comes stabuli*, as I have shown elsewhere)[35] – those who have been placed in the royal household to perform the ancient office of his marshals have taken the name esquire, as in the households of lords.

30. So the esquire was the noble servant who assisted the knight or lord in war and on horseback; and the valet was he who served him on foot in his household. We call the latter a 'man of the chamber', so termed as if it were *va-lez*, because he was closest to his master – his cutler and cup-bearer, 'attendant and bodyguard', as Cicero

---

[33] *Origines*, [fo. 32ʳᵒ].
[34] [*Recueil*, p. 274.]
[35] [*Offices*, IV. ii. 14–15.]

says.[36] Thus, among the servants or domestic officers of princes and lords the quality of valet used to be honourable. In Froissart, Gui de Lusignan calls himself valet of the count of Poitou.[37] In Villehardouin,[38] mention is made several times of the valet of Constantinople, who was the prince. So it is often found among the old Romans and on ancient tombs. Even the jack in a pack of cards testifies to this; and in the tarot cards there comes above him the knight, who is the middle degree of nobility, between the valet, who stands for the esquire or plain gentleman, and the prince.

31. Thus the king's chamberlains, who nowadays are called gentlemen of the chamber, were formerly called *valets de chambre*. But the French king saw that these offices had come to be exercised only by commoners, as at present are almost all the minor offices of the royal household which gentlemen of old considered themselves well honoured to exercise. He therefore introduced above them the gentlemen of the chamber, so that the name of 'valet' eventually became contemptible, and hence even became opposed to 'gentleman'.

32. By contrast, the name of 'esquire' has become fashionable, gentlemen of the sword having adopted it as a title to distinguish themselves from nobles of the town. So, in order to be reputed gentlemen, the minor officers of the royal household have almost all designated themselves esquires (like the officers of the stables), as anciently they would not otherwise have been appointed to such offices. Thus, those who used to be called 'valets-cutler' have wanted to be designated 'esquires-cutler'; the officers of the kitchen, formerly called master cooks, have called themselves esquires of the kitchens; and others likewise.

33. Hence we may gather that esquires were properly those among the gentlemen who gave themselves to the service of the greatest, and thereby were less highly regarded than those who lived on their rents. But now all country gentlemen have taken this name, evoking the military profession which undoubtedly is the most authentic source of nobility, in order to distinguish themselves from the nobility of the town which, ordinarily, proceeds from offices. Yet they have

---

[36] [*De lege agraria* II. xiii. 32.]

[37] [Untraced in Froissart; but the house of Lusignan was among the most illustrious of Poitou – hence the point of Loyseau's remark.]

[38] [Geoffroi de] Villehardouin [*Conquête de Constantinople*, ed. N. de Wailly (Paris, 1882), p. 42].

scarcely gained. For these officers have finally usurped the same name in order to appear as noble as gentlemen by lineage, even though they may never have borne buckler or shield.

34. As nobility is so eagerly sought, it stands to reason that the legitimate means of gaining it should be certain and limited; otherwise everyone would want a part in it, and it would finally fall into confusion. 'Bright honour certainly becomes vile in the multitude, and merit worthless in the eyes of the worthy when many possess it unworthily.'[39] Let us then consider how it is acquired. It seems that the question of nobility by lineage (which I called 'gentility' in the last chapter) cannot arise at all, as it has no commencement. Yet the great question has yet to be answered, whether it is acquired irrevocably 'by father and grandfather' – that is, by continual usage over two generations – when the earlier predecessors appear clearly to have been commoners.

35. The question results principally from the modern statute of 1600, concerning taxation. This[40]

> prohibits all persons to take the title of esquire and to insinuate themselves into the body of the nobility, except those descended from a grandfather and a father who engaged in the profession of arms without perpetrating any discreditable act nor derogating from their quality.

For gentlemen's valets, or those who have gone pillaging in the wars, or even those who have wanted to do nothing other than trail a sword, have deluded themselves into believing that if, through force and intimidation on their own part or on that of the backwoods gentlemen whom they serve as cup-bearers, cut-throats, even as murderers, they can escape for two generations from paying taxes, their descendants will become noble without any need of the king nor of ennoblement by him. They hold that nobility is acquired or prescribed by two generations.

36. In fact, almost all our doctors hold that nobility can be prescribed by possession time out of mind. Tiraqueau makes a mass of assertions about this;[41] and, indeed, it is a point.

37. Even so, I cannot hold with this new nobility of sword-danglers. I see disorder springing from the great crowd of people who nowadays

---

[39] [St Jerome: *PL*, XXII, cols. 642–3.]
[40] [(Article 25: Fontanon, II, p. 881.]
[41] *De nobil.*, p. 49.

want, by these easy means, to exempt themselves both from royal taxes and from the occupations of the people. They do so at the crushing expense of the common people who pay the taxes for them; at the expense of the public, to whom they contribute nothing by their labour and industry; and to the confusion and contempt of the true nobility. The position that seems to me more just and equitable is this. Given that there is clear and genuine evidence of the quality of the ancestors of someone who claims to have prescribed nobility by two generations, he cannot have acquired it by legal right without the prince's concession. For the definition of nobility is that it proceeds 'from possessing sovereign power'.[42]

38. Furthermore, that which concerns the rights of the king and the interest of the public is not subject to prescription, especially when it is without title and with bad faith, and when its origin appears faulty. This is still more emphatically the case with that which is beyond private commerce and the disposal of particular persons, as nobility is, given that even in respect of things that are trafficable the laws say that 'no one can sell to himself a position of his own possession, nor alter his own status'. How, then, can a commoner ennoble himself, and his descendants because of him, seeing that nobility is less easily acquired than freedom? And since usurpers of nobility are declared by the law[43] to be falsifiers and are punished by our ordinances, how can their usurpation have force and authority? Finally, in order to avoid surcharging the poor people the king by edict of 1598[44] has revoked all the ennoblements which he himself has conceded, even though these were verified in the sovereign courts and mostly given for money. Why, then, should those usurped without his concession be maintained?

39. Again, that statute of 1600[45] does not declare such persons to be precisely noble, and does not say that, should they otherwise appear to be commoners, they have gained and prescribed nobility. On the contrary, it assumes that their predecessors were of noble quality: witness these words, 'that they have never perpetrated acts derogatory to their quality'. Yet the truth is that authentic nobility has its commencement beyond the memory of men and, even so, can be proved

---

[42] [Unattributed, 1610; attributed 1701 to Bartolus [see above, ch. 4, note 59].]
[43] *Digest* 48.10.27.2.
[44] [Fontanon, II, pp. 876–8.]
[45] [Article 25: Fontanon, II, p. 881.]

only by possession. Therefore, this statute has ordained very justly that when nobility is called in question proof of its continuous possession from the father and grandfather serves as sufficient and conclusive presumption of authenticity, as long as there is no clear evidence to the contrary. But this is not the presumption that our doctors term 'of law and by law, against which proof is not admitted'. I fully agree with them, that nobility – or, rather, *ingenuitas* – is presumed certainly and decisively through immemorial possession 'which constitutes grounds of proof in law'.[46] But care must be taken that the possession in question is indeed immemorial, with neither memory nor proof nor, in consequence, certainty to the contrary.

40. Now such considerations do not apply to nobility proceeding from the offices of the father and grandfather, even though this seems in the same statute[47] to be reckoned equal to the former. The latter is gained by legal right at the third generation, because it proceeds in effect from the concession of the prince who confers offices. And this same statute signifies that great offices are the starting-point of nobility according to the customs of the realm. So much has never been said of engagement in military affairs, and still less so of those who merely trail a sword in their villages.

41. The fact remains that those who want to ground their nobility upon the way of life of their father and grandfather should have written proof of it: certificates of the captains under whom they served the king, extracted from the rolls in which they were included; contracts of marriage and division of property where they assumed the rank of esquire; and other similar documentary evidence. Proof by witnesses should not in itself suffice, even though it may be admitted to support documentary evidence, as that erstwhile oracle of the fiscal court (*cour des aides*), M. Le Bret, informs us.[48]

42. But in the case of benefices, the testimony of four witnesses suffices, according to the Concordat[49] and to King Louis XII's ordinance.[50]

43. As to whether a decree declaratory of nobility in such a case authenticates it thereafter, 'as long as everyone takes it to be the main

---

[46] *Digest* 43.20.3.4.
[47] [I.e., of 1600, as above, note 40.]
[48] Le Bret, fos. 208ᵛᵒ–209ʳᵒ.
[49] [I.e., of Bologna, 1516: Fontanon, IV, p. 401.]
[50] '1566' [rightly, 1510, art. 10: *Ord.*, XXI, p. 424].

point in the case',[51] Tiraqueau should be consulted.[52] For the rest, it is certain that a simple sentence of the district fiscal officers (*élus*), not ratified in the *cour des aides*, is not sufficient proof of nobility. Jurisdiction of first instance in cases of nobility lies with the said *cour des aides*, just as in cases of the royal domain it lies with the *parlement*. 44. To return to ennobling offices, they are almost all specified in my treatise on *Offices*,[53] where I have said that there are two kinds. One kind consists of those which not only ennoble the appointee, but also place him among the high nobility. Consequently, these have the power that solely through the father's dignity his children are ennobled with plain nobility, just as they are by means of letters of ennoblement which he obtained. I will say more in the next chapter about these offices, and also about ennobling lordships which have the same effect as great offices.

45. But there are other, lesser offices which ennoble only the appointee and ascribe to him only a personal nobility. These do not have the power of ennobling his descendants, if such offices or others like them were not held by the father and grandfather; in the latter case, nobility is acquired in perpetuity by the descendants.

46. The offices of counsellors in the sovereign courts are of this type. There is no edict expressly to the point, but it is grounded on the ancient laws and customs of the kingdom, as is said in the 1600 statute[54] and a privy council decree of 1602 on taxation in the Dauphiné, mentioned in my *Offices*.[55] This should not be thought strange, given Bartolus's conclusion[56] that 'nobility is annexed to an office in so far as it is commonly reputed to be so'.

47. However, royal secretaries do have an edict expressly to this point, and it also gives them the privilege that their children are noble as long as they should not have disposed of their offices otherwise than to a son or son-in-law. Likewise, several good towns of France have this privilege by well-authenticated royal charters, that their mayors – and, in some cases, their aldermen too – are ennobled,

---

[51] *Digest* 1.5.25.
[52] *De nobil.*, p. 254.
[53] I. [ix].
[54] [Article 25: Fontanon, II, p. 881.]
[55] I. [ix. 24–5].
[56] *Operae ... omnia* [(Basle, 1588–9), IV, pt. iii, p. 120, col. 2].

together with their descendants. This privilege is grounded on the claims of the decurions of Roman towns to nobility.[57]

48. As for military offices, from which nobility ought indeed to proceed rather than from any others, there is no doubt that the offices of governors of provinces and towns, captains and the leading men-at-arms of the royal ordinance companies, ennoble those who are thus honoured. Formerly it was even thought that all places in these companies, together with those of infantry captains, lieutenants and ensigns, should have the right of ennobling. But this statute of 1600[58] has determined the contrary, declaring them merely to be exempt from direct taxes as holders of simple privileges and as long as they continue in service, except that after twenty years' service they obtain the privilege of veteran. It adds that in future commoners who hold these positions shall enjoy no exemption until they have served ten full years, and as long as they continue to serve. Even so, it enjoins captains of the men-at-arms to fill their companies with gentlemen.

49. Here a noteworthy rule applies, that offices or charges assigned to plain nobles do not ennoble the appointee if he should turn out to be a commoner. It is true that as long as he is tacitly allowed to hold such a position he is presumed noble; and, if the father and grandfather have successively held such offices, this is a proof of nobility for those of the third generation. The statute which I have just interpreted is relevant here.

50. We must also distinguish boldly between, on the one hand, plain nobles with privileged exemption from direct taxes, such as privileged minor officers of royal or princely households; and, on the other, officers of the main tax districts and the like. The former are only semi-noble and are not taken for noble in any respect other than exemption from direct taxes. Even when these offices have been held for six generations, they endow descendants with neither nobility nor exemption.

51. So much for ennoblement which proceeds implicitly from offices or lordships. As for express ennoblement, this is conceded by letters from the prince. True nobility proceeds from virtue, of which honour is the greatest reward. A man's virtue is more fitting than that of his

---

[57] [Cf. *Digest* 50.2; *Code J* 10.32.]
[58] [Articles 27, 28: Fontanon, II, pp. 881–2.]

predecessors to produce honour for him; as Antigonus said,[59] man-like behaviour ought rather to be rewarded than father-like behaviour. So it is most reasonable that the sovereign prince should honour with the title of nobility someone whom he sees to be endowed with a distinct virtue, and thereby reward his particular merit and stimulate virtue in everyone.

52. But, be that as it may, this ennoblement can be conferred only by the prince whom God (from Whom all honour proceeds) has made distributor of the divine gift in this world. This, together with the fact that ennoblement diminishes the rights of the sovereign, is why dukes and counts have rightly lost the power to make knights and even to ennoble, which they formerly had usurped amongst other rights of sovereignty.

53. Even those amongst them who enjoy rights of sovereignty have been excluded and prevented from exercising this one: witness the old decree against the count of Flanders in 1280, recorded by Pithou:[60]

> It was declared that, notwithstanding the usage to the contrary proposed on behalf of the Count of Flanders, he neither could nor ought to make a commoner a knight without the authority of the king.

Likewise, this right has by numerous ordinances been withdrawn from governors of provinces, even of those claimed to have been not quite united and incorporated with the kingdom, such as Provence and Dauphiné, whose governors therefore pretend to have more authority than those of other provinces, as I have said elsewhere.

54. The formulary of letters of ennoblement is discussed at length by Bacquet,[61] and Thierriat[62] records three of them. Here the most notable point is that, as with redemption of inheritances, so with ennoblement of persons, the king should be indemnified through payment of a certain sum of money, fixed by his *chambre des comptes*, in consideration of the ennobled person's descendants' being freed from paying subsidies.

55. His Majesty is deemed to have given only what concerns honour,

---

[59] [Antigonus II of Macedon: see Plutarch, *Moralia* 183D.]
[60] Pithou [p. 1].
[61] Bacquet, pp. 43–4.
[62] [Florentin de] Thierriat [*Trois traictez* (Paris, 1606), pp. 168–82].

without diminution of his rights – unless the letters of ennoblement contain express release and quittance from such payment, a clause which nowadays is rarely omitted.

56. Yet, while the king may remit payment of his own indemnity, other considerations apply to the surcharge which reverts to the people through the exemption of the ennobled person and his descendants in perpetuity. This is why payment is due of a small sum of money by way of a charitable donation, which the masters of accounts likewise fix when they verify the ennoblement. The king remits this donation less commonly than his own indemnity, because it concerns the poor; nevertheless, he does sometimes remit it, and there is no doubt that he can do so.

57. For the rest, these letters of ennoblement should be verified both in the *chambre des comptes* owing to the diminution of the king's rights, and in the *cour des aides* owing to the exemption from direct taxes. Even so, because of the exemption from dues for frank-fee and, above all, because of the different right which various customs have introduced for the nobles, the surest mode of verification is in the *parlement*, the seat of ordinary and natural justice in respect of the king's rights and of sovereign justice in respect of his subjects' persons. In fact, the same Pithou records[63] a decree of 1543 ordaining that the inheritance of someone who had obtained letters of ennoblement which were verified not in his lifetime, but only by his widow after his death, should be divided like that of a commoner.

58. Nobility proceeding from ennoblement, express or implicit, is extended easily enough to the children, as it affects the blood and lineage: for, as Aristotle defines it,[64] 'nobility is virtue of lineage'. It even embraces those born before the ennoblement, following the provision of Roman law,[65] and above all the law which says:[66] 'It makes no difference whether the senator begot his son when already confirmed in senatorial rank or did so after attaining it'.

59. The later law[67] does not contradict this. As Cujas says,[68] it must be understood only in relation to offices subject to payment, and not

---

[63] Pithou [p. 1].
[64] [*Politics* 1283ᵃ37.]
[65] *Digest* 48.19.9.
[66] *Digest* 1.9.5.
[67] *Code J* 12.1.11.1.
[68] [Cf. *Opera C*, II, pt. ii, col. 273.]

to honours, as these terms show: 'Children should not be excluded from the honours enjoyed by their fathers'. It is thus a perpetual rule in law that the son of a senator or of a decurion, born before his father attained his position, should have the relevant honours and privileges, but not the duties and liabilities.[69]

60. In Roman law nobility of office and its privileges do not extend beyond the third generation of descendants, called 'great-grandsons',[70] as all the doctors hold on the relevant law.[71] Nevertheless, in France, where all our nobility is ultimately ascribed to that of lineage, all the descendants of ennobled persons are noble. Some even think that true nobility begins only with the third generation, as Budé says[72] on another relevant law.[73] Be that as it may, among us this nobility certainly is strengthened and always grows from generation to generation.

61. When I speak of descendants I mean those born in lawful marriage, and not bastards. Without exception, all our French doctors, such as Chasseneuz,[74] Guy Pape,[75] Bohier,[76] Benedicti,[77] Imbert[78] and Rebuffi,[79] hold it to be a general custom in France that the bastards of gentlemen are exempt from direct taxes. Nevertheless, the contrary is the case, as we learn from that statute of 1600, the words of which are these:[80]

> Although bastards may be born of noble fathers, they cannot assume the title and quality of gentlemen unless they obtain our

---

[69] *Digest* 50.2.2.2.

[70] *Code J* 9.41.11.

[71] *Code J* 12.1.1.

[72] [*Opera B*, III, p. 76.]

[73] *Digest* 1.9.12.

[74] [Cf.] *Consuetudines* [*ducatus Burgundiae* (Frankfurt, 1574), cols. 1182–3].

[75] *Decisiones* [*parlamenti Dalphinalis* (Lyon, 1593), p. 877].

[76] [Nicolas] Bohier, *Decisiones* [*Burdegalenses* (Lyon, 1566)], p. 221, col. 1.

[77] [Guillaume] Benedicti, *Repetitio* [. . . *in cap. Raynutius de testamentis* (Lyon, 1575), fos. 2ᵛᵒ col. 1–4ᵛᵒ col. 1. In fact, Benedicti shows how bastards are disqualified from enjoying various privileges.]

[78] [Jean] Imbert, *Enchiridion* [*ou brief recueil du droict escript* (Paris, 1603)], fo. 112ʳᵒ. [Imbert ascribes the position in question to Bohier, himself adding: 'This opinion ought not at present to be held in view of the recent ordinance' – i.e., of 1600 on direct taxes (*tailles*) from which he quotes the passage that Loyseau proceeds to cite.]

[79] [Pierre] Rebuffi, *Concordata* [(Paris, 1538)], pp. 76–82: [gloss, *s.vv.* 'cum vero probatio nobilitatis'. Yet Rebuffi's position is that privileges ascribed to the nobility should be understood 'of nobles legitimately born, not of bastards who by law are not nobles' (p. 77)].

[80] Article 26 [Fontanon, II, p. 881].

letters of ennoblement grounded on some great consideration of their merits or of their fathers', and verified as appropriate.

62. It is even held that, although they may be legitimatised by the king, they do not thereby become noble, as M. Le Bret tells us,[81] because letters of ennoblement are other than those of legitimation. As for nobility by lineage, it should come from father and grandfather. Now, a bastard legitimatised through his father's action is none the less not legitimatised or recognised as offspring by his father's father. That is why, when the bastard of a plain gentleman obtains his letters of legitimation, he must ensure that the clause of ennoblement is inserted there.

63. However, I consider that this rigorous ordinance must be construed strictly according to its terms, for it is undoubtedly contrary to the ancient custom of France, verified by all our doctors. And, given that it refers explicitly to gentlemen only, it should not be extended to the bastards of lords, for that last reason does not apply to them. The children of those of the high nobility have no need to prove that their grandfather was noble. Further, it is still evident enough at present that the bastards of lords bear the arms of their fathers' houses, with no difference other than the bar sinister; and who will say that the bastard of a great lord should pay direct taxes?

64. I have read somewhere a most equitable solution in this matter, as follows. Since it is not reasonable that bastards should be equal in dignity and degree of honour to legitimate children, they ought always to be placed one degree lower than they. Thus, the bastards of kings are princes, those of princes are lords, those of lords are gentlemen, and those of gentlemen are commoners, so that concubinage should not have as much honour as lawful marriage. I do not understand this to apply to persons legitimatised through subsequent marriage, for they are in every respect equal to those born in lawful wedlock.

65. To revert to bastards, however, the question may arise whether they can at least presume on their mothers' nobility. 'It is a law of nature that whoever is born out of lawful wedlock should follow the mother';[82] and 'when by some dispensation the mother's place of origin is taken into account, the son too is generally examined as to

---

[81] Le Bret, fos. 202vo–3ro
[82] *Digest* 1.5.24.

his mother's place of origin'.[83] But these laws speak 'of status, or of family, which is never traced from the mother, but proceeds solely from consanguinity on the father's side'.[84] This is why we say in France that 'the belly liberates and the rod ennobles'.[85] Thus, even the legitimate children of a noble mother and a commoner are commoners: as the law says,[86] 'In cases of children, even one born of a senator's daughter, we must judge the status of the father'. For, far from transferring her nobility to her husband or to her children, a noblewoman married to a commoner loses it herself, as it is a perpetual rule that the wife follows her husband's quality.[87]

66. True, the customs of the province of Champagne – specifically, of Troyes, Sens, Meaux, Chaumont, Vitry – expressly state that in order to be noble it is enough to be descended from a noble father or a noble mother. (This originates in a privilege given to the Champenois after the battle of Fontenay, near Auxerre, between King Charles the Bald and his brothers, according to some, or at Jaunes, near Bray, according to others, where most of the nobility of Champagne were killed.)[88]

67. But M. Pithou,[89] who has discussed this question fully, tells us that this custom is still observed only in respect of customary issues, and not for exemption from direct taxes. This was adjudicated in a decree of the *cour des aides* in 1566 and ordered to be published at the fiscal court of Troyes; though Thierriat records another of 7 August 1583,[90] to quite the contrary.

68. Further, the gloss to the Pragmatic Sanction[91] which, in certain cases, requires nobility on the side of both father and mother, says that this is to speak improperly, because there cannot be nobility on the mother's side. However, the truth is that the nobility of someone

---

[83] *Digest* 50.1.1.2.

[84] *Digest* 1.9 [especially 1.9.10 (paraphrased)].

[85] [1701 adds: Care must be taken that everything which occurs under natural being, which is liberty, is measured on the mother's side, and what occurs above proceeds from the father's stock.]

[86] *Digest* 1.9.10.

[87] *Digest* 1.9.8.

[88] [Battle of Fontenay, 25 June 841. 1701 adds: The privilege is similar to those mentioned in Roman law.]

[89] Pithou, pp. 2–4.

[90] [Rightly 1483: the source, as noted in 1710, is Bacquet (p. 35), not Thierriat.]

[91] [Cosme Guymier, *Pragmatica sanctio cu[m] concordatis . . . commentarius* (Lyon, 1532), fo. xcv^vo.]

born of a noble father and a noble mother is reputed more pure, through not being tainted by mingling with commoner blood. Such nobility is required of knights of the Order of the Holy Spirit, by the edict of their institution.

69. So much for those who are noble. Let us now see what rights they have. Tiraqueau[92] and Thierriat[93] (who has only translated him summarily) cite more than twenty fantastic and ridiculous ones, mostly false. If our petty country noblemen were to be believed, they give themselves so many privileges that a separate law, a separate country in this world and a separate paradise in the next would have to be designed for them. The insolence of the petty country gentlemen is so great (I do not speak of all those who have been raised at court, and especially of the great) that there is no living peaceably with them, and they themselves cannot live harmoniously with each other. They are birds of prey whose sole concern is to harass peaceful persons, to live off someone else's substance and, in a word, to pester each other.

70. Here, then, are the true rights of nobility. First, as to power I said in the first chapter that orders, unlike offices, have none in particular, but that they produce only an aptitude for offices, benefices and lordships. This is confirmed principally in the order of nobility, there being many offices particularly earmarked for the nobility.

71. The offices earmarked for the nobility are – to deal first with the royal household – all the chief positions and many of the rank and file: the gentlemen of the chamber, the one hundred gentlemen, the serving gentlemen, the esquires of the stables, the gentlemen of the hunt and falconry, and some others, as I have said in my *Offices*.[94] Secondly, so too are all the main military commands both of places and of companies, especially those of the cavalry, even down to simple membership of the ordinance companies. As for infantry captaincies, gentlemen again are preferred for them. Likewise, the edicts intended to refurbish the nominating of offices of judicature indicate that gentlemen are here preferred to commoners.

72. As for benefices, although the ecclesiastical order is distinct from the noble, yet there are many cathedral churches and even a number

---

[92] [*De nobil.*, pp. 65–89.]
[93] [*Trois traictez*, pp. 32 *et seq.*, 210 *et seq.*]
[94] IV. iii. [11, 19].

of abbeys where the dignities and simple canonries and places of the religious are earmarked for gentlemen. In general, however, gentlemen are favoured in the church through dispensations from restrictions of age, or of pluralism of benefices, or even of the period of study needed to attain the degree of doctor or licentiate.

73. Finally, in respect of lordships it is claimed that fiefs are reserved from time immemorial to nobles, and that today commoners are capable of holding them only by dispensation, for which they pay the king the subsidy of frank-fee: that is, reserved for the free-born and for gentlemen. Be that as it may, it is true that even nowadays only gentlemen are capable of holding great and middling lordships. The king's procurator and the feudal overlord himself can require a commoner to give them up if he has not been knowingly invested with them by the king, as I will show in the next chapter. Indeed, M. Choppin on the custom of Anjou[95] tells us that at the assembly of the Estates at Blois the nobility demanded in its lists of grievances that plain lordships, meaning those of high justice and fiefs held by knight's service, should be reserved for them, to the exclusion of commoners.

74. So much for power. As for the honour appertaining to nobility, it is the true effect of orders to produce a rank of honour, as the name indicates. So it is reasonable enough that nobility, which risks its life for the defence of the state, should be honoured by the people as its protector. With us, therefore, it is an established right that those of the order of nobility should precede and go before those of the third estate.

75. To this there are only two exceptions, both concerning offices of established status. First, in the district of their power all those who are magistrates take precedence over gentlemen, because of the command which they have over them. Consequently, all those residing within their territory can be described as their justiciable subjects, for magistrates have power to adjudicate upon such persons' goods, honour and lives, should occasion arise. Secondly, those who hold ennobling offices, such as the officers of the sovereign courts, the king's secretaries and others, should on all occasions take precedence over plain gentlemen by lineage. For, beyond the fact that they too

---

[95] Choppin, [I, pt. i, p. 212].

are nobles, they have the advantage of being officers of the king and so of having public power and an excellent function, which plain gentlemen do not have.

76. In respect of other marks of honour, nobles have the right to style themselves esquires and to bear timbred coats of arms, even if they should be townsmen and of the long robe and ennobled only by their offices.

77. Otherwise, all nobles except those of the long robe have the right to bear the sword as the insignia and mark of nobility. Seyssel says[96] that in France they may even bear it in the king's chamber – though by the statute of the Emperor Lothair[97] they are prohibited from bearing it in the palace of the counts without leave. I will deal with this right in the next chapter.

78. But the question arises whether commoners are duty bound to salute them, as they make out. The contrary is the case. As I mentioned in my *Offices*,[98] the salute is a recognition and duty of subjection. It is therefore due by way of formal behaviour only from subjects to those who have command over them by virtue either of property (as their lords) or of function (as their magistrates).

79. But honour and propriety dictate that salutation be given to those of the high nobility: to wit, great lords and officers of high dignity, and all those who have the right to style themselves knights. By the same propriety we salute those of our kin who have a degree of superior kinship over us. Even the most well-bred and most civilised salute all persons of honour, just as, from simple civility and courtesy, one salutes one's equal kin and one's friends. Even so, these last two points 'consist not in law, but in custom'.

80. As for pecuniary profits and emoluments, I have already said that pure orders have none. Yet the privileges of nobility are very great: to be exempt from direct taxes and all other personal payments levied for war. The privilege is indeed very reasonable, that those who contribute their lives for the state should be exempt from contributing their goods. In the same way, gentlemen are exempt from billeting soldiers, an obligation called in the ancient ordinances the

---

[96] *La Monarchie de France*, [ed. J. Poujol (Paris, 1961)] p. 121.

[97] [Lothair I (840–55): rightly, 'of the Emperor Frederick' I (1122–90) *De pace tenenda* [in *Operum C*, III, col. 1908; cf. below, section 87].

[98] I. vii. [18].

droit de gîte, and in Roman law 'the requirement of undertaking lodgings'.[99]

81. Gentlemen also have the privilege of hunting in places, in seasons, of game and with equipment which are not proscribed. This is justly prohibited to commoners for fear that they might thereby abandon their ordinary occupations, to the disservice of the public. It is rightly reserved to nobles so that in peacetime they may keep up an exercise similar to war, as hunting is: as Cicero says,[100] 'That they might engage in hunting, in resemblance of military discipline'. Yet in the law of Rome (where the nobility did not enjoy such advantages, nor was hunting so much used as has always been the case amongst the French, which Tiraqueau proves[101] from many fine authorities), hunting was permitted to all and sundry, in consequence of natural liberty. Nevertheless, the ordinances of France, ancient and modern alike, concede it only to gentlemen. Benedicti discusses this fully and observes, following Gaguin,[102] that one of the main causes of that memorable civil war called the War of the Public Weal was King Louis XI's prohibiting the nobility to hunt, which, he maintains, could not be done justly.

82. On the other hand, he refers to King Charles VI's ordinance of 1496[103] by which hunting is permitted not only to gentlemen, but also to honest burgesses living on their rents.

83. This seems to tally with King Henry IV's statute of hunting of 1601.[104] It specifically permits gentlemen and nobles to hunt and to shoot the arquebus, and prohibits these only to 'merchants, artisans, tillers of the soil, peasants and other such kinds of commoner persons': these, and not all commoners indiscriminately, are the terms of the statute. Hence it is easy to infer that honest burgesses living on their rents, notably those who have the right to style themselves noble men (whom I will specify in the last chapter), may, according to this statute, hunt and shoot the arquebus.[105]

---

[99] [*Code J* 12.40.10, cf. 12.40.4.]

[100] [*De natura deorum* II. 161.3.]

[101] [*De nobil.,* pp. 271–3.]

[102] *Repetitio* [. . . *in cap. Raynutius*], fo. 121ʳᵒ, col. 1; [cf. Robert] Gaguin [*De origine et gestis Francorum* (Lyon, 1497)].

[103] [Rightly, 1396/7: *Ord.,* VIII, pp. 117–18.]

[104] [Fontanon, II, pp. 340–1.]

[105] [1701 adds: As Pliny puts it, 'the condition of those who enjoyed descendants among the nobility is not inferior to that of those who had noble parents' [Pliny the Younger, *Panegyricus* lxx. 2].]

84. Gentlemen also have the privilege that when they happen to commit some crime they are not punished as rigorously as commoners. Tiraqueau has proved this with several citations,[106] to which I will add these lines from Prudentius:[107]

> Lest he sentence a man of distinction to vulgar punishment.
> Every man is punished according to his status,
> And it matters a great deal whether he is meanly or nobly born:
> The prisoners' rank dictates the form of torture.

85. This applies both to the severity of the condemnation and to the type of penalty. (There are penalties to which gentlemen are never condemned – to wit, the lash and the noose. Conversely, commoners are never beheaded, at least in this *parlement*.) Again, nobles obtain pardon and remission from the prince more readily than commoners obtain them.

86. But there are two exceptions to all this. The one concerns offences repugnant to nobility, such as treason, theft, perjury, falsehood. These are aggravated and augmented by the dignity of the person: 'for then the crime is increased by the status, rank and type of service', say the laws.[108] The other is that in respect of corporal punishments gentlemen are more delicately chastised, but in respect of fines or pecuniary penalties they ought to be punished more rigorously, as Tiraqueau demonstrates.[109] This is often observed in customs which lay down rates of fines.

87. Gentlemen also reckon it a privilege that they are not bound to engage in duels with commoners. This is true: it is contained in the statute of Federic [*sic*] on which Cujas[110] and other interpreters have commented. They say that the commoner ought to provide the noble whom he wishes to challenge to a duel with someone of equal status, or a noble champion. But I do not consider this a privilege, for divine and human laws indiscriminately prohibit all persons to duel. However, among our nobility 'this mischief is always prohibited and always retained'. This may be an act of divine providence that, just as in nature the most harmful animals exterminate each other, so it

---

[106] *De nobil.*, p. 78.
[107] [Aurelius] Prudentius [Clemens, *Peristephanon* x. 115, 118–20].
[108] *Digest* 49.16.2; 48.19.14.
[109] *De nobil.*, p. 80.
[110] *Opera C*, ii, cols. 757–8 [Rightly, 'Frederick' – cf. above, note 97].

is with our nobility who are surely at once the most valiant and the most violent and insolent in the world.

88. It remains to consider how nobility is lost. First, the great and important question arises, whether it is lost by ignominious condemnation, as is commonly held. Tiraqueau settles this in a general way with several fine citations.[111]

89. However, in my view we must be more specific about nobility. In the case of nobility of office, Tiraqueau's arguments lead me to think in general that it is lost through infamy, like the office on which it is grounded, as I have shown in my *Offices*.[112] In this connection Pithou cites[113] a memorable decree of 1534 by which the Sieur de Crem, Master of Accounts, was prohibited from styling himself knight because he had had to undergo a degrading public ritual (*amende honorable*) as a sign of his guilt. In the case of nobility which proceeds from lordship, the lordship is not lost through simple ignominious condemnation without confiscation of property. Baldus says[114] that such nobility is not lost through infamy because 'something is retained in consequence which could not be retained in principal'. I therefore think that when a commoner, who would have been ennobled through investiture with an ennobling lordship knowingly made him by the king, has lost his nobility through infamy, he can be further constrained to surrender the lordship by those with an interest in it. But, in so far as he is tolerated, he is reputed noble, as in the next chapter I shall say about the commoner who holds an ennobling lordship without royal investiture.

90. Yet as for nobility by lineage, which is native and – as it were – natural to man, I hold against Tiraqueau that it is not altogether lost through infamy. 'Rights of blood cannot be nullified by any civil law';[115] and 'a rule of civil law cannot destroy natural rights'.[116] There is only one exception to this: when the condemnation pronounces that the gentleman is declared a commoner or degraded from nobility, as is ordinarily done with the crime of treason and with every genuine

---

[111] *De nobil.*, pp. 99–101.
[112] I. xiii. [81].
[113] Pithou, [p. 5].
[114] [*In quartum et quintum Codicis ... praelectiones* (Lyon, 1561), fo. 174ʳᵒ, col. 1: on *Code J* 5.9.1.]
[115] *Digest* 50.17.8.
[116] *Digest* 4.5.8.

crime of *lèse majesté*. Furthermore, I said in the first chapter that order is not as easy to lose as office.

91. However, it seems that an infamous person cannot use the honorific rights of nobility. The laws say that 'infamous persons cannot make use of honours which are only conferred upon persons of worth';[117] and that 'the infamous shall be cut off from all honours';[118] and that 'a question of infamy takes away honour'.[119]

92. That is why I think that rank and precedence in the quality of a gentleman may justly be disputed in the case of a gentleman who has undergone a degrading public ritual as a sign of his guilt. But I believe that he retains the privileges of nobility, and so that he cannot be subjected to direct taxation; nor can his inheritance be divided commoner-fashion.

93. What, then, shall we say of someone who has obtained letters of ennoblement? For my part, I consider that in this respect he must be placed among the gentlemen by lineage. The king has purged and put out from him every commoner stain and mark, and has placed him in such rank and dignity as if he had been born of noble blood. Budé calls these letters 'restitution of birth',[120] as I said in the last chapter.

94. Further, there are two particular reasons, which do not apply to express ennoblement, as to why nobility by office is more liable than nobility by lineage to removal through infamy. The first is that nobility by office is indirect, accessory and accidental,[121] bestowed upon the person not because of himself, but because of his office or his lordship. Therefore it does not adhere as strongly as ennoblement which is conferred directly and immediately upon the person because of his own merit. The second is that nobility by office is grounded upon the office, and office is not compatible with infamy; while nobility which proceeds from ennoblement is grounded upon the absolute power of the prince who has wished to confer it upon the ennobled one.

95. A still greater difficulty arises over whether the children of a father who has quite lost his nobility – such as when a gentleman by

---

[117] *Code J* 10.59.1.
[118] [Cf.] *Digest* 48.6.
[119] *Code J* 10.31.8.
[120] [*Opera B*, III, p. 76.]
[121] *Code J* 12.2.1, *gl. ord. s. l.* 'q' [*Corpus iuris civilis* (Paris, 1576), V, pt. 2 (*Tres posteriores libri Codicis*), col. 222].

lineage is degraded from nobility – lose it for the same reason. This difficulty arises from an unsound reading of the words of the following law:[122]

> It was decided by the divine Marcus that the descendants of men designated 'most eminent' and 'most perfect', to the degree of great-grandsons, should not be subject to the penalties inflicted on plebeians, if no stigma of violated honour attached to children of a nearer degree through whom the privilege was transmitted. The most learned man Ulpian alleges in his books of *Disputations* on public law that this rule shall be observed in respect of decurions and their sons.

Cujas proves[123] that 'shall be observed' must be read 'shall not be observed', for the passage from Ulpian's *Disputations* is recorded at length elsewhere,[124] and there he says, following Papinian's opinion, that 'a son whose grandfather was a decurion shall not be dishonoured through censure of his father'.

96. The matter is resolved still more acutely in this law:[125]

> If a man had both a father and a grandfather of senatorial rank, he is considered to be both the son and the grandson of a senator; but if his father lost that dignity before his conception, it may be asked whether he ought still to be considered the grandson of a senator although he may not be a senator's son. The better opinion is that he ought, so that his grandfather's dignity may advance him rather than his father's misfortune hold him back.

97. However, I cannot altogether endorse Cujas's reasoning as to why the children of decurions retained their grandfather's privilege even though their father had fallen into infamy, and that the reverse was the case with the grandchildren of those called 'most perfect'. His reasoning is[126] that greater uprightness is required 'in the descendants of the most perfect than in those of decurions', the latter being of lesser quality. The law just cited says as much of senators 'who were most renowned' and therefore were of still higher degree than the 'most perfect', as I shall prove in my penultimate chapter.

---

[122] *Code J* 9.41.11.
[123] *Opera C*, III, col. 637.
[124] *Digest* 50.2.2.2.
[125] *Digest* 1.9.7.2.
[126] [Above, note 123.]

98. But, with all due respect to so great a personage, I consider it more reasonable to hold that the 'most perfect' were those who had this title of dignity because of their offices. Now it is certain that, excepting only exemption from liability to torture or to the punishments suffered by the populace at large, the privileges of offices are not passed on to children.[127] Even that exemption is not passed on if the impediment of infamy should intervene. On the contrary, it was peculiar to the orders of senators and decurions that they should transfer their dignities almost entirely to their descendants who also remained bound by the responsibilities thereof, as I said in the second chapter: so that this was, as it were, a particular condition of their lineage.

99. Here is the answer to our question. Nobility is transmissible to descendants, still more so than the orders of senator and decurion. Children who have lost nobility otherwise acquired through their father do not lose it through his offence. Thus, someone seeking to vindicate his nobility may produce the decree whereby his father was condemned to be beheaded.

100. There are those holding nobility only from their father – such as persons invested with offices of high dignity, or even with simple ennobling offices – who nevertheless have treated the penalty as void, and have transferred the nobility to their children on the grounds that their grandfather possessed a similar office. Yet a distinction must be drawn between children conceived before the father's misfortune (who do not lose the order of nobility through his offence, as they had it from their conception), and those conceived subsequently.[128] However, this opinion is extremely doubtful in respect of those who hold their nobility 'from father and grandfather', for the statute of 1600 requires[129] both father and grandfather always to have lived nobly, without derogating from their nobility.

101. Then since nobility by lineage is not altogether extinguished by crime, it follows still more emphatically that it should not be lost through exercising the mechanic arts. And yet (strange as it may initially seem), while crime does not deprive a gentleman of exemption from direct taxes, it is none the less well known that base and mechanic practices do deprive him of it. The explanation is the

---

[127] *Code J* 9.18.7.
[128] *Digest* 1.9.7.2; 50.2.2.2 *et seq.*
[129] Fontanon, II, p. 881.

declaration in the tax commissions that the exempt and the non-exempt shall be assessed except, amongst others, nobles living nobly. Accordingly, it is not enough to be noble unless one lives nobly. Furthermore, the people who pay more because of the gentleman's exemption are recompensed, in that the latter do not share in the profits from commerce and crafts.

102. However, this point must always be borne in mind: that nobility is not totally obliterated through such derogating acts, but is only suspended.

103. Thus, the gentleman is always poised to recover his nobility when he chooses to abstain from derogating from it.

104. However, without a public declaration of it such a gentleman's intention would not be known. Therefore, the practice in this case is to take out letters of rehabilitation from the king. These are legal letters, issued without cognisance of the case, and not normally refused; but they have only been contrived so as further to exalt the king's power. It could still be held that they are not at all necessary for a gentleman by lineage who has derogated from his status, nor for his descendants, for it is common law that rights of blood and of nature cannot be lost by civil means. But I consider that these letters are absolutely necessary to a gentlewoman by lineage who is the widow of a commoner; for without the prince's grace she cannot revert to her former condition, which she lost through placing herself by marriage in a commoner family. These letters are also necessary to children whose father and grandfather have derogated, because, since the nobility of the descendants is presumed through the noble life of the father and grandfather, it apparently should be lost through their ignoble life, if the prince does not re-establish it.

105. M. Le Bret holds[130] such rehabilitation to be sufficient, provided that the derogation has not continued to the seventh degree, in which case an entirely new ennoblement is necessary. In my view, this should also apply to the son of someone ennobled by office who derogated from his nobility without being rehabilitated in his lifetime. I think that his nobility is entirely extinguished, and still more so – for the reason just stated above – in the case of a person who pretends to nobility because of his father's and grandfather's ennobling offices.

106. The occupations derogating from nobility are those of prosecuting attorney, clerk of a court, notary, serjeant, clerk in general, mer-

---

[130] Le Bret, fos. 215ro–17vo.

chant, and artisan of any trade, except hunting. However, as M. Le Bret tells us,[131] the last of these does not bring nobility and is not assigned to nobles, as some think.

107. All this applies when one does such things for profit. It is base and sordid gain that derogates from nobility. The proper course for nobility is to live on one's rents, or at least not to sell one's efforts and one's labour.

108. And yet, judges, advocates, doctors and professors of the liberal [sciences], do not derogate from the nobility which they otherwise have, even though they gain their livelihoods through their positions. Beyond the fact that it proceeds from the work of the mind and not from the labour of the hands, this profit is rather honorary than mercenary: 'strictly speaking, they receive not wages, but fees for services rendered'.[132] This has never been doubted in respect of judges.

109. As for advocates of the sovereign courts, there is the common decree of Maître Anne de Terrières, sieur de Chappes, which Luc records.[133] And, for those of the lower courts, Pithou records[134] for us a privy council decree, given at Paris on 4 March 1547, between the noble denizens and the representatives of the third estate of Rennes. By this decree the king quashes the levy imposed upon nobles exercising offices of judicature, pleading for parties and taking salaries for it. He declares that they do not contravene their noble status, and so orders that what they have lost be returned to them. This should be understood only of those who plead, such as advocates, and not of those who act as solicitors, as advocates do in many courts, following the ordinance of Roussillon,[135] for the place of a solicitor even in a sovereign court is undoubtedly base and derogates from his nobility, as Tiraqueau proves.[136]

110. But, despite common opinion, the practice of tillage does not derogate at all from nobility. This is because of its utility, but more especially because no activity in which the gentleman engages for himself and without drawing money from someone else is derogatory.

---

[131] *Ibid.*, fos. 218ro–25vo.
[132] *Digest* 50.13.1 [paraphrased].
[133] [Jean du] Luc [*Placitorum summae apud Gallos curiae, libri* XII (Paris, 1553), p. 85].
[134] Pithou, [pp. 4–5].
[135] [1564: Isambert, XIV, pp. 161 *et seq.*].
[136] *De nobil.*, pp. 114–15.

If he should take farms to exploit, there is no doubt at all that he does not derogate, *pace* the law on rights of patronage.[137] This is understood to apply to farms for long terms, which we call 'rents' and the English, to whom this law refers, call 'farms', as I showed in my *Offices*.[138] Nobles are not prohibited from taking share-cropping leaseholds in perpetuity, for long terms of years, or for lives; because in these leases the rights of utilisation over the land are transferred to the taker,[139] so that from then on the gentleman is said to work his land and not that of someone else.

111. Much the most difficult question that I know in this matter, and perhaps the least discussed, is to establish whether foreign gentlemen living in France enjoy the privileges of nobility, especially exemption from direct taxes. One's initial impression is that they do not: as they are not citizens of France, still less can they be noble, given that nobility is the second degree of the French people, which presupposes the first.[140] And when they are made citizens by letters of naturalisation, these letters do not make them noble: as I have said, legitimation does not encompass ennoblement. Further, how should foreigners be free and exempt from the subsidies which natural citizens pay, given that in times past they paid a particular subsidy for the licence to reside in France, called *estrayere*, as it were *estrangere* (stranger), as Bacquet tells us?[141]

112. Further, it is certain that among the Romans nobility could appertain only to citizens of Rome. Foreigners, and even the inhabitants of other towns subject to Rome who were noble in their own country, were called *domi-nobiles*: that is, nobles at home or in their own way. 'From many towns and colonies, men of noble rank at home', says Sallust.[142] The term occurs more than ten times in Cicero (for brevity's sake I will not cite them in detail), and so Erasmus has included it in his *Proverbs*[143] – though he interprets it badly, saying that a *domi-nobilis* is someone 'who is not celebrated to such a noble degree for his works and power, but is of noble descent'. Care must

---

[137] *Decretales* 3.38.7.
[138] v. ii. [11–13].
[139] *Digest* 6.3.1.
[140] [I.e., membership of that people, not the 'first estate'.]
[141] Bacquet, [I, pp. 8–9].
[142] *Bellum Catilinae* [XVII. 4].
[143] *Adagiorum* [IV. ix. 49 (*Opera omnia*, II (Hildesheim, 1961), col. 1155)].

be taken that all these passages from Cicero, in Nizole's collection[144] where the term is used improperly, do refer to foreigners, or at least to others than inhabitants of Rome: above all, the passage in a letter[145] where he recommends to his brother Quintus 'Marcus Orphinus, a noble man at home and well regarded also outside his home'.

113. But the French are most courteous towards foreigners (though the latter do not reciprocate the treatment). I therefore have no doubt that foreigners who are certainly noble in their own country, and especially from states which are friendly and allied to this realm, will be taken for nobles in France and shall be exempt from all commoner subsidies. Surely it is a very fitting and useful thing in the society of men, primarily among Christians and above all among allied states, to acknowledge one's neighbour reciprocally in one's own house according to the quality which he enjoys in his country.

114. This is so when the foreigner is not naturalised, for in that case he remains in the quality of his country. It is also so when he has been made a citizen of the realm, for he is presumed to have been received there in his proper and pristine quality. This depends upon his making his quality clear, for otherwise he lies in vain who comes from afar, as the saying is. While the proof is often difficult, in my view the difficulty is more of fact than of law. But if it should appear by conclusive proof or well-attested fact, as when the son of a great lord from a foreign country has come to live in France, shall we make him pay direct taxes, or make him purchase his ennoblement?[146]

115. Even so, I take all this to apply to true and perfect nobility, proceeding by the means recognised in France: antiquity of lineage, concession of the sovereign, or great offices. There is no doubt at all that in no country in the world does nobility enjoy greater advantages than in France. Almost everywhere else it is only honorary, with no particular franchises. Direct taxes do not ordinarily fall only on the third estate, as in France; but subsidies are levied indiscriminately, upon all the people. Hence its easier concession, being rather an adornment than a charge upon the country, and a comfort to the people rather than a burden upon them.

---

[144] [Mario Nizzoli, *Nizolius, sive Thesaurus Ciceronianus* (Basle, 1568).]
[145] *Epistularum ad quintum fratrem* II. [xiv. 3].
[146] [1701 adds: Nobility is a quality inherent to the person and thus is borne everywhere: 'Those who hasten across the sea change their horizon, not their spirit' [Horace, *Epistularum* I. xi. 37].]

116. As Thomas Smith shows very well,[147]

> Gentlemen are made cheap in England. For whoever professes
> the liberal sciences, whoever can live comfortably on his rents
> without manual labour and bear the port, countenance and
> charge of a gentleman, shall be called a gentleman and taken for
> a gentleman. And for further assurance of his nobility, the king
> of arms will give him, in return for money, newly devised coats
> of arms, and will tender him letters indicating that these arms
> are given him for his merits; and then he can be called esquire.
> Such persons are often called derisively gentlemen of the first
> head.

He goes on to show that this convention is very useful to the country.
117. Now I do not think that such ennobled persons coming to reside
in France ought to enjoy the privileges of nobility. Aristotle settles
the matter excellently: there are those who are noble properly and
entirely, 'absolutely', and others who are so only improperly and in
some sort, 'relatively'.[148] The former, he says, are noble everywhere,
and wherever they go they take their nobility with them. But the
others, whose nobility is peculiar to their country and not indifferently
received everywhere, are not recognised as noble in another country.
Jerome Orose[149] has managed to make good use of this passage:

> On the one hand, nobility is unconditional everywhere; on the
> other, it in fact has its place only at home. Change of location
> never entails loss of the former: among whatever people it may
> be it always holds fast with deep and immovable roots, and has
> the same dignity among all nations. But the latter flourishes only
> in its own country and among its own people, rather by common
> opinion than by the luminous merits of true dignities.

118. And it is instances of the latter that the Romans termed *domi-
nobiles*, terms adapted to the inhabitants of other towns subject to
Rome and signifying the descendants of those who, in such towns,
had held offices corresponding to the great offices of Rome. As for
foreigners, the Romans called them likewise *domi-nobiles* – that is,

---

[147] *De Rep. Angl.*, [pp. 71–2]
[148] [Cf.] *Politics* 1255ᵃ33–7. [As Dr Lionel North reminds me, the quoted terms have
dialectical implications: see Aristotle, *Topics* 115ᵇ12–15.]
[149] '*De nobilit. civ.* lib. 1 cap. 4' [cf. Jeronimo de Oroz, author of *De apicibus juris civilis
libri quinque* (Lyon, 1661)].

nobles in their own homes. This was because the Romans claimed to be lords of the whole world, and so did not want to acknowledge that foreigners had any legitimate sovereignty even in their own country to establish a perfect nobility there. Be that as it may, the Romans did not countenance in any way that such persons should have any participation or communication of honour with them.

119. But in France all these considerations are void. On the one hand, all our towns are equal and none has any command over another; all are subject to our king, all are part of our monarchy. On the other hand, we hold that sovereign states are bounded according to the limits which God has imposed upon them, that they are all legitimate within their own boundaries. Accordingly, we make no difficulty about recognising as perfectly noble both those of the least significant village of France, and those of foreign countries who are reputed noble in their countries, especially if nobility is established there in the French form.

CHAPTER SIX

Of the high nobility

1. The closing remarks of the last chapter put me in mind of an amusing question which Chasseneuz and Tiraqueau raise:[1] whether the common saying of our country gentlemen can be sustained, 'that they are as much gentlemen as the king'. Both of them reject it, partly on the strength of the passages from Cicero and Aristotle that have just been cited, but above all because, as is well known, there are many degrees in the order of nobility.

2. For my part, I freely confess that this comparison of the subject with his king is odious, insolent and well-nigh blasphemous. Yet I consider it to be inherently true, given that whoever is absolutely and perfectly a gentleman cannot be more so, as that passage from Aristotle clearly states. It is also the case that true order is a substantive quality, positive and – as with substance in dialectic – not susceptible of increase nor of decrease. Thus, it is true to say that the lowest priest is as much a priest as the greatest bishop; and the lowest bishop, so to speak, is as much a bishop as the pope. This is the solution to the famous passage from St Cyprian which those of the so-called reformed religion allege against us: 'the rest of the apostles undoubtedly formed, with Peter, a community equal in both honour and power'[2] – that is, to the extent that they were apostles.

3. But the difficulty with the proverb in question arises when someone says, 'I am as noble as the king'. If this word 'noble' is understood as an adjective, signifying 'excellent', the proverb is apparently false;

---

[1] [Barthélemy de] Chasseneuz, [*Catalogus gloriae mundi* (Frankfurt, 1579), fo. 202ᵛᵒ; *De nobil.*, pp. 13–14].
[2] [*PL*, IV, col. 515.]

if as a substantive, like the word 'gentleman', signifying someone who has the order of nobility, the proverb is true, apart from the improbity of the comparison. Likewise, it would be false to say that an unlearned (*indocte*) doctor is as learned as the most learned; but it is true enough to say that he is as much a doctor as the latter.

4. So, just as there are degrees that enhance the order of the priesthood, there are likewise degrees that enhance the order of nobility. Yet, while the degrees of priesthood are consistent throughout Christendom which is governed by one and the same head, nevertheless the degrees of nobility differ in accordance with the diversity of states or sovereignties from which they depend.

5. Here I will say a word about the practices of our principal neighbours. A Spaniard[3] who has commented on the rules of chancery identifies six degrees of the nobility of Spain:

> Petty, lesser, least; great, greater, greatest. The petty have no official dignity, but merely jurisdiction; the lesser have no jurisdiction, but merely noble blood; the least are not noble by birth, but live nobly, on their rents. The great are barons; the greater are dukes and counts; the greatest, finally, are kings and emperors.

6. As for the English, they have plain nobles or gentlemen; then esquires (whom they generally distinguish from plain nobles, terming esquires specifically those who live in the country and engage only in the profession of arms); knights; and, finally, lords or 'my-lords' – to wit, dukes, marquises, earls, viscounts and barons. Beyond these, they do not recognise princes any more than Spaniards do, at least in the sense of a formal order, as in France; they call 'prince' only the king's eldest son.

7. It is noteworthy that in England only the lords are of the high nobility. As for gentlemen, esquires and knights, they are of the order of the common people: in fact, they are commingled with the people in the same chamber in assemblies of their parliament. These are their estates-general which we used to call by the same name before we reserved it for the sovereign judicial body. Thus in England there are only two estates or orders, namely the high nobility and the common people, just as in Rome there were at first only the 'Senate

---

[3] [Unidentified.]

and the People of Rome'. The order of the clergy constitutes no part
of the state in England, any more than it did in Rome, and unlike
our most Christian France. The archbishops alone have the right to
speak and to sit among the lords in the chamber of the high nobility,
and the bishops have the right of entry but not of speaking there; so
Thomas Smith tells us.[4]

8. But in France we think more highly of the nobility. We do not
commingle it at all with the humbler sort. In accordance with Bartolus's definition noted in the last chapter,[5] we hold it to be an order
entirely separated from the people. We even place the princes among
the nobility; and there is now no gentleman too insignificant for a
prince to object to receiving him in his company and at his table –
though in former times, when we were mixed with the English, it
was said that 'no one should sit at a baron's table unless he was a
knight'. In short, just as there is no nobility in the world more brave
and valiant than that of France, so there is none more honoured and
more advantaged.

9. And yet, we have more degrees of nobility than there are in England. Apart from our having, as they have, knights and lords of various
kinds, we have also the princes – to wit, those who issue from a
sovereign house. These again are of several kinds, so that we might
well lay claim to as many degrees of nobility as that Spanish commentator does. But, because the most perfect division is into three
species, I have divided our nobility – more to the purpose, as it seems
to me – into plain, high and illustrious. By plain nobility I mean that
which is not enhanced by any other degree of honour; by the high
nobility, that which is raised and improved by some dignity, whether
knighthood, great office, or lordship; and, finally, by the illustrious
nobility, that which proceeds from illustrious and sovereign blood,
close to the sovereign prince by kinship and capable in status of
succeeding to the sovereignty.

10. And because this general division comprises all the degrees of
nobility which are much more numerous than three, it is necessary
further to subdivide those of the highest degrees. In respect of the

---

[4] [Cf. *De Rep. Angl.*, pp. 79–85. Smith's point is that, while the bishops sit on one side
of the House of Lords and the lay peers on the other, it is the judges, master of the
rolls and secretaries of state, seated on the woolsacks in the middle, who 'have no voice
in the house'.]

[5] [Above, ch. 5, note 42.]

high nobility, which is our particular topic in this chapter, it can be subdivided in three: to wit, knights, great officers and lords. This is more especially the case as the high nobility proceeds from three divers sources: the order of knights, of great offices, and of lordships of dignity.

11. Yet all three of these species ultimately relate to the same titles of dignity by which all members of the high nobility call themselves well-nigh indiscriminately: knights and lords. On the one hand, those who have great offices and lordships of dignity, as well as those who have the order of chivalry, call themselves knights in their titles. On the other hand, knights and great office-holders call themselves lords, or *messeigneurs*, as do those who possess great lordships.

12. We have therefore to explain these three sorts of high nobility one after the other. Our modern writers compare that of knighthood, which is the least of the three, to those honorary militia whom Suetonius says[6] to have been devised by the Emperor Claudius. He terms them 'fictitious military services, performed *in absentia* and in name only', or 'for show' as Lampridius describes them.[7] But it is an abuse always to think of relating the ways of Rome to our own.

13. The fact is that the order of chivalry is a quality of honour which kings and other sovereign princes ascribe to those whom they wish to distinguish above other gentlemen, as the most stout and valiant. They do so with certain ceremonies in order to draw attention to the recipients and make them appear more impressive. The ancient Romans specify these ceremonies for us better than any books.

14. Briefly, the ceremonies are that after the recipients had kept watch at prayer all night in church and had then offered public and solemn prayers, the king gave them the accolade. Some take this to mean that he struck them on the shoulders with the flat of his sword, as Thomas Smith[8] and Du Tillet[9] observe. Thus were Roman slaves who received their freedom struck by the praetor with his rod, called the *vindicta*. When bishops confer the order of the tonsure or the degree of doctor is conferred in the universities, the promoted person is given a blow or a buffet.[10]

[6] *Divus Claudius* [xxv. 1].
[7] *Alexander Severus* [xv. 3].
[8] [*De Rep. Angl.*, p. 69.]
[9] *Recueil*, pp. 316–20 [especially 319].
[10] [1701 adds: as the last blow to be received by someone who enters into a quality exempting him from any such treatment thereafter.]

15. Alternatively, the accolade is the embrace which the new knight receives from his king or sovereign prince. Thereby he is afterwards reputed the king's friend and favourite, risen from his side. He is the king's knife-bearer, 'protector of the latter's side', if he is a knight at arms – or, if a knight at laws, counsellor and assessor at the sovereign's side, as the cardinals call themselves 'at the pope's side'. And as a mark and memento of the sovereign prince's accolade they thereafter wear a collar or a shoulder sash, so that this neck (*col*) or these shoulders which have once felt the friendly touch of majesty should always be adorned with his livery.

16. Now in my view it is very likely that this kind of accolade was copied from the magnificence of the Roman emperors who allowed only the most valiant men to salute and adore them,[11] notably those who had passed through all the military degrees, whether of the armed militia or the imperial guard. So much may be gathered from the following law:[12]

> Those who belong to the retinue of eminent officials charged with the annual collection of taxes shall be permitted each year to appear before the emperor and pay him reverence; these apart, none of those who hold provincial offices shall have the right to do reverence to our serenity, all such privileges being summarily abolished.

Additional laws[13] further confirm that if others took it upon themselves they were punished. Thus Spartianus says of the Emperor Severus that[14]

> he ordered a fellow-townsman who was once his comrade and, being a plebeian, had embraced him, to be beaten with clubs, and commanded a herald to announce that no plebeian should presume to embrace a legate of the Roman people.

17. This is called 'reverencing the emperor, or reverencing the purple', and is found more than ten times in the last three books of

---

[11] [1701 adds: Thus Dio Cassius says of the Emperor Claudius that 'he used to kiss very few, and to most even of the senators he only offered either his hand or his foot for homage'. This is more or less what Pliny says: 'lowering the embrace to his feet and returning the kiss with his hand' [Dio, *Rom. hist.* LIX. xxvii. 1; Pliny the Younger, *Panegyricus* 24. 2]. 1610 continues with matter occurring in section 19 of 1701.]

[12] *Code J* 12.53.1.

[13] *Code J* 12.11.1, 12.3.4, 12.52.1, 12.17; *Code Theod.* 6.24.3.

[14] *Severus* [II. vi].

Justinian's *Code*. Those who saluted the emperor got on their knees, as Zonaras tells us:[15]

> But when he was now in the presence of the ruler Belisarius persuaded Gelimer to throw himself on to the ground and in that posture to render obeisance to the emperor. With tears in his eyes he did as he was bidden. And Belisarius himself flung himself on the ground, showing Gelimer that he had been asked to do this not because he was a prisoner, but because this was the way in which obeisance was customarily done to the Roman emperors.

18. It was first made an ordinary practice by Diocletian. 'He', says Eutropius,[16] 'was the first to introduce a form of royal usage over and above Roman freedom and ordered that he be reverenced, whereas formerly the emperors were merely saluted'. However, Lampridius tells us[17] that it was Elagabalus who was the first to have himself reverenced: 'Alexander Severus forbade anyone to worship him, whereas Elagabalus had already begun to receive reverence in the manner of the kings of the Persians'. And Capitolinus describes[18] how Maximinus II

> was most haughty at his levees: for he both extended his hand and allowed his knees to be kissed. The elder Maximinus never allowed this, saying: 'May the gods forbid that any of the free-born should kiss my feet'.

19. The fact is that the practice came from the ancient manner of doing things in Rome where great lords were daily saluted ceremonially by their clients and friends. Likewise, those who were allowed to salute the prince were reputed to be his friends and favourites, which was considered a great honour and privilege.[19]

20. Our knights have borrowed yet another notable ceremony from the Roman emperors. In conferring the order of chivalry upon them, the prince gives them a sword and buckles it on: 'he gives a sword-

---

[15] *PG*, CXXXIV, col. 1245.
[16] [*Breviarum historiae Romanae* (London, 1821) IX. 26.]
[17] *Alexander Severus* [xviii. 3].
[18] *Maximini Duo* [xxviii. 7].
[19] [1701 adds: Furthermore it was permitted only to men of mark and the most valiant ... Again, Capitolinus tells us that when [the elder] Maximinus was a tribune he was not allowed to salute the emperor his predecessor: 'never did he come to take the emperor's hand, never did he greet him' (*Maximini Duo* [v. 1]).]

belt with the band passing over the shoulder'. We call this a baldric; under the Roman emperors it was the common insignia of dignities whether of the armed militia or of the imperial guard. In fact the belt is commonly taken in law to stand for the dignity; by Suidas' interpretation,[20] 'a belt is a sign of rank'. The baldric or military belt marked the distinction of rank or degree of honour held by those who had the same titles of simple honorary dignities, as in the law[21] which I will explain very shortly.

21. Now here, in my view, is how this practice developed gradually in Rome and came from Rome to us. It is quite certain that Roman soldiers dressed differently from citizens residing in towns, and their principal distinguishing feature was to bear the sword, 'to wear a sword', 'to be girded'. Just as the Romans were particularly careful of their toga, or garment of peace, so was it only those who were actually soldiers, that is to say enlisted, who had the right to bear the sword, which Suidas calls 'wearing a sword'.[22]

22. At first not all governors of provinces had that right. Thus, by the division which Augustus made, governorships of proconsular provinces were left to the senate, being considered the most peaceable; Dio has observed[23] this more satisfactorily than any other author of Roman history. Be that as it may, the right of bearing the sword at times other than war was ascribed at first only to eminent dignities: witness Herodian's comment on Plautius,[24] that 'he always wore the broad stripe, and he bore a sword and all the other badges of the highest ranks'.

23. However, as time passed everyone wanted a share of the privileges of the soldiers because these were very great. So all officers of the imperial household and many others again wanted to bear the sword and to have the military belt, even though this was the soldiers' insignia, 'the characteristic mark of being in the army', says Zonaras.[25] Hence their girdle signifies an office or public charge, for all those

---

[20] *Suidae* [*Lexicon*, ed. A. Adler (Leipzig, 1931), part II, p. 513 (141). The *Suda* was in fact a collaborative compilation, partly lexicographical, of the later Byzantine period (tenth century).]

[21] *Code J* 12.8.2 [see below, section 25].

[22] *Suidae* [*Lexicon*, part III, p. 497 (72)].

[23] *Rom. hist.* [LIII. xiii. 2–4].

[24] [*History* III. ii. 2.]

[25] *PG*, CXXXVII, [col. 273].

who had honourable offices bore the sword like men at arms, as the law shows.[26]

24. Again, after the Empire had been transferred to Greece and Greek ambition had established itself in the imperial court, everyone desired more and more dignities and ranks of honour, and the available offices were hardly enough to suit and accommodate all those who wanted them. So the emperors invented plain dignities: that is, they gave the titles and qualities of office to those who had never been officers, and these were termed 'vacant or honorary dignities'. In order that these honorary dignities might appear more convincing, they conferred ceremonially upon those whom they honoured the insignia of the dignity or office of which the latter received the title – and, notably, the military belt which thus became the common insignia of all dignities.

25. This is clearly explained in the law[27] where the emperor specifies the rank of dignities of the same title. He places in the first rank those who had had the actual exercise of the office. He then makes several ranks or dignities of those who had never had that exercise, but were plain honorary officers. In the second rank he places those who were at court and to whom the emperor had given the military belt; in the third, those to whom he had simply sent it in their absence; in the fourth, those to whom the belt had never been given at all, but to whom, being at court, the emperor had simply given the letters of dignity; and in the fifth and last, those to whom he had sent these simple letters in their absence. Thus, among these honorary officers, those who had had the military belt took precedence over those who had only simple letters; and amongst these, the ones who had been honoured in the imperial presence were more highly esteemed than those to whom either the military belt or the letters of honorary dignity had been sent in their absence.

26. Hence there arise several points of great relevance to the practice of our knights. First, the military belt was solemnly conferred upon persons of merit who had no office nor public charge, and it ascribed to them the right of continually bearing the sword

---

[26] [Cf.] *Code J* 12.33.5.2.
[27] *Code J* 12.8.2.

and consequently of enjoying the privileges of men at arms. Secondly, receiving it from the emperor himself was more of an honour than if it were simply sent. Thirdly, having the military belt even when simply sent by the emperor was more of an honour than having simple letters of dignity.

27. Likewise in France, those whom the kings recognised to be of great merit, or at least whom they wished to raise in dignity when they had no office to confer, were made knights: that is, the kings declared such men to be honorary men-at-arms, to enjoy the privileges of men-at-arms although they were not enlisted in the armed forces. Most of our French officers in fact term the knight in Latin *militem* and not *equitem*; but more particularly they pronounce them mounted men-at-arms (*de cheval*), because principally in France they are much more highly regarded than foot-soldiers.

28. And as a sign of their being made men-at-arms, the kings gave them with their own hands the baldric or military belt, with those splendid and noteworthy ceremonies which I have just recorded. For maximum effect these ceremonies were performed with such magnificence and expense that in order to meet the costs, as many customs show, lords had the right to levy taxes on their vassals, tenants and those subject to their jurisdiction, when they or their eldest sons were made knights, just as when they married off their eldest daughters, or when they paid their ransoms. In our customs this is termed 'the right to tax in the four cases'.

29. Furthermore, not only enlisted soldiers, but also plain gentlemen as soldiers born and destined for war have in France the right to bear the sword at all times and in all places, even in the king's cabinet, as I said in the last chapter. Therefore knights, who enjoy a degree of dignity above that of plain gentlemen, have had to be given insignia or a badge more peculiar to their dignity. This is to have gold spurs and all other chivalric apparel which, formerly, only knights were allowed to wear, as Boutillier has well observed,[28] and Du Tillet after him.[29] That is why some of our modern writers term knights 'gilded horsemen'.

30. But because of these beautiful ceremonies and magnificences which took place on the creation of knights (the more especially as

---

[28] [Jean] Boutillier [*La Somme rural[e]* (Lyon, 1500), fo. clxxviii^{ro}: 'De anoblir ung homme'].

[29] [*Recueil*, p. 318.]

the king most often took the trouble to buckle on their swords), not only plain gentlemen, but also lords, princes and even the royal children wanted to have this knightly dignity. They thought that receiving the sword at the king's hands would be not only an honour for them, but also a favourable portent and even an assurance of valour and prowess. So we see in our annals that King Charlemagne buckled on the sword of Louis the Pious, his son, in readiness to go to war against the Avars; and that the same Louis the Pious did as much for his son Charles the Bald, according to Aimon.[30] Similarly, the good St Louis made his eldest son Philip III a knight, and the latter his three children. And history records that in performing these acts the kings had their crowns on their heads and held plenary court and kept open table.

31. Again, it was the ancient practice to make knights either before a battle or an assault so as to encourage brave gentlemen to conduct themselves valiantly, or after the battle or the capture of the place so as to reward those who had done good service. Monstrelet gives a fine example,[31] as does Froissart[32] in his account of the Knights of the Hare which Du Tillet likewise recounts[33] in his chapter on knights.

32. They were also made at the marriages of kings or royal children to reflect honour on the tournaments which were held. In my view, Knights of the Bath are of that kind, so called by the Romans and in other old books because they were made on emerging from the solemn bath which was customary before marriage. Alternatively, Du Tillet suggests[34] that persons knighted in circumstances other than war were called Knights of the Bath because, among other ceremonies, they were required to bathe before receiving the order of chivalry.

33. At all events, nobles of the two other degrees – that is, plain gentlemen and princes – have their quality by nature, at least from their birth, against the common rule of other dignities. Yet knighthood maintains the common rule of orders: that no one is born a knight, but this order or quality must be actually conferred upon the

---

[30] Aimoinus, [*Historiae Francorum, libri V* (Paris, 1567),] p. 621.

[31] *La Chronique d'Eugerran de Monstrelet*, [ed. L. Doüet-d' Arcq, III (Paris, 1859),] pp. 137–8.

[32] *Chroniques de J. Froissart* [ed. S. Luce, vol. I (Paris, 1869), p. 182].

[33] *Recueil* [p. 319].

[34] [*Recueil*, pp. 317–18.]

person. While princes are above knights, yet princes are not true knights unless they have received the order of chivalry. Even royal children are not born knights, as Choppin demonstrates;[35] witness the examples which I have just recounted of our kings who, with great solemnity, made their children knights. The same Choppin records[36] an ancient decree of the *parlement* of 1334, which states that the king has the right to levy a tax on his people when he knights one of his sons.

34. It is even doubtful whether emperors and kings are themselves knights before receiving the order. In fact, Petri de Vineis tells us[37] that King Conrad, son of the Emperor Frederick II, wrote to the inhabitants of Palermo that he had wanted to be made a knight:

> It is lawful, by virtue of the noble blood with which nature endowed us and of our official dignities as ruler by divine grace over two kingdoms, that the auspices of military honour should not be withheld from us; yet, as the military belt sanctified by venerable antiquity had not until then sustained Our Serenity, we chose on the first day of the present month of August to adorn our body therewith, observing the solemnity of a young soldier's first campaign.

Likewise, we read in Sigebert[38] that Malcolm, king of Scotland, wanted to be knighted the king of France, Henry I; and in our annals, that after the battle of Marignano King Francis was knighted by Captain Bayard, who buckled on his sword.[39] Du Tillet tells us[40] that immediately after his coronation King Louis XI submitted to being knighted by the Good Duke Philip of Burgundy,

> especially (says he) as it is a mark of prowess in arms and every other virtue and honour that sovereign princes should voluntarily descend from their eminence and majesty to be in fraternity and companionage with some of their most pious and virtuous subjects, preferring merit and the virtues to all the advantages of fortune.

---

[35] *Traité du domaine* [*de la couronne de France*, in Choppin, II], p. 565.
[36] *Ibid.* [pp. 565–6].
[37] [Piero delle Vigne] *Epistolarum libri VI* [(Hamburg, 1609)], pp. 410–11.
[38] [Sigebert of Gembloux's *Chronicon* (Paris, 1513), fos. 91ᵛᵒ–96ʳᵒ, contains no mention of this; cf. also *PL* CLX, cols. 205–13.]
[39] [1515: cf. *Le loyal serviteur*, ed. J. Roman (Paris, 1875), p. 246.]
[40] [*Recueil*, p. 316.]

35. Yet the truth is that the royal dignity comprises in itself all dignities. All dignities proceed from it, just as all the light of the world proceeds from the sun. Thus, the wish of some kings to be made knights was rather to honour the order of chivalry, or else the person of the one at whose hands they received it, than themselves to have an increase of honour. We also see that, by the institutions of the particular orders of knights which I will discuss hereafter, the princes who instituted them have ordained that they and their successors in their states should remain their heads in perpetuity, those princes having no need of the order's conferment upon them for the purpose. 36. Besides, the rule that knights are 'made and not born' applies only to true knights and the true order of chivalry. As with all dignities, there are some which are only honorary and held by title, as I will consider in the last two chapters. Accordingly, there are many honorary knights only by title – that is, who do not have the order of chivalry: to wit, all those who possess high lordships and great offices. In sum, all those of the high nobility call themselves knights, just as knights reciprocally call themselves high lords although they have no high lordship.

37. As was noted earlier, whoever is knighted by the king, even someone who has a lordship or an office to which the title of knight appertains, is absolutely noble, both himself and his posterity; for knighthood is a degree above plain nobility and is compared to the Roman patriciate 'which washed off all stain of birth',[41] as M. Choppin proves.[42] Du Tillet discusses the matter elegantly:[43]

> In knighting a commoner the king ennobles him and gives him knighthood all at once. Some, wishing to take ennoblement separately so as to have good assurance of it (*d'en avoir belle lettre*), as they say, have themselves knighted by the king. For the letter of chivalry conveys nobility, without owning to commoner status. But if a commoner is knighted by someone other than the king, who alone has the power to ennoble, they ought both to acknowledge their guilt by public ritual.

38. We have here a very notable distinction. For when the dukes and counts of France had usurped almost all the rights of sovereignty,

---

[41] *Code J* 12.3.5.
[42] Choppin, 1 pt. i, pp. 341–2.
[43] [*Recueil*, p. 300.]

they took it upon themselves to confer the order of knighthood. Distinguished captains and knights made others, to the point where young lords thought themselves lucky to be made knights at such hands, as the Romans tell us. This was tolerated as long as persons thus knighted were nobles by lineage, for the faculty of ennobling the commoner has always been reserved to pure sovereigns. In fact, the ordinances and ancient experts that record royal rights and cases of sovereignty do not include amongst these the power of making knights, but include only the power of ennobling. This is also what we gather from the ancient customs of Paris and Orléans:[44]

> If anyone who is not a gentleman on his father's side should be so on his mother's side and should suffer himself to be made a knight, his lord can make him cut off his spurs on a dunghill.

The ancient decree of the *parlement* of Whitsun, 1280, says:

> that not withstanding the resolution to the contrary on the part of the Count of Flanders, he could not make a commoner a knight without the authority of the king: therefore, just so of nobility.

[Yet] Du Tillet[45] and Pithou[46] relate an old extract from the Chamber of the Treasury which states that in Provence and at Beaucaire burgesses can be knighted by the barons, and even by ecclesiastical prelates.

39. This faculty of making knights, coupled with our kings' eventual practice of making as many as presented themselves (to the point where Charles VI at the siege of Bourges made as many as five hundred in one day before the gallows of that town, says Monstrelet),[47] was the cause that, in order to refurbish the order and dignity of chivalry which fell into contempt owing to the numbers admitted to it and the scant merit of some of those admitted, it was necessary to extract from this multitude the principal and most notable knights and to reduce them to a little band or company.

40. Certain new orders or militia of knights were therefore devised, and in these only persons of great merit by valour or lineage were

---

[44] [Claude Fauchet, *Origines des chevaliers, armoiries et heraux*, in *Les oeuvres de feu M. Claude Fauchet* (Paris, 1600), fo. 512[vo].]
[45] [*Recueil*, p. 320.]
[46] Pithou, pp. 1–2.
[47] *La Chronique* [II p. 272].

retained. It is remarkable that even today only those who have the title of plain knight are received into them. To make them more august and deserving of veneration, they were obliged to observe certain religious ceremonies and so converted into the form of confraternities.

41. Further, in order to render knights of these orders more worthy of note and distinguishable amongst plain knights, they were made to wear a golden collar which the king gave and laid upon them when conferring the order. This was instead of the accolade of the old knights, or else it resembled the golden collars given, amongst military prizes, to distinguished Roman men-at-arms who thereafter were called *torquati*, says Vegetius.[48] The invented name comes from the collar given to Manlius Torquatus for having luckily killed in a duel that bold Gaul who had come to defy the Roman army.

42. Because of this collar our knights of the order are vulgarly called in Latin *equites torquatos*. But in as much as they would find it inconvenient to wear the collar continually, they reserve it for ceremonial occasions, and instead of it they wear daily on their clothes some mark or visible sign of their order.

43. The first order (at least to have lasted, for there was the Order of the Jennet instituted by Charles Martel, which did not last) was that of the Knights of the Virgin Mary, instituted in 1351 by King John at the Château Saint-Oüen near Paris, now called Clichy. They were called Knights of the Star because they wore a star on their hoods, and then on their cloaks after the use of hoods was abolished.

44. The second was the Order of St Michael instituted by King Louis XI, in honour of France's guardian angel. In order to ennoble it farther through nullifying the former, he gave the badge of the star to the knight of the guard at Paris and his archers.

45. Finally, the late King Henry III – a great inventor and lover of new ceremonies – instituted the Order and militia of the Holy Spirit in commemoration of his having been born and made king on the day of Pentecost. In addition to the badge of their order which they wear on their cloaks, these knights also wear another, hung around the neck on a blue taffeta ribbon.

46. Following the example of the kings of France, other kings and sovereign princes (or pretending to be such) have also made orders

---

[48] [Flavius] Vegetius [Renatus, *De re militari libri quatuor* (Lyon, 1592), p. 31].

of knights. The kings of England have made the Order of the Garter; those of Castile, the Order of the Belt or Sash; the kings of Sicily, of the second branch of the house of Anjou, the Order of the Crescent; the dukes of Burgundy, the Order of the Golden Fleece; the dukes of Savoy, that of the Annunciada; the dukes of Orléans, the Order of the Porcupine; and so, too, with others which I will not indulge myself in recording.

47. Now, before the invention of these knights of the orders, plain knights who had the means of raising a banner – that is, who had enough vassals dependent upon their lordships to form a full company of horsemen – were called knights banneret. This was considered a great honour, and so they raised their banners with great solemnity, as Froissart reports.[49]

48. As for other knights who did not have the means of raising a banner and therefore had to march under the banners of others, they were called bachelors. So some say, and notably Du Tillet[50] who shows that they were contrasted to bannerets. Be that as it may, it is certain that the quality of a bachelor was above that of an esquire and below that of a banneret: for Du Tillet cites several authorities from whom it appears that a banneret had two bachelors' pays, and a bachelor two esquires' pays.

49. But it seems very likely that bachelors were young men of good family, issued from lords and knights, who aspired to the order of chivalry. The bachelor was thus on a lower rung of knighthood. Similarly with academic degrees, a bachelor is one who has set himself on the way towards becoming a doctor; and in the mechanic arts, a bachelor is one who is ready to be passed a master of his trade. In the old French language which the Picards still retain, a bachelor is the suitor or lover of a nubile girl; and she in turn is called *bachelete*, meaning that she aspires to become mistress of a household, once married.

50. I consider this etymology more likely to be true than all those of our doctors of law and our modern French writers who have racked their brains over the matter. Some of them derive bachelor from *baculo* or *bacillo* because a baton was placed in the hands of those permitted to give public lectures, and because certain fiefs were

---

[49] *Chroniques de J. Froissart*, [I, p. 54].
[50] [*Recueil*, pp. 318–19.]

invested 'by the staff' (*per baculum*) as may be seen in books of fiefs. Others derive it from 'laurel berry' (*bacca lauri*), and thereby turn it into the Latin *baccalaureum*. Others again trace it to *buccellarii* who were the knife-bearers and bodyguards of Visigothic lords as may be seen in their laws and in the gloss to the *Basilics*.[51] Still others derive it 'from those *buccellariis*' who were certain horsemen mentioned in the laws:[52] Cujas,[53] Alciato[54] and Turnebus[55] should be consulted on this. Finally, Fauchet says[56] that bachelors signify a kind of low-grade knight (*bas-chevaliers*); he offers no proof, but he might be helped by a passage in Froissart[57] who uses the term *bas-chevalereux*.

51. Nevertheless, I cannot abandon my own etymology that bachelor comes from *bas-échelon* signifying someone on the lowest rung or degree who is on the way towards ascending to higher ones. So a bachelor signifies someone who is in the process of becoming a knight, a doctor, a master of a craft or trade, or the father of a family. In all walks of life there are ordinarily candidates or postulants who have the aptitude and ability and await their actual admission. In Greek they are called 'those about to be (μελλοντες)', says Budé;[58] in Latin, *candidati*; in the last three books of the *Code*, 'supernumerar-ies'; and with us, 'retainers' whom I will discuss later, in the penultimate chapter.

52. In respect of nobility, then, the bachelor figures in two ways in the old books.

53. The first is when he is contrasted to the knight; in this case the term signifies someone awaiting or seeking the order of chivalry. The second is when he is contrasted to the lord or the banneret; and in that case the term signifies someone who is the son of a great lord, can succeed to his lordship, and meanwhile enjoys a portion of its lands with the same rights and prerogatives as the principal lord.

---

[51] [Early tenth-century compilation of Byzantine law in sixty books, with supplementary *Novellae*.]

[52] *Code J* 9.12.10.

[53] *Opera C*, II, pt. ii, cols. 657–8.

[54] [Andrea] Alciato, *Dispunctionum* III. 20 [in *Opera* (Frankfurt, 1617), IV, col. 192].

[55] [Adrien Turnèbe,] *Adversariorum* [III (Paris, 1573), p. 54].

[56] *Origines de chevaliers* [fo. 510ᵛᵒ].

[57] *Oeuvres de Froissart: Chroniques* [ed. Kervyn de Lettenhove, II (Brussels, 1867), p. 35; cf. *Chroniques de J. Froissart*, ed. S. Luce, I, p. 225].

[58] *Opera B*, IV [col. 1258].

54. So much do we learn from the customs of Anjou[59] and Maine,[60] the terms of which are these:

> There are in the said country some other lords who are not counts, viscounts, barons nor castellans, and yet have castles, fortresses, great houses and places which are part of the counties, viscounties, baronies or castellanies. Such persons are called bachelors, and they have the same or similar rights of justice as those of which they are part; and in this they are grounded upon law and custom.

Hence, perhaps, the origin of 'peers' (*pairs*) of fiefs, and of *parages*. Such peers are the younger sons of great houses to whom certain member or dependent lands of high lordships were given as a share, to hold with rights and prerogatives of honour equal to those of the eldest who held the chief place and principal member – and, none the less, to hold them 'in parage' of him.

55. This brings us to great lordships and fiefs of dignity from which high nobility likewise proceeds. It also proceeds from great offices. I have discussed the latter fully enough in my treatise on *Offices*,[61] and so I will say no more about them here, except that to my earlier enumeration of offices which produce high nobility must be added governorships of provinces and towns, and captaincies in chief of the companies of the ordinances maintained in peace and in war. Some hold that even lieutenancies of those companies qualify, although these are not offices, but simple commissions. Yet they are permanent, as we see, and not normally revoked; and furthermore, it is the property of nobility to arise from and to be increased by military valour.

56. Just as captaincies signify high nobility, so do principal lordships. Originally these were captaincies, for when the Franks or Franconians of Germany had conquered the Gauls they distributed almost all the lands of the latter to their captains. They gave to such and such a one an entire province with the title of duchy; to another, a frontier territory with the title of marquisate; to another, a town and its adjacent territory with the title of county; and, briefly, to others castles

---

[59] [Art. 63:] *Coustumes du pays et duché d'Anjou* [ed. C. Pocquet de Livonnière, I (Paris, 1725), cols. 148–9].

[60] Art. 72: *Les coustumes du pays et comté du Maine* [eds. Thibault Baillet and Jehan le Lieure (Le Mans, 1581), fos. 19vo–20ro].

[61] I. ix.

or villages with the title of barony or castellany. This was done according to each one's particular merits and to the number of soldiers that each captain had under him. The arrangement was made as much for him as for his soldiers, and on condition of including them by title of fief, so that the soldiers should always remain obliged to assist their captain in time of war. Furthermore, he was the head, governor and judge of the entire territory allotted to him, because in former times arms and justice were not separated.

57. That is why these principal vassals are called 'captains of the king or of the realm'. As the Book of Fiefs indicates:[62]

> Duke, marquis and count are properly called captains of the realm or the king. They and others are those who receive fiefs from such personages. They are properly termed vassals of the king or realm, but nowadays they are called captains.

This passage has been very badly interpreted. The 'personages' in question have been taken to refer to the duke, the marquis and the count, although the reference should be to 'the king or realm', as I have proved in my treatise on *Seigneuries*.[63] What it signifies is that at first only the dukes, marquises and counts were captains of the king or of the realm, and that the others holding fiefs of them did not have those titles and were called simply 'vassals of the king' or 'of the realm', but not 'captains'. Nevertheless, with the passage of time these too were called captains. That is why in the law,[64] after the definitions of duke, marquis and count, the plain captain is defined as 'he who is invested by the prince from the position of commoner or the multitude'.

58. Hence it follows that these captains are properly those whom we formerly called the barons of France. As Du Tillet says,[65] 'baron' is a general term comprising all those who hold their principal lordships immediately of the crown with all rights save sovereignty. In as much as there were then many fiefs depending from the crown which were not duchies, marquisates or counties and had no title of dignity other than the general term 'baron', it has come about with the passage of

---

[62] [*Operum C*, III, col. 1789; the 'Book of Fiefs' refers to *Feudorum libri cum fragmentis*, ed. Obertus de Horto, upon which Cujas commented extensively.]
[63] [vi. 3–9.]
[64] [*Operum C*, III, cols. 1841–2.]
[65] [*Recueil*, p. 341.]

time that the term has been taken for a particular species of dignity. Dukes, marquises and counts wishing to usurp the rights of sovereignty have ceased to call themselves barons because a barony is not capable of sovereignty. On the other hand, vassals depending not from the crown, but simply from the king through the reunion of ancient duchies and counties to the crown, have wished to be called barons, as I said in my *Seigneuries*.[66]

59. Thence it seems to follow that lords who, not being captains, are below the barons, ought not to be of the rank of the high nobility. Yet, owing to the great congruity and affinity which castellans have with barons (castellans being lesser barons, and barons great castellans), and also because in matters of dignity one always ascends with the passage of time, they have gained this point of being of the high nobility. Therefore it must be held that every lordship or fief of dignity which has a particular name and title, as do all the great and intermediate lordships, carry high nobility. So only plain lordships or jurisdictions do not have this advantage.

60. It may seem that intermediate lordships which do not depend from the king ought not to carry high nobility, because only those which depend from the king could be called captaincies. Nevertheless, the false interpretation which our doctors have given the passage in question has conferred this advantage upon intermediate lords depending from dukes, marquises and counts: that they have been placed in the rank of captains and, consequently, of the high nobility.

61. Here, however, care is needed. If the possessor of an intermediate lordship, such as a viscounty, vidamy, barony and castellany, depending from another than the king is noble by lineage, he enters the ranks of the high nobility through the investiture which his suzerain gives him: just as it was formerly allowed that dukes and counts might knight those who were nobles and not commoners.

62. But, far from placing him in the ranks of the high nobility, investiture of a commoner with such lordships by another than the king does not even ennoble him. For it is an infallible rule that no one other than the king can confer nobility. Even when a commoner has been invested with a great or an intermediate lordship depending from the king by his local officers or even by the *chambre des comptes*, he is not thereby ennobled. Ennoblement is a royal right and a case of sovereignty which is inseparable from the king.

[66] [vi. 32 *et seq.*]

63. The strongest doubts are certainly tenable as to how a piece of land or a lordship could ennoble a man. Rather, it ought to be the man who should ennoble the land belonging to him; God has created it for the service of man. It is also repugnant that nobility should be bought indirectly, in buying a fief of dignity. Yet it cannot be denied that, according to the customs of the Lombards,[67] not only do fiefs of dignity ennoble their possessors, but so too do all the ancient fiefs depending from captains or great vassals.

64. This may be gathered 'in the converse sense' from what is said in the law cited above,[68] that acquirers of new fiefs 'are none the less commoners', and that 'by those fiefs they have no parage (*paragium*)'. The word should be read thus, as Cujas reads it, and not as *paradogium* or *pedagium*, in the vulgar way. For the ancient vassals of captains or great vassals were peers of their courts, assisting their lords both to command lesser vassals in war and to judge cases in their fiefs; and by virtue of this power and authority they were noble in Lombardy.

65. But in France we have always taken care that the king alone should ennoble. He does so in three ways: either by express letters of ennoblement, or by granting great offices, or by investiture with fiefs of dignity. And then, be it well understood, it is neither the money given to obtain the letters of ennoblement, nor yet the office nor the fief of dignity that ennobles, but the king, by his sovereign power. He exercises it in giving letters of nobility, or provision to office, or investiture with a fief.

66. Although in France certain fiefs are called noble, they are not called such 'by effect, but rather by particular quality'. That is to say, it is not because they have the power to ennoble their possessor, but because of their proper dignity they are assigned to persons already noble, and cannot be held by commoners. It would indeed be contrary to reason that a commoner should be lord of a fief of dignity which carries knighthood and high nobility. So a commoner invested by someone other than the king himself can be sued either by the king's proctor, or by his feudal lord (albeit other than the one who invested him), or his heir, and even by vassals of the fief, to surrender it to a capable person. Thus, following the law,[69] things are related to persons, and not persons to things.

---

[67] [*Operum C*, III, cols. 1841–2.]
[68] [Note 64.]
[69] *Digest* 21.1.44.

67. As it is repugnant that the possessor of a fief of dignity should be a commoner, there are some apparent grounds for holding that those who possess these fiefs are presumed noble. To that extent they are in possession of high nobility. Therefore, if the father and the grandfather have possessed such fiefs consecutively, nobility thenceforth is prescribed for their descendants. This follows from the statute of 1600 concerning taxation.[70]

68. Now let us turn to the rights and prerogatives of the high nobility. First, it undoubtedly takes entire precedence over plain nobility, and consequently over all officers except those that are also of the high nobility. There are some grounds for holding that knights and lords ought to walk before judges and magistrates by whom they are justiciable when the latter are of no higher degree than plain nobility.

69. However, when they are actually exercising their authority they represent the king's majesty directly. They exercise justice for him, even for God Who is the author of justice. Therefore, they then give way to no one.

70. That is why I cannot take the side of the doctors who say that the judge should go to seek notable gentlemen in their houses in order to interrogate them, as a certain law suggests.[71] This law does not say that the judge himself should go, but only that he should send there. So, if the judge goes there himself and rouses them to come to his abode, this is from civility and not because he must do so. Further, in this law I would not interpret the phrase 'by distinguished persons' to signify all those of the high nobility, but only princes, dukes and counts, or great officers who hold the rank of counts, called in Latin *magnati, primores, proceres*.

71. For in the high nobility there are several subordinate ranks and degrees. The lowest of these is the knights. Du Tillet concludes[72] that they have absolutely no established status, saying that they are created as proof of valour rather than as a rank. For these terms I refer you to the subject of his book, which is a treatise on the ranks of the great. You will thus understand that among the great, who are those of the high nobility, the knights have no prerogative. In the case of two counts, the one who is a knight of the order shall not on that account be warranted to walk before the other. But a plain baron

---

[70] [Fontanon, II, p. 881.]
[71] *Digest* 12.2.15.
[72] [*Recueil*, pp. 316–20.]

ought to walk before someone who has no dignity other than that of knight: witness the old lawyers' saying, which Choppin records,[73] that 'no one should sit at a baron's table if he is not a knight'.

72. As for lordships, there are almost as many degrees as there are divers kinds and names. However, they can all be reduced to two classes: the great lordships which can be called royal fiefs or dignities, participate in certain honours of sovereignty, and are capable of being sovereign; and intermediate ones which are not so favoured. I have demonstrated this fully in my treatise on *Seigneuries*[74] where I have recorded the particular rights and prerogatives of each of them.

73. But what they all have in common is that their possessors have every right to call themselves 'knights', 'lords' and 'messires', and to call their wives 'mesdames', as I will explain more fully in the last chapter. Further, they enjoy the right to have noble persons as pages and esquires in their retinues, and their wives to have ladies as attendants; and the right to wear gilt harness, specifically spurs, and all other equipage for war and cavalry.

74. Yet this is something that plain gentlemen, even commoners, take on themselves these days without contradiction. Likewise, they presume to surmount their coats of arms with crests, although this was formerly a right of high nobility while the plain nobility bore them unadorned and uncrested, and commoners did not bear them at all.

75. But now the plain nobility timbre their arms with helmets. Even so, these ought not to be gilded or open, for such arms should be reserved to those of the high nobility: gilded in the case of knights, and open in the case of captains. The latter have the visor raised so that they may keep an eye on their soldiers, and above the helm they also place some animal or other device.

76. As for those who have great lordships – dukes, marquises and counts – they place a crown on their crests with the ducal or count's cloak, and their device.

77. But the wives of all those of the high nobility may indiscriminately bear their arms quartered or emblazoned on a lozenge, as a sign that their husbands are captains, with a banner. This, too, I have explained more fully in my treatise on *Seigneuries*.[75]

[73] Choppin [I, pt. i, p. 300].
[74] [vi and vii.]
[75] [viii. 8–9.]

CHAPTER SEVEN

Of princes

1. Cicero makes much of a great case which was pleaded in his time before the hundred judges of Rome between the patrician families Marcellus and Claudius, on the question of their lineage. He says[1] that in order to relate what was due by right of lineage and gentility it was necessary 'to discuss the entire law of lineal descent and kinship'. But to examine the ancestries and sovereign houses of princes issued from a monarch and sovereign prince is far and away a higher discourse than to consider patrician ancestries such as those of the most noble of Rome, descended from a plain senator. Such a discourse is still more difficult, even more hazardous, than it is elevated. Yet, my project commits me to it absolutely, for, having undertaken to discuss orders and dignities, I cannot omit that of princes which among us is the first and highest of all.

2. For the supreme degree of our nobility appertains to those whom we call princes. Communicated to them by honours and as a title of honorary dignity is the name of prince which in effect belongs only to the sovereign. According to its true etymology, 'prince' signifies the supreme head, that is, he who has the sovereignty of the state; and this is how we understand it when we speak simply of the prince.

3. This prince, who is the lively image of God, 'God's living image', says Menander,[2] is so august and so full of majesty that those born of him or related to him by male kinship deserve particular respect

---

[1] *De oratore* I. [xxxix. 176].

[2] Menander [of Laodicea: cf. *Menander Rhetor*, eds. D. A. Russell and N. G. Wilson (Oxford, 1981), pp. 76–95 ('Basilikos Logos'). Also cf. Budé, *Annotationes in Pandectas* (Basle, 1557), p. 69; the phrase, by Loyseau's time, amounted to a cliché.]

and a status above his other subjects. Further, this lieutenancy of God on earth, and this absolute power over men, which we call principality or sovereignty is so perfectly excellent that it must leave a great impression and be of great effect upon anyone who approximates to and has hope of it. The ancient emperors created offices or honorary dignities with which they titled and qualified those who were not officers but deserved to be such, in order to assign to them a rank among the genuine officers. In the same way and with more right reason, our kings have been able to communicate to their kin this honorary title of prince, although they do not enjoy true principality, which is sovereignty, but only the aptitude to attain it – they or their posterity – in their degree of succession.

4. I single out our kings. For there is no kingdom in the world, so far as I know, where there is a formal and established order of prince as there is in France, in respect of title or of rank.

5. As to title, we find the name of prince in the oldest authors, notably Holy Scripture. There, however, it signifies only personal primacy or first dignity, and does not relate to extraction. Be that as it may, 'prince' normally signifies there only the principal or first in dignity. It is sometimes translated from the Greek 'great man', or 'great men' in the plural, a term which Suetonius, Tacitus and Ammianus Marcellinus have used in Latin. In fact, Erasmus translates as *primatibus* these words from St Mark,[3] 'Herod made a dinner for his great men', although the common version says *principibus*.

6. But from the time when the Roman emperors called themselves princes, the term signified in Latin no longer simple primacy, but sovereign power. That is why sovereign princes, jealous of their proper title, now only communicate it to their eldest son. In some respects this has always been so: to wit, in erecting one of their lordships to the title of principality assigned in perpetuity to their eldest. Such cases are, in England, the principality of Wales; in Castile, that of Asturias; in Aragon, that of Gerona. Thus, they were not at first called princes absolutely, but prince of such and such a place.

7. Nowadays the practice is established in almost all the monarchies of Christendom that the son of the sovereign is called prince without qualification, just as his father is called the king or the duke, and as the son of the emperor of Constantinople was called δεσποτης

---

[3] vi.[21].

('lord') – 'doubtless because he was accounted lord in his father's lifetime', as the Roman law says.[4]

8. As for their collateral kin, the monarchs in question still did not communicate this august title of prince to these. If we do sometimes find in our history that it was ascribed to them (for example, when Commynes says[5] that in three years eighty English princes were executed), we must be careful that he speaks in the French manner. Camden[6] and Thomas Smith, who have amply described the orders of England, do not place that of the princes amongst them.

9. So much for title. As for rank, it is certain that in other monarchies of Christendom the matter always has been and still is regulated according to personal dignities – to wit, high lordships and great offices – and not according to houses or ancestries. It is true that sovereigns confer the premier dignities on their closest kin, and by virtue of these the latter take the first ranks which would not belong to them by virtue of their extraction alone, as with our French princes.

10. Yet hence ensues absurdity. In elective monarchies it is not reasonable, and above all not secure, to establish the kin of the sovereign in the rank of princes, given that they do not inherit his sovereignty. In respect of hereditary monarchies, they change families so often through regular inheritance in the female line, as Bodin proves,[7] that if all the matrilineal descendants of sovereigns capable of succeeding were to be recognised as princes, so many princes of divers names and divers families would be found there that they would be both costly and dishonourable to the state, and even to their quality; for amid so great a multitude many of them would inevitably be poor.

11. On the other hand, another inconvenience arises if descendants only in the male line were to be recognised as princes of the blood (and in good jurisprudence rights of family and dignities of lineage ought to come only from fathers, as I showed in the fifth chapter; and principality above all is not spun out on the distaff). The incon-

---

[4] [Cf., for example, *Leg. Nov.*, Nov. Arthemius. 2. On the significance of the term δεσπότης see below, ch. 11, section 42.]

[5] [Cf. *Mémoires de Philippe de] Commynes* [ed. B. de Mandrot, I (Paris, 1901), pp. 194–5].

[6] [Cf. William] Camden [*Britannia* (London, 1637), pp. 163–4: 'The States and Degrees of England'].

[7] *République* [pp. 1001–2].

venience is that, as often happens, the descendants of daughters are the nearest to and most capable of the succession to the state. Those excluded from succeeding would thus be taken for princes, and not those who would be the successors. In such a case it would even happen that the former would, as princes, walk before the latter who would expect in due course to command them.

12. But in France we have a very particular reason for giving the title and rank of prince to those who are of the royal line. The crown is destined to each of them in his rank and degree of consanguinity. It is destined, I say, [not] by heredity, which transfers the right of the deceased to the nearest heir and, consequently, the responsibility for his acts and promises as representing the person of the deceased. Rather, it is destined by right of blood and in the successor's own right, without right and title of heir. By its proper nature and peculiar establishment, called its fundamental law, the kingdom is assigned to the princes of the blood. It is the same with fiefs which by their condition and first investiture are assigned to certain houses or left as fideicommissa to families.[8]

13. Hence it follows that males of the house of France have a right or claim to the crown equal to that of heirs in tail to assets tied by entail. This is a much stronger right than the hope of a simple kinsman to inherit from those of his lineage. Here indeed is a fine device. It prevents the kingdom from being transferred to a foreign dynasty. By the same token, the princes to whom it is assigned are obliged to be careful of its conservation, in their own interest. That is particularly why in France males issued from our kings are called princes, and notably princes of the blood. They are of that blood to which the principality and sovereignty are assigned; and they are also princes of the blood as entailees of the crown. This, I believe, is not the case in any other state in the world, and so I consider that only in France are there true princes.

14. Even so, it is not long since they called themselves princes by virtue of their extraction. Indeed, they first took this title because of the duchies and counties that they possessed. As Du Tillet has shown,[9] the dukes and counts of France had long since called themselves princes because they had usurped the rights of sovereignty.

---

[8] *Digest* 35.2.54.
[9] [*Recueil*, p. 224.]

Thus they were really subject princes, which is one of the four species of princes by lordship that I have noted and explained in my book on *Seigneuries*.[10] Hence it will not be irrelevant to resume this discourse from its beginning and to explain the title and rank which the princes of the blood have taken from time to time, as I think, in this kingdom.

15. In the first place, there can be no doubt that in the first two dynasties of our kings those of their lineage were greatly revered. They all succeeded together to the kingdom: or at least, each of them had his share by partible inheritance, in perfect sovereignty and with royal title. Therefore, all the royal children were already tantamount to kings by certain expectation, during their father's lifetime. What made them more revered was that during the first dynasty they wore their hair long as a sign of sovereign domination, while serfs were shaven as a sign of perfect subjection.

16. However, it cannot be said that this particular veneration accorded to the king's children in France during the first two dynasties was ever communicated to their collateral kinsfolk. This could not be, given that the royal children were all kings after their father's death.

17. If those collaterals had had children, they too would have been kings in the same way, and there would have been as many kings – or, to be more exact, as many parts of the realm with the title of kingdom – as there were males descending from kings. If this had continued under the third dynasty, those of the royal line whom we now call princes of the blood would all have been kings.

18. But at the end of the second dynasty Charles, the younger son of Louis d'Outremer (and surnamed the Young as he had another, older brother named Carloman), was not able to have a share of the kingdom owing to the understanding which the wife of Lothair, his elder brother in turn, had with Hugh Capet, mayor of the palace. So he fled to Otho, emperor of Germany, his cousin german, who gave him the duchy of Lorraine.

19. For this reason he was utterly excluded thereafter from the crown, and it was transferred to the third dynasty.

20. This dynasty, more crafty and more prudent than the two previous ones, paid attention from the outset to maintaining the kingdom

[10] ii. [13 *et seq.*].

in its entirety. Younger sons were excluded from the succession, following the later practice of the previous dynasty, whence its advancement came. Only appanages were given to them – that is, sustenance and maintenance. Two things helped it greatly in this. First, the initial kings of this dynasty never failed to have their eldest sons consecrated and recognised as kings with them in their lifetimes. The eldest son thus found himself upon his father's death fully established and recognised throughout the kingdom, as Lothair, the last king of the second dynasty, had done in respect of his son Louis, with the same end in view: fear that his uncle Charles the Young would trouble him.

21. Secondly, owing to the usurpations of the counts, the kingdom had left hardly any domain upon which younger sons might set foot. It consisted in an abstract right of superiority and authority, and almost as a simple expression of vassalage by the dukes and counts. Such a right was not as easy to partition and to encroach upon as a material domain would have been.

22. Being so closely allied together to maintain their usurpations, these dukes and counts were inclined all together to recognise as their king the eldest son of the late king, to whom they were bound by fealty and homage during his father's lifetime. Thus it is true to say that the usurpation and cantonising of the dukes and counts saved France from a much more dangerous division and dismemberment, from which its entire ruin would inevitably have ensued.

23. It was undoubtedly these dukes and counts who were then called princes and who were the first in France to be called by this title, because of the rights of sovereignty which they had usurped. Further, they were then the greatest lords of France after the kings and the latter's eldest sons who were recognised as kings during the father's lifetime.

24. The younger sons, having only their appanages or maintenance (which from the very beginning could not be given them in land, for the king had scarcely any domain for himself), were not disposed to challenge and to dispute precedence with those lords. On the contrary, the usual scheme of these younger sons was to place themselves on a par with the latter through forming alliances with them and marrying their heiresses, by the king's favour and the commendation of their lineage. Hugh, the younger son of Henry I, did so when he married the daughter of the count of Vermandois. So did Robert and

Pierre, younger sons of Louis the Fat, who married, respectively, the heiress of Dreux or, as some say, Brenne; and the heiress of Courtenay.

25. In doing this they took the names and the arms of their wives; and they took more account of these than they did of the arms of the house of France which belonged to them by lineage.

26. Philip, younger son of Philip Augustus, called the Conqueror, was the first to alter this custom, though only in part. He took the name of Boulogne through having married the heiress of the county of Boulogne. His daughter, Jeanne de Boulogne, bore the name after him; but he retained the arms of France, charged only with a lambrequin.

27. What emboldened him to do this was that the house of France began at that time to gain greater authority, as Du Tillet has observed.[11] His father, King Philip Augustus, had conquered and reunited many of these duchies, by virtue of journeys to the Holy Land and other good opportunities which he knew very well how to exploit. Yet in his time younger sons of the house of France still did not hold the rank of princes of the blood and did not walk before dukes and counts. So much may be gathered from the decree which he gave for the homage of the county of Champagne and Brie. All the dukes of France, and even Guillaume de Ponthieu who was neither a prince of the blood nor a peer of France, were appointed to do this before Robert, count of Dreux, and Pierre, count of Brittany, grandsons of King Louis the Fat.

28. But, as Du Haillan has remarked,[12] it was mainly in the reign of Louis VIII, father of St Louis, that the younger sons of France acquired greater credit and authority. This king had five younger sons, three of whom were well provided for and given appanages; and they had ample descendants and founded great houses. So those of the house of France were increased in number and in power. Conversely, the dukes and counts were much reduced, and well-nigh all exterminated. It was then that those of the royal house gained the upper hand. Apparently, it was also then that they took their quality

[11] [Jean II Du Tillet, *Chronique abbregée*, fos. 47ʳᵒ–50ʳᵒ (appended to *Recueil*).]
[12] [Bernard de Girard, seigneur] du Haillan [*De l'estat et succez des affaires de France* (Paris, 1571), fo. 98ʳᵒ; cf. du Haillan *L'Histoire de France* (Paris, 1576), p. 556. Neither of these fully bears out Loyseau's point.]

of princes of the blood, to fill the place of those princely usurpers whose lordships had been reunited to the crown.

29. They called themselves princes because, like the usurpers, they had duchies and counties; and princes of the blood because they were, furthermore, of the blood of France. However, one scarcely finds in that time that they styled themselves princes, but only lords of the king's lineage.

30. The advantageous effect of this style became apparent above all when Philip de Valois, first prince of the blood, succeeded to the crown after the deaths of the three brothers, his cousins german, who were kings one after another. It was still more striking in contrast to the English – the reason why the Salic law had to be researched, and the right and pre-eminence of males descended from the kings, who are our princes of the blood, had to be established once and for all.

31. However, they were not able peacefully to gain precedence over the survivors of the old dukes and counts who enjoyed rights of sovereignty; nor even over the peers of France afterwards created, these being the crown's first and principal vassals even though they did not have rights of sovereignty.

32. In this respect the princes of the blood did themselves harm. When two princes of the blood met one another, the one who was farther removed from the crown claimed precedence over the other – even the younger over the elder – through his quality as peer or by his seigneurial prerogative. At Charles VI's coronation banquet Philip, duke of Burgundy, did so on the pretext of his quality as peer of France, seating himself above the duke of Anjou, his elder brother. Under the same king there was a lawsuit over precedence between the count of Alençon and the duke of Bourbon who claimed precedence as a duke although he was farther removed from the crown. In this lawsuit the royal council directed that they should take precedence in turns. As the count of Alençon was not content with this, his county was erected into a duchy-peerdom, and so the difficulty between them was settled.

33. Nevertheless, the general dispute remained unresolved until our own day. So did that of peers claiming precedence over princes of the blood, at least when they performed their office as peers – specifically, at royal coronations and in the *parlement*. In fact, in order

to avoid it after the death of King Henry II, the late Queen Mother dressed her younger sons in the robes of peers at the time of the coronation of Francis II, her eldest son, and so made them walk first, as Fauchet has recorded.[13] And from then on the ancient peers which are suppressed and reunited to the crown have been represented by the princes of the blood; and so there is scarcely cause any longer for dispute or discontent.

34. But in order altogether to settle disputes over precedence between prince-peers and the other more ancient peers who still contested it with the former in those two acts of peerdom, King Henry III made a notable ordinance in 1576. Its words are these:[14]

> We ordain that the princes of our blood, peers of France, shall precede and, according to their degree of consanguinity, take precedence over the other princes and lords peers of France of whatever quality they may be, as much at consecrations and coronations of kings as at sessions of the courts of *parlement* and other solemnities, assemblies and public ceremonies whatsoever: without any dispute or controversy on grounds of titles and priorities in creations of peerdoms of other princes and lords, or otherwise for whatever cause or occasion there may be.

35. However, this applies only to the status of princes of the blood who are peers, and not of those who are not such. It seems that in the latter respect the difficulty would remain greater than before. Even so, it can be said that the ordinance was conceived in these terms because its purpose was only to determine the rank of peers of France among themselves. The matter was debated at the time in connection only with the acts of their office of peers: whether in that regard they ought to be ordered in accordance with the title and antiquity of their peerdoms, or according to the rank of their lineage. But this ordinance was not intended to determine the other great question: whether the princes of the blood who are not peers and find themselves assisting extraordinarily, and as quasi-supernumeraries, at royal coronations or at the *parlement*, should take precedence over the peers who are there as genuine and natural officers.

36. Be that as it may, now that the status of the princes of the blood is better established than ever, there is no longer any doubt that even

---

[13] *Origines*, [fo. 48ʳᵒ].
[14] [Fontanon, II, p. 32.]

though they may not be dukes or counts they should walk everywhere before dukes and counts, even before the peers; and that amongst themselves they should likewise have precedence according to their proximity to the crown, and not according to the title of their lordships.

37. Other lordships are no longer comparable with them. So many have reverted rapidly and almost unexpectedly to the crown, at least in the collateral line, as with Kings Louis XII and Francis I, Charles IX and Henry III, and, above all, our great King Henry IV who was twenty-one degrees removed from his predecessor. So the princes of the blood now undoubtedly constitute a separate body and an order of supreme dignity, and surpass by far all the other dignities of France.

38. The first of this order is the king's eldest son. He is called 'Monseigneur le Dauphin' because the lordship of Dauphiné in Viennois is ascribed to him. At least, he is required to bear its title, the more especially as it was sold or, as some say, given on this condition to King Philip of Valois, by Humbert the Dauphin.

39. Some say that he should be called simply 'the dauphin' and not 'my lord the dauphin', as one says 'the king' and not 'my lord the king'. Nevertheless, the contrary usage has prevailed. In my view this arises from the fact that, as the Dauphiné is a lordship claimed to be separated from the kingdom, its title signifies no acknowledgement of sovereignty over the French unless the quality of 'my lord' or 'monsieur' is put in front of it. This was the ancient title of the eldest son of France before he was called dauphin, similar to the name 'despot' in the empire of Constantinople, and that of prince in other sovereign kingdoms and principalities. For the son is a participant not of the power, but of the honour of the lordship in his father's lifetime, 'and he lacks only the administration' as our doctors say, following the canon law.[15]

40. This is the reason why Monseigneur the Dauphin calls himself in his letters patent, 'By the grace of God, eldest son of France, dauphin of Viennois'. These are terms that only sovereigns can use, for they alone are vassals and feudatories of God.

41. Again, it must be observed that the quality of eldest son of France is prefixed not only to that of dauphin, but also to the titles of

---

[15] *Decretum* 24 q. 1 c. *ult.*; *gl. ord.* see under 'rex'.

kingdoms. So Du Tillet[16] and Belleforest[17] prove, by the example of those who were kings of Navarre before being kings of France and in their letters placed the title 'eldest son of France' before that of 'king of Navarre'.

42. King Francis II did as much after marrying the queen of Scotland, although his contract of marriage stated that he would take the name of king of Scotland. That is why he was called King Dauphin during his father's lifetime, because all the eldest sons of France are obliged to bear the title of dauphin.

43. So I am astonished, just as Du Tillet finds it strange,[18] that they should place the title of dauphin before that of duke, saying that it is a greater thing to be a duke than to be dauphin. This might be true if the duchy of which the eldest son of France took the name were a sovereign duchy. But the Dauphiné, being a sovereign lordship, is undoubtedly a higher title than that of any subordinate ones. Formerly things might be done otherwise: sovereign duchies and counties were not yet sufficiently distinguished from subordinate ones, as all dukes and counts pretended to sovereignty. But since our kings have taken care to reduce their encroachments, it was with good reason that when King Henry II was dauphin he called himself dauphin of Viennois and duke of Brittany, to show that the duchy of Brittany was not sovereign.

44. Now although the dauphin of France places his quality of eldest son before those of kingdoms which he holds, yet he gives way to foreign kings; Du Tillet presents some examples.[19] He does so outside France from duty and common right, but within France only from honour, hospitality and courtesy, which are customary to the French. For right reason dictates that even if a foreign prince were emperor he should not walk before the dauphin in France, owing to the latter's participation in the honours of the crown. Likewise, in little lordships no gentleman ventures to walk before the son of the lord of the village. I have discussed the point fully in my treatise on *Seigneuries*.[20]

16 [*Recueil*, pp. 212–13.]
17 [*Annales*, fo. 7ᵛᵒ.]
18 [*Recueil*, pp. 212–13.]
19 [*Recueil*, pp. 212–13]
20 [Cf. *Seigneuries*, xi. 14.]

45. This participation is recognised in Roman law. It is sufficient in itself as far as simple honour is concerned, without any need for our kings in their lifetimes to have their sons consecrated or otherwise acknowledged kings, as they did at the commencement of the dynasty in order to establish their sons more securely. But now that the latter are established through such a long succession, it is more secure not to give them the title of king during their father's lifetime, for fear of a quite contrary inconvenience. However, all our doctors whose opinions are collected by Tiraqueau[21] hold that the eldest son of the king can call himself king during his father's lifetime.

46. Even so, when the eldest son of France wields sovereign command, whether as regent of the kingdom or as lieutenant-general to his father the king, he gives way to no one in the realm. And when in this capacity he goes to the *parlement*, he is accorded the same honours as the king, with these exceptions noted by Du Tillet:[22] that he does not sit on the *lit de justice*, but in the highest place adjacent to it; that decrees given in his presence are expressed in the name of the court; and that advocates address the court.

47. In respect of the younger sons of France, who are the trunks of the branches and founders of the families of the princes of the blood, Du Tillet says[23] that formerly they bore the surname of France. But Du Haillan assures us[24] that they no longer bear it. Indeed, as their father has no surname, so they themselves cannot have one from their birth. In fact, they sign only with their own names; and in their letters patent this is the only title they give themselves, immediately adding the quality 'son of France' without inserting 'by the grace of God', for they do not participate in the honour of sovereignty as their elder brother does.

48. For the same reason, if they have some kingdom they place its title before that of the son of France. Thus Charles, king of Sicily and brother of St Louis, called himself 'Charles, king of Jerusalem, Naples and Sicily, son of the king of France, count of Anjou, of Provence and Forcalquier'. Likewise another Charles, younger son of King Philip III, having been invested by the pope with the

---

[21] *De jure prim.*, pp. 392–4.
[22] [*Recueil*, pp. 212–13.]
[23] [*Recueil*, pp. 206 et seq.]
[24] [*De l'estat et succez*, fo. 105ʳᵒ.]

kingdoms of Aragon and Valencia, titled himself 'king of Aragon and Valencia, son of the king of France, and count of Valois'.

49. Even in ordinary conversation, the younger sons of France were formerly referred to only by their own names. To these was added the title 'Monsieur', such as 'Francis Monsieur', 'Henry Monsieur', at least before they had some definite appanage; and afterwards they were addressed by the title of the appanage. But because the baptisms of the younger sons of the present king have been postponed, they have been given the names of Orléans and Anjou, although these have not yet been granted them in appanage. I consider it an error to think that these are assigned to them as the Dauphiné is to the eldest.

50. Here I will say nothing about these appanages, for in this book I am dealing only with orders and ranks of honour, and not with lordships or inheritances. I will only say that formerly such appanage land was readily erected into a peerdom by its letters of concession. But it is held that the arrangement is no longer needful, now that the princes of the blood are better established than they were in the past; and that [even] without a peerdom they have all the same rights and privileges as the peers of France. As for their appanages, since these always remain parcel of the crown's domain there is no doubt that they should be directly under the jurisdiction of the *parlement*, an arrangement vulgarly termed 'holding in peerage'. This is especially so now that, by sound agreement, the practice has begun of treating the justice of lands in appanage as remaining royal and exercised in the names of the king and the appanaged prince jointly, as I have said in my book on *Offices*.[25]

51. The daughters of France are all called 'mesdames' and bear the surname of France which is given only to the king's daughters. Those of Monseigneur the Dauphin are called 'mesdamoiselles' and bear the surname of the appanage, or at least of their father's principal lordship, unless and until he becomes king; then they take the title of 'mesdames' and the surname of France. There was a time when they were called queens, both before and after being married; yet they still ranked below kings, as I will show more fully in the last chapter when I deal with honorary titles.

52. Be that as it may, it is quite certain that neither they nor the other princesses lose their status and title of princesses through being

---

[25] [IV. ix. 35–9.]

married to men of lesser quality. Principality is a quality above all others. It places those so titled in a status separate from other men, into whose ranks they never return. And this quality is so illustrious that it illuminates by its splendour those associated with it, rather than losing its lustre and brilliancy through contact with a weaker light.

53. Nowadays the children of France, both male and female, ordinarily have a fine privilege which only Monseigneur the Dauphin used to have. It is that their household officers are privileged like those of the king. In 1539 King Francis himself granted privileges to the household officers of the queen of Navarre, his sister, even though she was not a daughter of France. So too, in 1549, did King Henry II to those of Madame Marguerite, his sister; and the present king granted them to those of Madame the Duchess of Bar. Monseigneur the Dauphin enjoys yet another, higher privilege, which is to have a chancellor and other great officers. The younger sons of France do not have this privilege, unless they become the second persons of France.

54. So much for the king's children. When kings have none, they are accustomed to give the heir presumptive to the crown letters as first prince of the blood or, as Du Tillet says,[26] the second person of France. They do this as much to obviate dangerous disputes over the royal succession that could arise after their deaths, as to gratify him and elevate him in honour during their lifetimes. Du Tillet records several examples. These tell us that our kings have such confidence, as much in the piety of princes of the blood as in their subjects' fidelity, that they do not entertain the doubts which foreign princes have over designating their successors – which the late queen of England called placing a funeral bandeau over one's eyes.

55. Even minor officers and holders of minor benefices have a horror of such designation. The Romans feared it so much in respect of private inheritances that, in order to remove all assurance of it even from those who were called by nature to inherit, they brought wills into ordinary usage, and then even hid those wills so that the witnesses knew nothing of the contents and their own children should be in doubt as to whether they were the heirs.

56. In consequence of this declaration or designation, the first prince of the blood has once in his lifetime the right to grant one, two or

---

[26] [*Recueil*, p. 220.]

three letters of mastership of every craft or trade in all the towns of France, even in those of lords. The privilege is ascribed at present to all the younger sons of France. They do not enjoy it themselves, any more than Monseigneur the Dauphin does: it is the queen who enjoys it and grants these letters in their stead, immediately after their births. The household officers of the first prince are also privileged, like those of the younger sons of France; and he retains that privilege throughout his life, even though the king should afterwards happen to have children – as is manifest at present in the person of Monsieur the Prince of Condé.

57. If the first prince of the blood is the son of a king of France, he is recognised as the second person, having the relevant privileges as soon as occasion arises. Unlike other, more distant, kin, he has no need of a royal declaration: at least, they need it in order to enjoy the relevant privileges. In respect of the title, some hold that he may take it without letters. They draw a distinction between the first prince of the blood, who, they say, is the first in the royal line, after the children of France; and the second person of France, who is the younger son of the son of France, capable of succeeding when his elder brother the king has no children.

58. He is then called 'Monsieur' absolutely and without any addition, as the eldest son of France was formerly called; and, like the latter, he can have great officers, as in the case of Monsieur the Duke of Anjou, lately deceased. I consider this to apply only for as long as he remains heir presumptive to the crown, because this title of 'monsieur' and to have great officers are marks of participation in the honour of sovereignty.

59. But the first prince of the blood who is not the king's son retains only the name of his appanage, like the other princes of the blood. It is a general rule that all the descendants of the younger sons of France have the name of their father's appanage and not the name of France, but only the arms, and these not plain, but charged.

60. Now the other princes of the blood undoubtedly walk after the first, down to the last, before all the other subjects of the king. To this there are no exceptions, whether of the king's natural children, or foreign princes, or church prelates, or dukes and other great lords. The princes of the blood even precede the great officers, except when these last are performing their main official duties, for then they are representing directly the royal person under whose authority they

perform those duties; and even then they often yield honorary precedence, deferring as much of their function as may be to the princes of the blood. But I consider in this case that the deference is only from honour and not from duty.

61. To turn to the rank which the princes of the blood have amongst themselves, I say, in the first place, that their quality conceals and obscures all the other qualities which they otherwise have, as it is the most honourable and illustrious that the subject of a sovereign prince could have. So it is now a settled point that they themselves walk in order not according to the titles of their lordships, nor according to the antiquity of their peerdoms, nor according to the status of their offices (except when, as has just been said, they are actually performing its main functions), but according to the prerogative of their blood: as the ordinance of 1576 puts it, 'according to their degree of consanguinity'.[27]

62. Princedom consists in their being the king's issue, kinsfolk of the reigning king. Above all, they are capable of succeeding to the kingdom in their turn, or of engendering children who will succeed to it. So it is certainly easy to understand that the closer they are to it, the more they are illuminated with the rays of sovereignty. However, in respect of nobility the contrary is the case, that it is the more highly esteemed when it is the more ancient. The reason for this difference is that nobility consists in remoteness from the scum of the people, and principality in proximity to sovereignty.

63. Even so, when the question arises of the status of entire houses proceeding from divers stock and otherwise being in the same relation to sovereignty, the more ancient takes precedence by the prerogative of time, 'and because', as an old head says, 'those near to God approach the immortal'.

64. Yet this rule of the ordinance of 1576, that 'the princes of the blood walk according to their degrees of consanguinity', is very difficult to interpret. If these words 'degrees of consanguinity' are taken to mean 'degrees of persons', accounting them in the form of right according to their order of proximity to the king (as the words seem literally to signify, and as is observed with private successions), it follows that a nephew, son of the eldest, should be preceded by his uncle, given that he is further removed than the latter from the king

---

[27] [Fontanon, II, p. 32.]

by one degree. Furthermore, it seems that superior kinship gives the uncle rank and authority over his nephew. In fact, Du Tillet gives us some examples[28] of how the uncles of kings have taken precedence over their brothers. Hence it follows that, as this is observed when uncles are farther removed than nephews, it ought by all the more reason to be observed when they are nearer.

65. Nevertheless, the present well-known practice is that a nephew who is the son of the eldest son walks before his uncle. He is the head of the family, or branch, and consequently has its name and arms: and not merely the name, but also the lordship of the appanage which, according to French law, belongs unfailingly to him as his father's successor, or else as the latter's representative by right of primogeniture. For in France we observe even amongst plain gentlemen that the younger and their descendants always yield first place to their elder, and to the one among his descendants who is head of their name and arms and is ordinarily lord of the principal land of their house.

66. In fact, this is expressed in the form of a proverb used among our doctors of law, as is noted by Iserni,[29] Decius,[30] Matthaeus de Afflictis[31] and Paulus Paris[32] 'to live or to succeed in the manner of the French'.

67. Thus in France, successions among gentlemen even to fiefs, which are at present patrimonial, are bestowed according to proximity of kinship, to males and females alike. The only exceptions are the legacy to which the eldest in the direct line is entitled before division of the estate, and that in collateral successions males exclude females in the same degree. Often enough, therefore, the lordship of a house falls by way of daughters to another family. Often enough, too, someone who is not the head by name or arms, but is descended from the younger, excludes the descendants of the elder when he occurs nearer than they in degree of kinship.

68. However, the kingdom is not handed down according to the order of ordinary successions and according to degrees of kinship,

---

[28] [*Recueil*, pp. 221–2.]

[29] [Andreas de Rampinis ab] Isernia [*In usus feudorum commentaria* (Naples, 1571)], fo. 266ro (sec. 35).

[30] Philip Decius, *Consilia* [*sive responsa* (Venice, 1570)], p. 471.

[31] [Matteo d'Afflitto] *Dec[isiones sacrii consilii Neapolitani* (Lyon, 1552),] pp. 220–2.

[32] '*consil. 72, col. ult., lib. 4*' [? Paulus de Castro, *Consilia*, though not traced in Frankfurt, 1582, edn.].

but according to the order and prerogative of branches and families derived from the house of France. Each one of them is placed according to the prerogative of persons, with the elder ones always preferred as heads of the branches or families.

69. So God Himself terms them: in Exodus,[33] 'they are the heads (*principes*) of their fathers' houses', and 'heads of their houses by their kindred'; and in Chronicles[34] they are called 'princes in their families and in the house of their fathers', and 'heads of their fathers' house'. In these passages it may clearly be seen that the prerogatives of primogeniture extended successively to the heads of each branch. For the law of primogeniture is established by the law of God Who said in Genesis:[35] 'The first-born shall be lord of his brothers'; that 'his mother's sons were bowed down before him'; and that 'the first-born sat according to his birth-right, and the youngest according to his youth'. In France we now adhere to this for the succession to the crown, in consequence of the graduated entail (*substitution graduelle*) established in perpetuity by the fundamental law of the state, whereby the crown is conveyed by degrees to the branches which are the last to issue from it and, therefore, are the closest to it. And in every branch the succession is conveyed to its head, from the eldest to the eldest successively, be this to the thousandth degree, as Baldus has said,[36] specifically of the house of Bourbon.

70. For the learned Benedicti teaches us[37] that this kingdom was established almost like that of the people of God.

71. Now it was in this perpetual pre-eminence over the younger sons, called by Philo the Jew[38] 'the rights of the eldest to respect and power', that the effect of the blessing of the eldest properly consisted among the people of God. Its visible sign was the robe of primogeniture, specifically called *primogenita*. Being perfumed, this was the

---

[33] vi. [14, 25].

[34] 1 Chronicles iv. [38], v.[15].

[35] [Cf.] xxvii. [29]; xliii. [33].

[36] [For Baldus on primogeniture in respect of royal succession (though with no specific mention of the house of Bourbon), see *Prima Baldi super Digesto veteri commentariorum* (Lyon, 1540), fo. 10ᵛᵒ (*tit. 'De iustitia et iure', lex 'Ex hoc iure'*).]

[37] [Cf. Guillaume] Benedicti [*Repetitio . . . in cap. Raynatius de testamentis* (Lyon, 1575)], fo. 17ʳᵒ, no. 79. [Benedicti's point is that the French kingdom resembles the kingdom of Israel in debarring females from the throne – not the general position that Loyseau ascribes to him.]

[38] [Cf.] Philo Judaeus [*De sacrificiis Abelis et Caini*, 16–20].

cause of deceiving the good Isaac by its odour when he gave his blessing to Jacob who had put it on.

72. St Jerome,[39] following the Hebrew commentators, says that this robe was the robe of priesthood, because priesthood was exercised by the first-born of families, sanctified by God and dedicated to his service before Aaron had been designated priest of all the people. Likewise among the pagans, sacrifices were specific to houses and occurred in the presence of their heads.

73. We who have no private sacrifices have therefore given another mark to the eldest of the lineage, to distinguish him for ever from all the younger ones. It is that he bears the arms of his house plain (and so they pass from the eldest to the eldest), while the younger bear them charged and distinguished by some sign. In so far as new branches arise, so they are charged with divers marks by which every mutation of branches is always recognised. Thus is the eldest of each branch recognised; and thus are conserved perpetually the rank and pre-eminence of all those of the lineage.

74. So, if simple gentlemen defer and yield the arms of their family to its head although he does not always possess the principal land of the house by right of succession, how much more should this be the case with the crown. The crown is always consigned to the eldest of the house. It remains – in accordance with the ancient nature of the most noble fiefs – assigned to the head of the family, with graduated entail summoning forth into infinity the first-born of the eldest son of the house for its perpetual conservation. This was implemented quite recently in the person of our great present king, and again in the case of the prince of Condé. The latter was declared first prince of the blood as current head of the branch of Bourbon, although he was only the son of His Majesty's cousin and although he had uncles who were His Majesty's cousins german and thus nearer by one degree, if one were to count according to degrees of kinship as with ordinary inheritances.

75. I have discussed this very fully because of the importance and also the difficulty of the question. It was discussed by all sorts of characters at the commencement of the recent troubles during the life of the late Monsieur the Cardinal of Bourbon who pretended to the succession to the crown as the nearest kinsman according to the

---

[39] [*PL*, XXIII, col. 1030.]

ordinary degrees of succession, to the prejudice of our king who was the eldest of his branch.

76. Nevertheless, almost all of those who have discussed it have occupied themselves with the famous question of the uncle against the nephew, on which Tiraqueau[40] has left nothing more to be said. They have not noticed that this question has never been thrashed out except in relation to degrees of representation, equating the nephew with the uncle or prompting the assertion that he is to be preferred in respect of indivisible things. So they have not dealt with the true and particular point of law which concerns the crown of France: that it is assigned to the eldest from the eldest son. The princes of the blood, the officers of the crown and the greater part of the nobility of France have always held this to be the case. But above all, the great God of armies, by whom kings reign and princes are maintained, has decided it, not only in establishing our invincible king on his throne despite so many enemies and rebel subjects, but in making him flourish there and reign as peacefully and happily as ever any of his predecessors did – and, beyond all this and almost beyond all expectation, has given him so fine a progeny. 'These things would not be without the will of the gods'.

77. So, since the respect and status accorded to the princes of the blood stem from their being successors presumptive to the kingdom in their turn, it follows that the processional order amongst them ought to be the same as the successional order; for it would be unseemly if those farther removed from the crown were to walk before those who have the capacity to reign over them. Thus I consider that not only should the head of the branch walk before the younger even though the latter may be closer kin to the king according to the ordinary reckoning of degrees of kinship; but also that the last of the nearest branch that is, the branch most recently issued from the royal house and family – should walk before the heads of all the other branches; and so on, in sequence. And it is in this way that the rule of the ordinance of 1576[41] should be understood, that the princes of the blood walk 'according to their degree of consanguinity': that is, according to the rank and superiority of their blood.

78. This word 'degree' has two meanings in law, over and above the vulgar meaning which is to count each person as one degree. It

---

[40] [*De iure prim.*, p. 431.]
[41] [Above, sections 61, 64.]

often signifies the order and rank of divers species or qualities of propinquity, so to speak. Ulpian, explaining this rule of law that successions are conferred by degrees, says:[42]

> Possession of property upon intestacy is granted through seven degrees: in the first degree, to children; in the second, to right heirs; in the third, to the nearest cognate relations; in the fourth, to the family; etc.

Elsewhere in the law it is said:[43] 'The praetor made different degrees of succession: the first, of children; the second, of heirs at law; the third, of cognate relations, etc.'; and Justinian also says as much.[44]

79. Besides, when the ordinance says 'degree of consanguinity' the intention is not to say, 'of masculine kinship or agnation'. By 'degree of consanguinity' is meant the order and prerogative of the blood. Because of this, all these princes are called 'princes of the blood', and thus the intention is to prefer from degree to degree 'heads of houses by families, or heads of families by their cognate relations'.

80. So much for the rank of the princes of the blood. As for their other privileges, I will content myself here with a summary enumeration of the main ones, because Du Tillet,[45] Du Haillan[46] and others have discussed them. First, they are by birth counsellors of the king's privy council and likewise of his *parlement* – which was anciently the council of state – without being required to swear their oath there as the peers are. It is true that without the oath they have only the right of entry to the sessions of the *parlement*. Item, and in a word, all the prerogatives of the peers of France are theirs without exception; I have dealt in detail with these in my *Seigneuries*.[47] They are, moreover, exempt from all tolls, even from paying anything for the royal seals. They forfeit none of their status through entering the church; nor do their daughters through marrying those who are not princes of the blood.

81. They assist and advise at judgements upon the peers of France and other princes of the blood. They are exempt from duelling, and

---

[42] [*Fragmenti sive excerpta ex Ulpiani libro singulari*] *regulorum*, XXVIII. [7, in *The Institutes of Gaius and Rules of Ulpian*, ed. J. Muirhead (Edinburgh, 1904), p. 430].

[43] *Digest* 38.6.1.1.

[44] *Inst J* 3.9.

[45] [*Recueil*, pp. 218–25.]

[46] [*De l'estat et succez*, fo. 105ᵛᵒ.]

[47] vi. *passim*.

consequently ought to be exempt, after the king, from all challenges and defiances. They are even debarred from fighting at jousts and tournaments; on this I read somewhere that St Louis made an ordinance on the matter because his son Robert, count of Clermont, received in his youth so many blows with a mace at a tournament that he expected to die of them and was ill for the rest of his life. We may well consider what a misfortune it would have been for France if this prince had then been killed, for in that case the crown would have been vacant after the death of King Henry III without any prince of the blood to succeed to it, given that our great present king and all those who are now princes of the blood are the issue of this Prince Robert.

82. On this same point it must be noted that until now the blood of France has been so spared that no prince of the blood has ever suffered the death penalty by law, and there is only one who was condemned without being executed. This is not so much a privilege of immunity as, rather, a mark of their virtue and fidelity, or else of our kings' goodwill and affection towards them.

83. From all this it follows that the order of princes is now formally constituted and perfectly established in France, in respect of the title which they have in common with the sovereign prince; of their present undisputed status above all the great personages of the realm; and, finally, of those other great privileges which I have just recorded.

84. It follows further that in respect of the status of France's great personages more attention is now paid to their extraction than to their lordships. Indeed, dignity proceeding from lineage is of greater merit than that which proceeds from lordships, especially in the case of subordinate ones. For the former subsists in the person himself and immediately in his blood, naturally and inseparably; and the latter resides formally in a piece of land and is communicated to the person only accessorily, accidentally and separably.

85. Formerly lords walked in France, and in other monarchies they still walk, according to the prerogative of their lordships and not of their houses. It seems very likely that this originated and was first established at the time when dukes and counts enjoyed rights of sovereignty. They were then princes by lordship, for the title of prince has always implied precedence and the first rank in the state. But at present it is an undisputed law in France that the title and rank of prince can come only by lineage, princedom being not dative, but

native. So far is it from the case that those little lordships erected to the title of principalities engender the order and rank of prince that, on the contrary, duchies and counties take precedence without difficulty over them, as I have proved in my *Seigneuries*.[48] I remember an exchange between the count of Saint-Pol, prince of the blood of the house of Bourbon, and King Francis: when the latter asked his advice on the erection of such and such a princedom, he said that His Majesty could make princes only on the queen. As this rule is thus established amongst us, that the quality of prince and the first ranks are conferred according to the merit of the blood, everyone who could avail himself of his extraction to be installed in the order of princes has done so. So there are still found princes other than those of the blood royal. This can no longer be doubted. The aforementioned ordinance of 1576[49] speaks expressly of others. Prefaces to our kings' edicts ordinarily observe that on the affairs in question they have taken the advice of the princes of the blood and other princes and lords of their court.

86. First, then, the natural children of our kings, or of the princes of the blood whose branch has attained to the crown, and their descendants have maintained that, as the descendants of the legitimate children are legitimate princes, so they are natural princes of the kingdom.

87. Indeed, I will not shrink from saying, in the wake of Du Tillet,[50] that faithful recorder of the secrets of France, that under the first two dynasties of our kings, when a plurality of heirs were admitted to the kingdom, the bastard took his share with the true-born and even had his portion designated a kingdom. We gather from the annals[51] that Clovis, the first Christian king (just as Constantine was the first Christian emperor), was a bastard, nay, a bastard begotten in adultery, born of Basina, wife of the king of Thuringia; and Thierry, his natural son, succeeded to the kingdom with the three legitimate sons, and he was king of France with the title of Austrasia. Chlotar the Great was equally a bastard, according to the most common opinion; and Sigebert [I], his bastard, was also king of France in Austrasia. In the second dynasty, of which the founding

---

[48] [ii. 95.]
[49] [Above, sections 61 *et seq.*]
[50] [*Recueil*, p. 206.]
[51] *Annales*, fo. 16ro.

father, Charles Martel, was a bastard, Louis and Carloman, bastards of Louis the Stammerer, were kings together.

88. But the third dynasty has always abided quite rightly by the rule of excluding bastards from the royal succession, according to the common law established at present, as I believe, in all the states of Christendom where polygamy and concubinage are prohibited: though in ancient times bastards would succeed in company with legitimate heirs even among the people of God where these prohibitions did not apply.

89. Yet we do find, at the beginning of this third dynasty, the illustrious house of Montfort, descended from Amaury, natural son of King Robert. The king gave him the county of Montfort, near Paris, which is still at present called by his name, Montfort l'Amaury. From him are descended many great princes and lords, as is recorded by Du Tillet[52] who makes a branch of them as of princes of the blood. They include Boudouin and Amaury, kings of Jerusalem; Simon de Montfort who defeated the Albigensians; and another Simon de Montfort, earl of Leicester and brother-in-law of Henry III, king of England, who defeated the latter and took him prisoner in a fixed battle.

90. Since then our kings have feared lest natural sons should confront legitimate ones, or at least that they would one day claim the succession to the kingdom in accordance with the unjust practice of the two earlier dynasties. So the kings have made it their custom (I do not know whether I ought to say with Du Tillet)[53] not to avow them, but rather to put them out of the way and give them to the church, just as under those earlier dynasties monks were made of those whom one wished to exclude from the kingdom, or else as a more convenient and an easier way of advancing them whilst depriving them of all hope of progeny.

91. But now that this rule of their exclusion from the crown is established over so many centuries and such a long series of peaceable kings that anyone wishing to breach it would achieve nothing beyond making himself ridiculous, our kings no longer hesitate either to avow their natural children or to let them marry. They even legitimatise them in all things, except for the succession to the kingdom; and

---

[52] [*Recueil*, pp. 68–71.]
[53] [*Ibid.*, pp. 206 *et seq.*]

this by express letters which have the clause that they should walk immediately after the princes of the blood, letters which are verified in the *parlement*. So there is no doubt whatsoever that the kings' natural children and all their legitimate descendants have the title and rank of prince.

92. This is certainly very conducive to the extreme respect and reverence in which the people of France, more than all others, holds its kings and their blood. In the excellence of that blood no blemish nor corruption ought to be imagined. On the contrary, this royal blood purifies and ennobles all other blood with which it is mingled. For it must be acknowledged to be of much more noble and august material and quality than that of other men. Plato said [54] that by comparison with other men those who are born to command are made of another metal. More to the point, Aristotle said[55] that kings are of a mean genus between God and the people. As the poets call the bastards of the gods heroes or demi-gods, so can we say that the bastards of kings are demi-kings – that is, princes, the mean quality between kings and other men. And since we deprive them of the power of command, we ought at least to leave them the honour or honorary title of prince and the rank below that of princes who are capable of sovereign command.

93. Likewise, the good will and shrewdness of our kings have let the descendants of foreign sovereignties be installed in the order of princes. This is well done: for the practice yields much honour and security and increase to this kingdom. It yields honour in that a collection and accumulation of the sovereign houses of Christendom are seen at the court of France. It yields security in as much as for us these foreign princes are tantamount to voluntary and perpetual hostages for the alliances which we have with the heads of their houses. And it yields increase because they bring into France their means, their credit and their friends, and above all their own gentle persons who are so many captains in case of need; and in truth it must be allowed that they have done the realm some signal services.

94. They are also very well rewarded for it. For they rarely stay in the grandeur and opulence of France without being appointed to

---

[54] *Republic* III. 415A.
[55] [Cf. *Politics* 1284[a] 3–11.]

principal charges and endowed with principal lordships, or finding advantageous marriages. So it cannot be denied that they are advanced here much more than they could be in their own countries.

95. Here, then, are two kinds of princes recognised in France apart from those of the blood: French princes and foreign princes, or else natural princes and naturalised princes. Yet neither the former nor the latter are as truly and properly princes as those of the blood. The principal mark of a prince is to be capable of succeeding to the sovereignty: I mean, the sovereignty of the place where he wishes to be recognised as prince. Lordships are limited; and, as the sovereign of another state is not sovereign in France, his kin are not perfectly princes here and by virtue of their own quality, but only in as much as it pleases the king to recognise them as such.

96. That is why the *parlement*, which is particularly jealous of the conservation of the rights of the crown and consequently of its princes, has not yet allowed [them] this quality, at least without limitation and without qualification in terms of their country. The perfect correctness of the words ought to be religiously kept in this, especially in matters of such importance.

97. This apart, I consider that one cannot fail to call them princes absolutely. The king, whose unvarnished word makes the law in such matters, honours them daily with this title in ordinary speech and in sober acts, and even maintains them in the enjoyment of prerogatives ascribed to princes alone. Furthermore, it is a rule of dialectic that the name of the genus can be used for all its species.

98. This is perhaps the reason why princes capable of the crown call themselves not simply princes, but princes of the blood, thereby using an adjective of more particular dignity. They do so in order to distinguish themselves from princes of foreign extraction (as indeed they are of a much more eminent degree). Likewise, in order to distinguish themselves from natural princes and the descendants of the latter, they call themselves princes of the crown.

99. In my view, what Du Haillan says[56] is not the case, that only the children of France can call themselves princes of the crown. They can take no more elevated a title than that of son of France; and, according to its true meaning, the title 'prince of the crown' applies

---

[56] [*De l'estat et succez*, fo. 105ᵐ.]

as well to their descendants, who are the other princes of the blood, as to them. Belleforest shows very well[57] that all the princes of the blood can call themselves princes of the crown.

100. But he says that it is otherwise with the king's kinsfolk on the female side. This is still farther removed from reason. Apart from their not being princes at all, it is common knowledge that the title of prince of the blood cannot in any case apply to them; and so this is enough to distinguish them from the latter. Consequently, we must reaffirm this truth that, in order to distinguish themselves from bastards and their descendants (without wishing to single them out by calling them prince bastards), the legitimate princes of France call themselves crown princes: that is to say, capable of succeeding to the crown. In this lies the true property or perfection of principality – the more especially as otherwise the title of prince of the blood can in some way apply to natural princes, in as much as the blood has to do with the effect of nature.

101. Now, just as natural princes, and naturalised ones too, have obtained the title of prince which they now enjoy in common with those of the blood, so have they found means of enjoying many of the pre-eminences of the latter. They walk in the rank of the princes and thus precede all the great lords and, likewise, all the great officers: save that great officers[58] do not give way nor defer to such princes as they do for honour's sake to the princes of the blood.

102. Those other princes walk amongst themselves not according to the merit of their subordinate lordships, but according to their degrees as princes. In this regard I will not spend time on deciding whether the natural or the naturalised should take precedence, nor on discussing the other great questions which arise on the rank of the former or the latter; because it is a matter for the king alone to decide these things.

103. As the princes of the blood who are the king's true kinsfolk are called by him either his uncles (if they are a good deal older), or his cousins (if they are much the same age), or his nephews (if they are younger); so are the other princes addressed in the same way by His Majesty. When dukes and counts enjoyed rights of sovereignty, our kings did them the honour of calling them their true kinsfolk;[59] [and

---

[57] *Annales* [fo. 9ʳᵒ].
[58] [1701 adds: when they are performing their official functions.]
[59] [1701 adds: and, reciprocally, the king's true kin.]

they] took the title of prince which had first been used by those sovereign dukes and counts of France. Hence comes it that His Majesty still bestows this same honour upon dukes although they are no longer sovereign: for in matters of honour one ought never to abase. This is also done in respect of foreign sovereign dukes and counts; and, as for the other kings of Christendom, ours, who is the eldest son of the church, calls them his brothers.

104. Likewise, as the princes of the blood are born counsellors of the council of state, the other princes also have gained the right of entry, sitting and speaking without needing a royal warrant for the purpose as the other counsellors do. But they do not have entry to the *parlement* as do the princes of the blood, unless they are peers of France. In this case they still keep the status of their princedoms and not those of their principalities, like the princes of the blood. The reason is that the princes of the blood assist there as princes, and those others only as peers.

105. Finally, they claim to be exempt from the duel. Indeed, as it is held that a gentleman is not bound in point of honour to fight with a commoner, so is it held that a prince is not bound to enter into a duel against a gentleman, whether he be a knight or a duke, because of the inequality of their condition, and in duelling one must deal with one's equal. But, setting aside the ordinances prohibiting duels, I consider there to be no difficulty about princes other than those of the blood fighting duels with each other. Yet duels between princes of the blood should not be sanctioned. That their blood be spared is of well-nigh as much importance for France as the sparing of the blood of France itself.

CHAPTER EIGHT

Of the third estate

1. In as much as order is a species of dignity the third estate of France is not properly an order: for, as it embraces all the rest of the people, apart from churchmen and nobles, all the people of France would have to be in dignity. But in as much as order signifies a condition or occupation or else a distinct species of persons, the third estate is one of the three orders or estates general of France.

2. Nevertheless, in ancient Gaul no account was taken of it, nor was it held in any respect or regard. So Caesar says:[1]

> Throughout Gaul there are two kinds of men who are in some rank and honour – on the one hand druids, on the other knights. For the common people are reckoned in the place virtually of slaves who undertake nothing by themselves and are never consulted.

3. M. Pasquier observes[2] very pertinently that in the first two dynasties of our kings there was no mention of the third estate, and that the common people were not summoned at all to the general assemblies convened for the state's constitutional affairs.

4. At those assemblies, which were then called *parlements* and are now called estates-general, there were only prelates and barons: that is, the principal members of the clergy and the nobility. Hence our courts of *parlement* are at present composed of clerics and laymen who were formerly nobles and men of the sword, as the old books testify.

---

[1] *De bello Gallico* VI. [xiii].
[2] [*Les*] *Recherches* [*de la France*] II. vii [in *Les Oeuvres d'Estienne Pasquier* (Amsterdam, 1723), I, col. 86].

5. Pasquier adds that in the third dynasty our kings had got into the habit of asking the common people for a relief or subsidy in money for the necessity of war. In order to obtain their consent (without which in that time no monetary levy could be made), they were thenceforth summoned to these assemblies which for that reason were called estates-general. That is why the common people are called the third estate, just as the order of Roman knights is called by [the elder] Pliny[3] the third order because it was added to the other two which were instituted long before.

6. This third estate of France is at present much greater in power and authority than it was formerly. For the officers of justice and finance are almost all in it since the nobility has despised learning and embraced idleness. I say the nobility as those from whose ranks the judges were chosen in ancient times – and, as Fauchet shows,[4] the chief officers of finance too: just as at Rome the knights were for a very long time the judges, and the principal tax-farmers and financiers were always of their number, while the quaestors or intendants of finance were most often taken from among the senators.

7. The term 'third estate' is more comprehensive than 'bourgeois' which includes only town-dwellers. Towns are called *bourgs* in Old French, as they still are in German· hence our term *fois-bourgs* for what lies outside the town. *Villes* formerly signified country houses, like the Latin *villae*. Hence most of the villages of the Beauce still retain the suffix *ville* appended to the name of their ancient lord; and in many country districts the villagers nowadays call their villages *villes*.

8. Again, the term 'bourgeois' does not properly include all the townspeople. Although nobles may reside in the towns, they do not call themselves bourgeois, because nobility is an order quite separate from the third estate to which the bourgeoisie belongs. That is why the noble is ordinarily contrasted to the bourgeois, as when we refer to the right of wardship of a minor as *garde-noble* and *garde-bourgeoise* [respectively]. Moreover, base persons of the common people do not have the right to call themselves bourgeois: and they have no part in the honours of the city nor voice in its assemblies, in which rights bourgeoisie consists.

[3] *Nat. hist.* XXXIII. [vii. 29].
[4] [Cf. *Origines] des chevaliers [armoiries et heraux*, in *Les oeuvres de feu M. Claude Fauchet* (Paris, 1610), fos. 506ro–512vo].

9. Furthermore, and to be precise, the bourgeois are to be found not in all towns, but only in privileged towns which have corporate and communal rights. For to be a citizen or a bourgeois, as Plutarch defines it very well,[5] is to participate in a city's rights and privileges. So, if a city is neither a commune nor incorporate and has neither officers nor privileges, there can be no bourgeois there. Therefore they are called in law 'townspeople deprived of offices', as Bodin shows,[6] arguing that in our language bourgeois has something, however inexpressible, more special than 'citizen'.

10. Now in France, as in Rome, there are several orders or degrees of the third estate. The Romans had 'paymasters', 'scribes', 'merchants', 'lictors', 'master-craftsmen', 'artisans' and 'the common crowd'. Likewise in France we have learned men, financiers, legal practitioners, merchants, husbandmen, servants of justice and workmen, each of which must be dealt with separately.

11. In view of the honour due to learning, I have placed learned men in the first rank. The Romans never made these into a separate order, but mixed them amongst the three estates. Further, the Romans did not have as many persons with learning as their profession and particular occupation as do we. Few though the Romans had of these, they were constituted formally into civil professions, offices which were virtually perpetual. So the Romans did them more honour than we do and gave them great privileges, as may be seen in the relevant law.[7] Also, there were only a certain number of them, whereas in France as many capable ones are received as present themselves.

12. Our learned men are divided into four faculties or principal fields of learning: theology; jurisprudence, in which I include civil and canon law; medicine; and arts, which embrace grammar, rhetoric and philosophy. In each of these four faculties there are three degrees – to wit, bachelor, licentiate, and doctor or master.

13. The bachelor (the etymology of which was explained earlier)[8] is he who, having completed his studies, is admitted to the classes of the faculty to aim for the doctorate or mastership. The licentiate is he who, having completed his classes and done all the requisite acts

---

[5] *Solon* [xviii].
[6] [*République*] pp. 73–9 [also providing the foregoing citation from Plutarch].
[7] *Code J* 10.53.6.
[8] Above, ch. 6 (sections 48 *et seq.*).

and tests, is declared capable of obtaining the degree of doctor or master; that is why he has almost the same advantages as the doctor. The doctor or master is he who, having formally received the marks and insignia of this dignity, obtains the power to teach others publicly and to confer upon them the same degree, a power which the simple licentiate does not have.

14. I will not indulge myself in noting here the ceremonies observed for the conferment of every degree. They are different according to the divers faculties, and again according to the divers universities in which these degrees are granted. The ceremonies were only devised the better to maintain the honour of learning through these outward shows. The fact remains that these orders or degrees are dignities of the school.

15. But there is another order or dignity of the learned which the magistrate confers publicly upon persons leaving the school. It is that of advocate which can be conferred only upon those who already have the degree of doctor or at least of licentiate in civil and canon law.

16. The Romans first called advocates those who assisted the parties by their simple presence when cases were pleaded by those called 'defenders of the cases'. Asconius says:[9]

> Whoever defends another in a court of justice is called either the defender if he is the orator; or a jurisconsult if he advises on the law; or an advocate if he lends his presence to his friend; or a procurator if he takes the affair upon himself; or a *cognitor* if he alters the case by his presence and so is examined as if it were his own affair.

But today we abuse these names, and we avow (*advocamus*) a defender, we implore or 'invoke' a judge, we challenge or 'provoke' an opponent, we call forth or 'evoke' a witness. So 'advocate' is the name given in general to 'all those who acted in pleading cases with some degree of application'.[10]

17. Nevertheless, to take advocates in their particular sense, they were distinguished from jurists, the former being pleaders in the courts, the latter being consultants. In Rome these were two quite

---

[9] [Quintus] Asconius [Pedianus, *In Ciceronis orationes commentarii* (Venice, 1498), sig. c. iᵛᵒ].

[10] *Digest* 50.13.1.11.

different occupations. The advocates or orators never became jurists as our pleaders become consultants. With us it is but a single occupation, so that pleading leads them to the consultant's work as they grow older and more experienced.

18. The orators and defenders of cases were the advocate-pleaders, reckoned so honourable a practice amongst the Romans that senators and other great personages spent their youth in it. In the Roman Republic to be a good advocate was the main way of attaining to great offices. By defending cases gratis, as they did, they bound many persons closely to them. Consequently they acquired a great many clients (as they called those whose cases they had defended), and so gained great support and authority amongst the people. This served them well to arrive at great offices, which were the summit of their advance. Further, those who knew how to declaim well had a great advantage in assemblies of the people who willingly let themselves be led by the ears: so that in republics advocates are the first in power and authority.

19. But under the emperors this authority was much reduced, as the author of the dialogue attributed to Tacitus says:[11] because popular favour was no longer any use to obtain great offices. This was when they became mercenary, as they could no longer be paid otherwise than in money. Nevertheless the emperors, not wanting them to be displaced altogether, constituted them into a civil profession. Thus they acquired all those fine privileges which soldiers had, and other peculiar ones again, notably that after performing their functions for twenty years they became counts.[12]

20. For in their capacity as defenders they became advocates of the treasury; and, having performed this function for a year and then two, they were no longer advocates as such.[13] This is what the law[14] calls 'the limit of the profession'; and it was then that they became counts, as being destined for great offices. It is thus that this vulgar passage in Tacitus should be understood: 'When pleadings end, the dignities of advocates then begin'.[15] True, as there were so few advocates in the time of Valentinian they were made perpetual.[16] This was

[11] *Dialogus de oratoribus* [xxxvi. 4, xxxviii. 2].
[12] *Code J* 2.8.1.
[13] *Code J* 2.7.8,12.
[14] *Code J* 2.7.17.
[15] [Cf. *Leg. Nov.*, Nov. Theodosius 10.2.]
[16] [Cf. *Leg. Nov.*, Nov. Valentinian 2.4.]

afterwards corrected by another fine law of Valentinian and Marcian, which Cujas records.[17]

21. As for the jurisconsults, in Rome they were not as esteemed during the Republic as were the orators, who carried off all the glory. The former were like ministers to the latter: 'counsellors and backstage advisers', says Budé,[18] 'who supplied the advocate with points of law and legal formulae by their assistants'.

22. The style came from the Greeks who called them 'pragmatics', as Cicero[19] and Quintilian[20] say. They were also called 'composers of writs' and 'pettifoggers' because they had invented certain formulae or secrets, unknown to the rest of the people, which they wrote in notes or ciphers, as physicians write their prescriptions, so that only those of their trade could read and understand them. Nevertheless, they had gained this point over the judges, that whoever mistook such a formula by a single syllable should lose his case. This is why Cicero calls them 'word-catchers',[21] quibblers. In short, they quite resemble our chicaners of the Roman curia who are also called practitioners.

23. But after Gnaeus Flavius had divulged and communicated their secret to the people,[22] many then applied themselves to philosophising more freely on the law. Thus, from among the wits of Rome, there shortly emerged a fine science; and those gifted in it were called 'persons learned in the law', 'jurisconsults' or 'jurisprudents' – or else simply 'wise' and 'judicious'. These in due course were greatly respected owing to everyone's need of them. Above all, the emperors gave them great authority when they ordained that the judges in judging should be bound to follow their advice, as is said in the *Institutes*.[23]

24. They had three principal functions: 'to warn'; 'to give an opinion on the law'; and 'to examine judicially or sit as magistrates'. To warn was to advise the parties, which was the only function of the old practitioners. To give an opinion was to advise the judges on a point of law, in a process ready to be judged. To examine judicially was to

[17] [*Opera C*, III, col. 509.]
[18] [*Opera B*, III, p. 337.]
[19] *De oratore* I.[xlv. 198].
[20] *Institutionis oratoriae* III. [vi. 59], XII. iii. [4].
[21] [*De oratore* I. lv. 236.]
[22] [Livy, *Hist.* ix. xlvi. 5.]
[23] *Inst. J* [*Prooemium.* 3].

be the magistrates' delegated assessors or commissioners, instructing and sometimes adjudicating the process whether with them or without them.

25. They had yet another authority which was that when some difficult question occurred in Rome they all met together to debate and agree. This conference was called the 'debate of the forum'; Cicero mentions it.[24] What they settled in such assemblies were called 'decrees or guarantees of decisions', and these were a kind of 'unwritten law', as Raevardus discusses very methodically.[25]

26. In brief, they also had this honour, that they were readily called to the emperor's retinue and council. This may be gathered from the following law:[26]

> Our best and greatest emperors provided that jurisconsults assisting the imperial council should be excused the offices of guardians since they were in attendance about the imperial person; and the honour so conferred had no certain limit either of time or of place.

Elsewhere it is said[27] that the jurisconsult Menander was excused from guardianship 'because he was engaged about the emperor', and in this connection he is called 'the counsellor Menander'. This began from the time of the Emperor Hadrian of whom Spartianus says:[28]

> When he tried cases he had in his council not only his friends or members of his retinue, but jurisconsults – in particular Julius Celsus, Salvius Iulianus, Neratius Priscus, and others; yet only those whom the whole senate had approved.

Lampridius says of Alexander Severus[29] that 'he was an excellent emperor because he ruled the state mainly in accordance with Ulpian's advice'; and, a little earlier, that 'he issued no definitive ordinance without involving twenty jurisconsults'.

27. But what began to bring them into greater vogue and celebrity was that Augustus enjoined them to take letters from him, and thus they were held to be officers of the emperor. Afterwards the Emperor

---

[24] [Cf. *Topica* xvi. 65.]
[25] [Jacobus] Raevardus, *De auctoritate prudentium* [(Antwerp, 1566)], pp. 128–37.
[26] *Digest* 27.1.30.
[27] *Digest* 4.4.11.2.
[28] *Hadrian* [xviii. 1].
[29] *Severus Alexander* [li. 4, xvi. 1].

Hadrian derided this with good reason, saying that it was not for the emperor to authorise the capacity required to be a jurisconsult, as Gaius records.[30] The fact remains that thereafter jurisconsults practising by the emperor's authority were like public officers and 'in perpetual civil office', at least as Manilius calls the jurisconsult:[31]

In his own house he is a lifelong magistrate of the people.

28. That is how the Romans arranged matters from time to time. But in France we have not separated the orators from the jurisconsults. We include them all in the order and under the name of advocates. Some are pleaders and the others consultants – the honourable retirement of their old age. For the reward for the labour of their past life is that those who can no longer bear the work and contention of pleading, and who have also gained more capacity and experience through years spent continuously amid affairs, should thenceforth give counsel to the younger ones. Further, in the sessions of the *parlements* these advocates have their bench apart and their seats on the fleurs-de-lis, like the provincial judges.

29. They also have their separate title in the ancient ordinances of the *parlement* where they are called 'advocate counsellors' as they are titled in various laws.[32] This title will be explained later. And from the old French lawyers one gathers that formerly the advocates were counsellors because it was they who counselled the judges in sessions of the court as in council.

30. This has yielded occasion for placing counsellors by right of office in their place. Since venality of offices was established, all sorts of honourable functions have been reduced to offices, so as to sell them; and these counsellors erected into offices have been called 'counsellor magistrates' as distinct from the former counsellors who were the ancient advocates, not officers. Du Moulin complains bitterly about this.[33] He says that formerly there were scarcely seen so many appeals because processes were judged by the old advocates, whereas now they are mostly adjudicated by young and ignorant counsellors, there being hardly anyone who buys these little offices apart from those incapable of being advocates.

---

[30] [Rightly, Pomponius:] *Digest* 1.2.49.
[31] [Marcus] Manilius [*Astronomicon* IV. 212, referring specifically to the jurist Servius Sulpicius Rufus].
[32] *Digest* 1.22.5; *Code J* 1.51.3; *Code Theod.* 1.34.1.
[33] [Untraced.]

31. In my view, after these learned men should come the financiers, in order. In Rome they held the first order of the common people; they were called 'tribunes or quaestors of the treasury', as I said earlier.[34] By the Aurelian law[35] the right of adjudicating cases with the senators and knights was ascribed to them.

32. In interpreting this, Dio[36] says that, as it had been decided that all three orders of the Roman people should participate in judgements, and because the order of the common people was too numerous, only the tribunes of finance were chosen, as the principal and most honourable of them, to act as judges with the senators and knights. Furthermore, the tax-farmers called 'publicans' were of the order of knights, and these are still gentlemen in Venice and in several other countries.

33. I term 'financiers' all those who intervene in the management of finance – that is, the king's monies – whether as officers or otherwise. For we are dealing here with orders, or rather with simple occupations which are compatible with offices. The truth is that formerly financial responsibilities were not offices, but simple commissions, as I have proved elsewhere.[37] In most instances they were conferred by the people. When they granted some levy of monies to the king, they appointed so many persons to divide and apportion it: first, by provinces, whom they called *généraux*; then, by parishes, whom they called *elus*; and finally, by the several inhabitants of every parish, whom they still call 'assessors'. Likewise, they deputed men of the parishes to be 'collectors'.

34. But since venality of offices came into use there is no financial function, however petty, which has not been made into an office. And because these offices ordinarily involve scant honour and scant power too, they have been accorded plenty of pay. Further, it is reasonable that, just as whoever handles pitch should keep some of it on his fingers, those who handle finance should take their share: which they scarcely ever forget willingly to do.

35. The lawyers or legal practitioners come next. They are mentioned in the law,[38] and by Juvenal:[39]

---

[34] Above, ch. 2 [section 81].
[35] [Law (70 BC) of the praetor Lucius Aurelius Cotta, by which juries were composed of equal numbers of senators, knights and tribunes of the public treasury.]
[36] [Cf. *Rom. hist.* XLIII. XXV. 1.]
[37] [*Offices*, III.i.62; IV.v.18.]
[38] *Digest* 48.19.9.4.
[39] [*Saturae* VIII.122–3.]

if one gold piece should fall to your lot
Some of it will drop off by bargain of the legal advisers.

They are all those who, apart from the judges and advocates, make their livings out of the legal affairs and processes of others. There are two kinds of them: those of the long robe – our clerks, notaries, attorneys – whom the Romans called 'scribes'; and those of the short robe – our sergeants, criers, valuers and others like them – who were particularly called 'apparitors, or public servants of the magistrates'. These constituted an order distinct from that of the scribes; for the order of the scribes took precedence over that of the merchants, but that of apparitors came after the latter. Likewise in France, practitioners of the long robe walk before the merchants, but those of the short robe come behind. Nevertheless, both kinds are included in the name of practitioners.

36. I have dealt amply in my *Offices*[40] with the clerks and the notaries. As for attorneys, here only those are relevant whom we designate 'for lawsuits' and not those 'for business' who in law are called 'administrators' or 'agents'. According to Budé,[41] attorneys for lawsuits were called in Rome *cognitores*. Cicero observes:[42]

> What is the difference between a man who litigates for himself and one who gives an attorney's services? Surely, he who begins an action in person claims for himself alone, no one can claim for another unless he has been appointed attorney.

37 However, Asconius in the passage cited above[43] distinguishes quite otherwise between a *cognitor* and an attorney:

> Surely an attorney is a person who undertakes the business of someone who is absent; a *cognitor* is a person who defends the case of someone who is present as if it were his own.

38. Be that as it may, the Romans certainly made use of attorneys 'for lawsuits', as numerous laws show.[44] Hence it is said in the *Digest*[45] that 'issue being joined, the attorney becomes the principal in the action'. True, they were not needed in all cases in Rome, no more

---

[40] II.[v].
[41] [*Opera B*, III, p. 73, cf. 141.]
[42] *Pro Quinto Roscio Comoedo* [xviii.53].
[43] [Section 16.]
[44] *Digest* 46.3.86, 2.14.13, 21.2.66.2, 2.7.4.3; *Code J* 2.24.1.
[45] *Digest* 49.1.4.5.

than in ancient French legal practice where the king's grace and privilege were needed in order to be admitted and to plead by attorney, as may be seen in the ancient procedural practice of the *parlement*.

39. But the practice or pettifoggery has since developed amongst us so that the parties are not constrained, as in Roman law, to appear in person at all hearings of the case, as long as they have given bail at the outset 'to appear in court after being bound over by the judge'; we call this 'to be at law'. So we have hit on this expedient to constitute in all cases an attorney who thenceforth may appear for us. We give these attorneys such authority and account them so necessary that nowadays the parties are not permitted to appear without them in the judgement of civil cases. The attorney's authority cannot even be revoked, once he has appeared and concerned himself in the case, unless another is constituted in his place by the same act of revocation.

40. As the use of attorneys has become necessary in all cases and for all the parties pleading, it is not surprising that today this should be a specific occupation, and a very lucrative one, given that the law says[46] that they are the masters of cases; and they certainly make this known. The fact is that, owing to the power which they have, it has been most necessary not to admit all kinds of persons indiscriminately to be attorneys, but to make of them a true order of chosen men, examined and found capable, and to restrict them to a certain number. For a multitude of attorneys signifies a multiplying and prolonging of legal process, especially as those who have few cases normally desire to multiply and prolong them; and, in so far as they wish it, they can easily do so.

41. I say, then, that attorneyship is truly an order and not an office, given that they have no public function, and although they are limited to a certain number, as were the advocates in the Roman empire. The senators of Rome and the clergy of the early church, 'whose number was fixed',[47] were none the less orders and not offices, as I proved earlier.[48]

42. It is true that in 1572 the attorneys were erected into an office. But this edict has never been executed in respect of those of the

---

[46] [Cf. *Digest* 3.3.]
[47] [*Nov. J* 3.]
[48] [Above, ch. 2, sections 18, 41, etc; 3, sections 1, 3, 4, etc.]

parlement. It was altogether revoked at the Estates of Blois.[49] After having been renewed, it was revoked a second time in 1584, and then re-instituted again in 1587. Nevertheless, it could not be executed upon those of the *parlement* which for this reason remained closed for more than fifteen days, all the attorneys concerned having resolved to quit their places rather than buy them; so that it was finally revoked for the third time. However, in most of the royal courts it has not ceased to be observed (even though I do not know that it has been re-instituted after that last revocation of 1587), and the attorneys' offices to be procured at the office of escheats (*parties casuelles*), whether they are vacant through resignation or through death. In that place money will always buy wax.

43. Yet in other courts the custom has never been adopted of procuring these places as offices at the *parties casuelles*. Nevertheless, as their number is limited, when an attorney wants to leave his office to his son, his son-in-law or his nephew, he does it not by a true resignation (which does not apply in the case of orders), but by a simple demission, discussed above.[50] However, this demission has almost the same effect as resignation, given that it has been adjudicated in several decrees that the judge can admit to the place only the person in whose favour the demission was made. Nor can he refuse the place to a competent person if the latter is close kin to the one demitting in his favour. No letters are requisite from the prince; and while the person so demitting retains the quality of attorney, yet he can no longer practise as such. Even so, advocates who have served their time may yet be admitted to plead for their closest kin.[51]

44. In order to show that the attorneys are an order and even a legal community, the ordinance of 1551[52] says expressly that a person wishing to be admitted as an attorney must be found sufficient by the other attorneys of the court. This is common form with communities of orders, and not with companies of officers. Besides, the requirement is that they should have been practised for at least five years, and for ten years in the *parlement*; then that [the court] be informed of the candidate's character; and finally that his capability be examined. This is common to offices and to orders of importance.

---

[49] [Fontanon, II, p. 586.]
[50] Ch. I [section 48].
[51] [*Digest* 2.7.2.2, 24.]
[52] [Fontanon, I, p. 335.]

And although an advocate may be admitted at the age of seventeen,[53] nevertheless the ordinances require attorneys to be twenty-five years old, because they daily deal with the parties and stand for them in judgement.

45. After the principal lawyers, in Rome and in France, come the merchants, as much for the utility – indeed, the public necessity – of commerce[54] as for the ordinary wealth of merchants which brings them credit and respect. Further, they derive a great deal of power in the towns by their means of employing artisans and workmen. The merchants are the last of the people who bear the quality of honour. They are called 'honourable men' or 'gentle persons and bourgeois of the towns'. These qualities are ascribed neither to husbandmen nor to sergeants nor to artisans, and still less to workmen who are all reputed base persons, as will shortly be shown.

46. But as for merchants, although Aristotle normally disparages them, yet in the *Politics*[55] he ranks them with honourable persons. Cicero speaks[56] of 'a suitable order of men of business, by good-will'. Callistratus says[57] that those who sell small commodities 'ought not to be kept among base persons, nor utterly kept away from honours'. That is why I said that they call themselves bourgeois because in the towns they participate in the privileges and are capable of holding offices which ought not to be given to artisans and mechanics. By the ancient ordinances only merchants seem to be capable of municipal offices, because royal officers and advocates and even lawyers are excluded from them. Perhaps this is why the first officer of the town of Paris is called the provost of the merchants.

47. In my opinion, the husbandmen ought to follow the merchants and to precede the legal practitioners of the short robe, just as at Rome they took precedence over the magistrates' apparitors. Aristotle, in the place cited above,[58] prefers them to merchants; and, as I said earlier,[59] at Rome 'the rustic tribes were more honoured than urban ones'. Likewise in France it is apparent that country life is the ordinary occupation of the nobility, and that of merchandise derog-

---

[53] *Digest* 3.1.3.
[54] *Digest* 50.11.2.
[55] 1290[b]37–1291[b]30.
[56] [Cf.] *Pro lege Manilia* [vii.17–18].
[57] [Cf. *Digest* 50.2.12.]
[58] [See note 55.]
[59] Above, ch. 2. [section 67].

ates from their status. It is true that by 'husbandmen' I mean those whose ordinary occupation is to work as farmers for someone else, an activity from which the nobility are as debarred as they are from trade of merchandise. But, be that as it may, there is no way of life of greater innocence nor of gain more in accordance with nature than that of husbandry. Philosophers have preferred it to every other occupation. On the other hand, in the public weal of France we have so disparaged husbandmen, and even oppressed them through taxes and the tyranny of the gentry, that it is amazing how they can subsist and how there are any to nourish us. Indeed, most of them would rather be man-servants and ploughmen for others than masters and farmers.

48. Be that as it may, we nowadays consider husbandmen and all other villagers whom we call 'peasants' to be base persons. In fact, according to Budé[60] the word 'villain' comes from *villa* and *villicus* [bailiff], not from *ville* as Bodin says,[61] except in so far as *ville* significs village which is its first meaning, as I have just said. Since Roman times the greatest have subjected villagers to themselves, calling them 'clowns and clodhoppers'; in France we used to call them 'villeins', 'persons in mortmain' or 'in mortgage'. Caesar provides a fine indication of this:[62]

> The common people for the most part declare themselves to be in servitude to the nobles as long as they are oppressed by debt, or by weight of tribute, or by injuries at the hands of the more powerful: the same laws apply to them as to slaves in relation to their lords.

49. The artisans or tradesmen are those who practise the mechanic arts, so called as distinct from the liberal arts: for the mechanic arts were formerly practised by serfs and slaves. We commonly term 'mechanic' that which is base and abject. Nevertheless, because much skill is needed for these mechanic arts they have given rise to masterships, as with the liberal arts.

50. By ordinance, three years of apprenticeship are requisite under the same master, on pain of commencing the apprenticeship afresh. One then becomes a 'companion', anciently termed 'bachelor' and

---

[60] [*Opera B*, III, p. 54.]
[61] [*République*, p. 73.]
[62] *De bello Gallico* VI.[xiii].

signifying a pretender or aspirant to mastership. Following three more years as a companion working for masters, one may be admitted master after having given public proof of one's sufficiency. This is termed a 'masterpiece', and by it one is found capable.[63] The arrangement is very well founded, so that no one shall be admitted master unless he knows his trade very well, and so that masters shall lack neither apprentices nor companions to help them with their work.

51. However, this fine arrangement is falling into disuse, at least in small towns, owing to masterships by letters which dispense from apprenticeship, bachelorship and masterpiece alike. The king grants them upon his accession to the crown; the queen, after her marriage; the dauphin and, nowadays, other royal children too, both male and female, after their births, or the queen on their behalf; and, finally, the first prince of the blood, after his proclamation. This arose because, just as these princes' household officers are privileged, so too the artisans whom they formerly chose from each trade to serve them were presumed worthy of being masters. It has grown to the point of allowing that these princes give a letter of retainer for each trade in each town where sworn gilds predominate (*ville juré*). Yet the king currently empowers them to grant two, and sometimes three; and so many new excuses continue to be found for giving these letters that in most trades there are not enough artisans to take them in the small towns. So in the end all artisans will become tantamount to officers of the king and the princes by means of these letters, if this disorder should persist.

52. Now, while artisans are properly mechanic and reputed base persons, there are nevertheless certain trades which are trade and commerce all in one. In as much as they are trades, reception into them is by the same means as with simple trades. But in so far as they participate in trade of merchandise, they are honourable; and those who practise them are not placed among base persons, but 'on the worthier side', able to call themselves 'honourable men' and 'bourgeois', as other merchants do. Such are apothecaries, goldsmiths, jewellers, haberdashers, wholesalers, drapers, hosiers, and others like them, as may be seen in the ordinances.[64]

53. On the other hand, there are trades which consist rather in phys-

[63] [Cf. ordinances of Villers-Cotterêts (1539), art. 189; of Orléans (1561), art. 98 (Isambert, XII, p. 639; XIV, p. 88).]
[64] [Cf. *Ord.*, XXI, pp. 364, 561, etc.]

ical labour than in commercial activity or in shrewdness of mind, and those are the basest. As Cicero says,[65] 'The baser are those which are paid for manual labour, not for artistic skill'. That is why the Romans distinguished 'artificers' from 'workmen'.

54. And with all the more reason those who engage neither in a trade nor in commerce and make a living by physical labour – those whom we therefore call 'hacks' or 'hired men', such as porters, masons' mates, carters and other journeymen – are the basest of the common people. For there is no worse occupation than to have no occupation.

55. Yet those who busy themselves with earning their livings by the sweat of their bodies, according to God's commandment, deserve to be supported, at the expense of so many sturdy beggars with whom our France is at present quite filled because of the immoderation of the taxes. This compels working people to prefer to leave everything and become vagabonds and beggars to live idly and carefree at the expense of others, rather than to work continually with no profit or return other than to pay their tax. Unless this is amended promptly, two inconveniences will follow through the enormous multiplication of this riff raff which occurs daily: to wit, that the fields will be devoid of men willing to work in them; and that travellers will no longer be safe on the roads, nor country folk in their houses.

---

[65] *De officiis* [I.xlii].

CHAPTER NINE

Of solemn deprivation of order

1. Just as order is different from office, so too is its deprivation different. Deprivation of office is called 'forfeiture'; that of order is commonly termed 'degradation', in as much as grade or degree is understood to be synonymous with order, although degrees are, properly, the ranks of a particular order. That is why, strictly speaking, the degradation which our jurisconsults call *de gradu dejectionem* and the laws of the *Code* call *regradationem* (for *degradatio* is not Latin) is not properly the absolute deprivation of order, as the vulgar think, but only a demotion or deprivation of a higher degree or rank, being put or thrown back to a lower degree whilst nevertheless remaining in the order.

2. In Greek this is called 'demotion', and in Latin *regradatio* where 're' either is a privative particle or signifies 'backwards'.

3. It is in this sense that St Jerome says[1] that 'Heraclius was demoted from a bishop to a priest'; and he says,[2] 'Let anyone demoted from the power of a tribune by his fault be deprived of every office of the service and be reduced to the designation of tiro'. He also says[3] that 'In the book of Ezekiel, priests who transgressed were demoted to sacristans and doorkeepers'. The passage in Ezekiel contains these words:[4] 'The Levites who strayed from the Lord after their idols

---

[1] 'in *Chronicis*' [untraced in Jerome's *Quaestiones Hebraicae in libros Paralipomenon*. (*PL*, XXIII, pt. ii, cols. 1431–70); possibly a reference to Heraclides, early fifth-century bishop of Ephesus who was deposed by the opponents of his patron John Chrysostom – see Sozomenus, *Historia ecclesiastica*, viii.6, 19, etc.].

[2] *PL*, XXIII [col. 386].

[3] *PL*, XXIII [col. 339].

[4] [Cf.] Ezekiel xliv. [10–11].

shall be ministers in the sanctuary of God and keepers of the gates'.
4. There is a notable example of this penalty in Lampridius where
he says [5] that in order to elect a new senator Alexander Severus
asked those in office for their opinions, 'so that whoever had spoken
falsely should be cast down to the lowest rank'. Another occurs in
Ammianus Marcellinus:[6]

> In order to show that he was content with a fairly mild punish-
> ment, Theodosius thrust to the lowest degree of the service all
> the knights who had defected to the rebel side.

Some laws[7] use the word *regradari*, others[8] the word *degradare*; and
in the *Theodosian Code* there occurs[9] the word *regradatio*: 'whoever
has acted against this decree will be punished by the humiliation of
demotion'.

5. But a still clearer example, together with the difference between
demotion and deprivation of order, occurs in [Justinian's] *Code*[10] 'If
anyone of the household retinue' (these were, as with us, the archers
of the royal bodyguard)

> should, without licence, neglect the duties of our Serene High-
> ness for two years, he shall be reduced five grades, if he is proved
> to have been continuously absent for three years, he shall be
> reduced ten (*regredictur*: Cujas reads *regradetur*); if he should be
> absent for four years, he shall be put in the lowest place; if he
> has been astray for five years, he shall be expelled from military
> service.

In another law of the *Code* it is said:[11]

> Whoever has been absent for six months after the expiry of his
> leave shall be reduced to a place after the five immediately below
> him; an absentee for a year, to the tenth place after those serving
> below him; a four-year absentee, to the fiftieth such place; and
> anyone absent for longer than that shall be struck from the rolls
> of the army.

---

[5] *Severus Alexander* [xix.2].
[6] [*Rerum gestarum*] XXIX.[v.20].
[7] *Code Theod.* 7.1.10; *Code J* 12.29.1.
[8] [Cf.] *Code J* 1.31.3.
[9] *Code Theod.* 8.5.2.
[10] *Code J* 12.17.3.
[11] *Code J* 12.42.2.

The same is again said in two further laws.[12]

6. Another notable example is to be found in the *Decretum*.[13] In order to suppress the great dispute over precedence which had previously occurred between priests and deacons, it is said that a deacon wishing henceforth to elevate himself above the priests 'is repulsed from his own degree and shall become the last of all in his order'. This shows that degradation, as I have described it, was practised of old in the church as it is still practised today in reformed religious houses, especially among nuns or those guilty of some notorious fault. These lose their former rank and sometimes are placed below the novices, even after the lay sisters.

7. But above all, in the Roman state this punishment was usual amongst soldiers, according to Modestinus.[14] Rehearsing the various kinds of military punishments in law, he includes these three – 'change of branch of the service', 'reduction in military rank', 'dishonourable discharge' – as being three different penalties, although they resemble one another. 'Change of branch of the service' was 'when a knight was made a foot-soldier, or when foot-soldiers were transferred into the ranks of the auxiliary slingers', as Valerius Maximus puts it.[15] And therefore, whatever the learned Faber may say,[16] this punishment was different from demotion: witness the law[17] that 'a peacetime deserter changes his branch of the service if he is a knight, and is demoted if he is a foot-soldier'.

8. 'Demotion' was when a soldier lost the degree or rank which he had in his company – 'made from an officer into a new recruit', says St Jerome following the aforementioned passage[18] – whilst none the less remaining a soldier. 'Disgraceful dismissal' was when he was altogether deprived of the military order 'and made from a soldier into a civilian', as in this passage from Lampridius:[19] 'He discharged entire legions, calling soldiers civilians'. In Lucan,[20] 'You, rabble of Rome, will now observe our triumphs', says the Emperor, speaking

---

[12] *Code J* 12.42.3, 12.7.2.
[13] *Decretum* D.[93] c.*ult.*
[14] [*Digest* 49.16.3.]
[15] [*Factorem et dictorum memorabilium* (Leipzig, 1888)] II.[vii.15].
[16] *Semestrium*, p. 155.
[17] [Cf.] *Digest* 49.16.5.1.
[18] [Above, note 2.]
[19] *Severus Alexander* [lii.3].
[20] [Marcus Annaeus] Lucanus, [*De bello civili* v.334].

to his soldiers; and, in another place,[21] 'Cowards and civilians, surrender our standards to men'. This is like a formulary for discharging
a company of soldiers.

9. For this depriving of military order 'by removal of military insignia'
is properly called 'discharge from military service': that is, depriving
of the authority and the dignity, just as deprivation of priesthood was
called in Rome 'desecrating'. While discharge in its general sense
signifies every dismissal of a soldier 'whether honourable, on grounds
of sickness, or disgraceful', as the same Faber proves[22] against Valla,
it is true that the term more commonly signifies disgraceful dismissal.

10. Likewise 'among the servants of heaven' discharge was very
common in the ancient church. In Greek it is called 'deposition' in
respect of clerics, meaning destruction or deprivation; and in respect
of laymen they called it 'exclusion', as if to say suppression, which is
our excommunication. Both of them differed from 'demotion' which
signifies plain down-grading or retrograding.

11. Let us revert to our deprivation of order, transferred as it has
been 'from armed to divine service' as the law says.[23] There were
two kinds of deprivation of the military, one by word of mouth 'when
the emperor pronounced a man dismissed by reason of ignominy',
the other by act 'when he removed the military insignia'.[24] Likewise
are there two kinds of deprivation of order, the one verbal and
properly called 'deposition', the other enacted and called
'degradation'.

12. Although this law says that verbal dismissal of a soldier is not
disgraceful unless it is expressly said to be for a disgraceful cause,
nevertheless the truth is that verbal deposition from other orders is
always disgraceful, as several laws declare.[25]

13. It must be understood that dismissal from armed service differs
from deposition or deprivation of the other orders. Soldiers were
dismissed not always for delinquency, but sometimes for an honourable cause, 'perhaps after a year's paid service', or for an allowable
reason such as an illness, a wound or the like. Delinquency is not to
be presumed when the dismissal is made indeterminately and without

---

21 [*Ibid.* v.358.]
22 [*Semestrium*, p. 165.]
23 *Sext* 5.9.2.
24 *Digest* 3.2.2.2.
25 *Digest* 50.13.5; *Code J* 2.11.3.

adding a cause; but if it is probably for delinquency it is disgraceful, even though the cause is not expressed.[26]

14. This last law seems directly contrary to the one cited previously.[27] So the learned Antonius Augustinus has wanted to correct it,[28] replacing a negative with an affirmative; and President Faber wants to interpret it[29] as enacted discharge, 'by removal of insignia', even though it speaks expressly of the three verbal dismissals, 'honourable, on grounds of sickness, and disgraceful'. That is why I say that when it says, 'those dismissed without mention of disgrace are nevertheless understood to be dismissed for ignominy', reference must be made to the preceding words and care taken that it particularly concerns those 'who are dismissed for delinquency'. Thus, what it means is that 'those dismissed for delinquency are disgraced; even though in their dismissal the established formula is not added, they are dismissed by reason of ignominy'.

15. Let us now reconcile clearly these two paragraphs and all the laws on this matter. In my opinion, discharge by enactment is always disgraceful,[30] and so is verbal deposition from all orders other than the military.[31] But verbal dismissal of a soldier without express cause is not disgraceful, apart from dismissal for delinquency which does entail disgrace even though it is not said to be 'by reason of ignominy'.[32] Thus I said in my *Offices*[33] that every criminal sentence involving deprivation of order or of office is disgraceful even though disgrace does not figure expressly in it.

16. Conversely, however, in order to discover whether every disgraceful sentence entails deprivation of order when this is not expressly said, I consider that orders which have an established rank of honour in the civil community must be distinguished from those which have none. The former are lost by disgrace, which is not compatible with civil and political dignity; the latter are not, given that there is no incompatibility. Having proved this fully in my *Offices*,[34] I

[26] *Digest* 49.16.13.3.
[27] Above, note 24.
[28] [Antonio Augustín,] *Emendationum* [*et opinionem, libri quatuor* (Lyon, 1544)], p. 32, [cf. p. 337].
[29] *Semestrium*, p. 165.
[30] *Digest* 3.2.2.
[31] *Digest* 50.13.5.
[32] *Digest* 49.16.13.3.
[33] I.[xiii.54].
[34] I.xiii.

will not spend time on confirming it here. For instance, a disgraced person (I mean true disgrace in law, such as that incurred particularly by sentence) cannot be an advocate, at least in a sovereign court, but may be an attorney.[35]

17. I said 'in the civil community', because ecclesiastical orders are not lost by infamy, owing to consecration which imprints an ineradicable quality. Likewise, degrees in the liberal and mechanic arts which have no established rank are not lost by disgrace. In my view, a further exception lies in orders proceeding from lineage or by nature, such as the quality of gentleman or prince. These are not lost by civil disgrace, 'because a rule of civil law cannot destroy natural rights',[36] unless the law or the judge's sentence should expressly say that the gentleman shall be degraded from nobility. But an order of chivalry is undoubtedly lost by disgrace: for any stain of dishonour is formally contrary to it.

18. So much for verbal deposition or deprivation. As for enactment, which we call 'degradation', this is more commonly practised in respect of orders than of offices, because it is more usual for orders to have some sign or visible mark of their dignity, whereas offices shine forth sufficiently through public power without need of visible ornaments.

19. I do not know that our offices have visible ornaments, apart from certain offices of the crown because of their eminence, and those of the *parlements* which retain them as a remnant of their having formerly been orders. In respect of these last we also find that solemn degradation was formerly practised. I have read somewhere that in 1528 Maître Pierre Ledet, clerical counsellor in the *parlement*, was solemnly degraded by its decree, his red robe removed in the presence of all the chambers, and he himself sent before the ecclesiastical judge. In my late father's collections I find that in 1496 a man named Chanvreux, counsellor in the *parlement*, having been deprived of his office for falsifying an inquiry, was stripped of his red robe in the auditory of the *parlement* and then underwent a degrading public ritual before the royal advocates and attorneys and at the marble table. And not long ago, at the time of Marshal Biron's execution, the Chancellor removed his collar of the order and then demanded his marshal's baton; but he replied that he had never borne it.

[35] *Inst. J* 4.13.
[36] *Digest* 4.5.8.

20. Thus Plutarch records [37] that the Praetor Lentulus, an accomplice in the Catilene conspiracy, was degraded from his office, having been required to remove his purple robe in full senate and to take a black one. Sidonius records that[38]

> Arvandus, prefect of the city of Rome, [an office] which he had held by reappointment for five years, was discharged and consigned to perpetual prison and made plebeian as one not added but restored to a plebeian family.

According to the *Code:*[39]

> Judges convicted of being defiled by deceitful and wicked acts shall be deprived of their badge of office and dignity and placed among the plebeians; nor shall they afterwards delight in those honours of which they have shown themselves unworthy.

In law, 'loss of the belt' often denotes deprivation of office. There are several examples.[40]

21. I have especially noted uses of degradation in respect of offices because it is neither usual nor necessary, in as much as deprivation of orders and offices should be governed by the rule of law: 'There is nothing so natural than that things bound in the same way should be loosed in the same way'. Just as the robe and badge of an officer are not solemnly given him upon his reception, so is there no need solemnly to remove them from him upon his deprivation. Conversely, in most of the orders insignia are publicly and solemnly given upon collocation, and so their solemn removal is customary upon deprivation. Thus, for example, in the order of chivalry, as was done in that execution of Marshal Biron when the Chancellor removed his order – to wit, his collar of the Order of the Holy Spirit.

22. Similarly, it was customary to strip Roman soldiers of their baldrics or military belts before executing them. 'He discharged and put to death ten of the soldiers who had fled', says Ammianus Marcellinus.[41] According to [the younger] Pliny,[42] 'Having sifted the evidence Caesar cashiered the centurion and also banished him'. According

---

[37] *Cicero* [xix.2].
[38] [Gaius] Sidonius, *Epistularum* i.vii.[11].
[39] *Code J* 12.1.12.
[40] *Code J* 12.17.3, 7.38.1, 10.27.2.
[41] [*Rerum gestarum*] XXIV. [iii.1].
[42] *Epistularum* VI. [xxxi.5].

to Lampridius,[43] 'Having discharged from the service a soldier who had inflicted injuries upon an old woman, he gave him to her as a slave'. Livy too observes[44] that the Samnites 'in the defeat of Caudium' stripped the Roman soldiers of their military ensigns before making them run the gauntlet.

23. We also have some observations on this in our law: 'traitors and deserters are tortured after being discharged';[45] 'a soldier who has come to an agreement with his wife's lover should be released from his oath and banished';[46] 'an outcast from military service is compelled to undergo appropriate punishments';[47] 'you should degrade the prisoners for dismissal with punishment';[48] 'those ejected from military service should undergo corporal punishments'.[49]

24. I have said that enacted degradation is usual in respect of orders, but it is not always necessary. In order to make a soldier it is not necessary to gird him publicly; nor, likewise, to ungird him solemnly in order to cashier or to banish him. Indeed, it has just been said that 'most soldiers were dismissed solely by verbal disgrace'.

25. But, by the rule which has just been cited, where solemnity is necessary in collocation to orders, it is also necessary in deprivation. Thus with sacred orders which, owing to their peculiar dignity, are conferred with certain mysteries and ceremonies in which the form of sacrament consists. It is even held that in these orders solemn degradation cannot eradicate the sacred quality altogether, for it penetrates to the very soul, as will presently be said.

26. With yet greater reason, then, is it beyond doubt that the priest who has only been verbally deposed – that is, simply deprived by sentence of the order of priesthood – nevertheless still remains a priest until he has been degraded by enactment. But it is a great question whether the law may execute him without prior degradation. In recent times the *parlements*, and even plain provost-marshals, have often been seen to execute priests without degradation; and I have heard tell that a great quarrel lately occurred about this between the *parlement* of Provence and the archbishop of Aix.

[43] *Severus Alexander* [lii.1].
[44] [*Hist.* IX.xv.7.]
[45] *Digest* 49.16.7.
[46] *Digest* 48.5.12.
[47] [Cf. *Digest* 49.16.5.]
[48] *Code Theod.* 6.27.18.
[49] *Code J* 3.2.3.

27. Those who hold that degradation of priests is not necessary ground their view on a false maxim, that 'the condition of being accused removes every dignity'. This is taken from the *Code*[50] where it is said that senators having committed rape should be punished at the place of the offence without being allowed to use their privilege of being sent to Rome: 'because', says the law, 'such an indictment removes every honour'. Thus it is evident enough that this is a special decision because of the atrocity of the crime, and a particular exception to the rule in the same law which ascribes particular judges to senators in all the latter's criminal cases.

28. If that mockery were observed indiscriminately one would have to conclude that in criminal matters all privileges, all honours and all respect towards officers and other privileged persons would cease. That is why the worthies of the *parlement* have this privilege of being judged in matters criminal only by the *parlement* in a body and with the chambers assembled, like the princes of the blood and the peers of France. Why is it that for the same crime commoners are hanged and gentlemen decapitated if not that the latter, as Xenophon says,[51] 'seemed to be the better death'? And what would come of the privileges ascribed by law to so many persons, such as nobles, municipal officers and soldiers, of not being put to the torture?

29. We also find that vestal virgins were never executed until they had been solemnly degraded 'by the high-priests, and their sacerdotal chaplets and other insignia removed', as I shall presently say in discussing the ceremonies of degradation. For the moment I will content myself with the evidence of Pomponius Laetus, speaking of their punishment:[52] 'Before this was done, the priests within the gate removed the sacerdotal garments and jewels'. And according to Festus Pomponius,[53] 'The vestal virgins were discharged before punishment'.

30. But, to speak in particular of our priests, Justinian has ruled plainly on this question:[54]

> It is perfectly clear that, if the governor of a province should find a cleric deserving of punishment, he should first be stripped of

---

[50] *Code J* 3.24.1.
[51] [*Anabasis* ii.vi.29.]
[52] [Giulio Pomponio Laeto] *De antiquitatibus urbis Romae* [in *Antiquitatum variorum autores* (Lyon, 1552), p. 594].
[53] [Untraced in Sextus Pomponius Festus, *De verb. signif.*; ? Sextus Pomponius, *De iuris origine.*]
[54] *Nov. J* 83.2.

his sacerdotal office by the bishop and then be placed in the hands of the law.

The question is resolved still more authoritatively in a fine passage from the book of Numbers[55] where God, having condemned the high priest Aaron to death for his unbelief, orders that he shall first be degraded from the priesthood. This is His commandment to Moses:

> Take Aaron and his son with him, and bring them unto mount Hor. And strip the father of his garments and put them upon Eleazar his son, and Aaron shall be gathered [unto his people] and shall die there: and Moses did as the Lord commanded.

31. In France there can no longer be any doubt about it, there being an express ordinance of 1571,[56] the words of which are these: 'Priests and others advanced to sacred orders shall not be executed without degradation'.

32. The reason for this is quite obvious. As we have proved that until degradation the priest still remains in his dignity and quality, is it not injurious to the order, to the church and even to God that an executioner should lay his hand upon His anointed?

33. Indeed, the Roman people were far more religious; for when the question arose of judging in full assembly a common man accused of a capital crime, and the criminal had prayed and called upon his gods to have pity upon him, thereafter no one would have dared to condemn him to death, he having placed himself under the gods' protection, unless the magistrate had first compelled him to revoke this prayer and adjuration. This was termed *resecrare*, says Festus on that same word.[57]

34. The Romans would not have dared to try to storm a besieged town unless, by means of certain ceremonies, they had first won over and summoned forth the gods worshipped there, for fear of injuring them. According to [the elder] Pliny:[58]

> It was customary at the beginning of a siege for the Romans to call forth the god under whose protection that town was and to promise him the same or a more splendid place among the Romans.

---

[55] xx.[25–7].
[56] [Fontanon. IV, p. 193.]
[57] [*De verb. signif.*, p. 353.]
[58] [*Nat. hist.*] XXVIII.[iv.18].

The formulary of this evocation is reported in Livy[59] and in Macrobius.[60]

35. Thus I conclude that it is much more seemly and more pious to degrade priests before delivering them to the executioner of high justice, given that as they are God's anointed it is strictly forbidden to lay hands on them in any way whatsoever. But when they are degraded this prohibition ceases, for the unction is removed and wiped away from them. It is the church itself which then gives them to the secular arm to be dealt with according to the laws, as common persons. For the rest, it is not reasonable that through having been dedicated to God they should be exempt from the world's laws and permitted to do evil without risk of punishment. On the contrary, it is likely that they should be punished more severely when they fail, as it is for them to show an example to the people.

36. That is why, to speak plainly, I cannot but censure two alleged qualms of conscience (let me not say mischiefs) which a few ecclesiastics – rather, worldly sages – have dragged up from afar, wishing to prepare a refuge and an immunity for their entire order and thereby making degradation extremely difficult, even well-nigh impossible. Having been thoughtlessly allowed, these have prompted secular magistrates to resolve to neglect and omit degradation rather than leave priests' crimes unpunished.

37. The first is that Boniface VIII – the author is notable – decided[61] that in order to perform degradation the number of bishops specified in the ancient canons (and which he himself shrinks from stating) is requisite: to wit, twelve to degrade a bishop, six to degrade a priest, and three with the local bishop to degrade a deacon. So much is said in these canons,[62] and the reason given in this chapter:[63]

> The difference between the corporeal and the spiritual is that the corporeal is more easily destroyed than made, and the spiritual more easily made than destroyed.

But, subject to correction, this reason does not prove that more bishops are needed to degrade than to consecrate a priest, against

---

59 [*Hist.* v.xxi.3.]
60 *Saturnalia* III.ix.[7–8].
61 *Sext* 5.9.2.
62 *Decretum* 15 q.7 c.3, 4, 5.
63 *Decretales* 1.7.2.

the rule of canon law. Rather, it implies that because the sacred orders are more durable degradation does not altogether eradicate them as it does with secular orders. This shall shortly be shown.

38. As for these ancient canons, care must be taken [to note] that they do not speak at all of the degradation of ecclesiastics, but only of the requisite number of judges to bring an action against them. Here are the terms: 'a bishop should be heard by twelve bishops, a priest by six, a deacon by three with his own bishop'; and the third of these canons adds, 'who should hear their cases'. Besides, they must be understood according to their time, for the ecclesiastic estate was anciently more aristocratic than monarchic, so that proceedings which led to the deposition of priests or of bishops could at first be determined only at councils or synods. So says the canon of the Council of Seville[64] which in the *Decretum* is placed immediately before, and again repeated after, the three canons of which we speak. In the same way at present, noteworthy chastisements of religious persons in the reformed congregations are ordinarily reserved to their chapters.

39. But because with the passage of time faults needing correction happened so often among the clergy that it was not convenient to tarry for the synod, the second Council of Carthage, from which one of those three canons is taken, decreed[65] that 'if there should be very great necessity so that many bishops could not be assembled' clerics should be judged by the number of bishops stated above, 'lest they should remain subject to accusation'.

40. Further, ecclesiastical justice was not then established with ordinary curial and jurisdictional status. Anciently, bishops had powers only of simple correction of the morals of persons of their order, and punishment only of ecclesiastical offences. Other misdemeanours were left to secular justice, as I said in my *Seigneuries*. But since the government of the church was established in monarchical form and its justice constituted into ordinary courts with their definite judges and their regular degrees of appeal, like secular justice, it is beyond doubt that a simple episcopal or archidiaconal judge can condemn the most skilful priest of his diocese to be deposed or degraded from his order. But bishops have retained this franchise of

---

[64] [AD 619, canon 6: *Conc. omn. gen.*, XIV, p. 430.]
[65] [AD 420:] *Decretum* 15 q.7 c.4.

being justiciable only by the Holy See. So that is why these ancient canons are not relevant to degradation.

41. Therefore it can be taken as certain that, just as a plain bishop can consecrate a priest, so can he degrade him. Thus is it observed in practice, notwithstanding the decretal of Boniface VIII and beyond all doubt. For the Council of Trent has decided[66] that not only a bishop, but even his vicar general in spirituals can perform a priest's degradation as long as he sends for six clergymen if that number can be found in the town, or else six notable persons appointed to the ecclesiastical dignity.

42. The second qualm of conscience is that when an ecclesiastic has been condemned to death by a secular judge in a privileged case there are bishops who make difficulties about degrading him without bringing a fresh action against him. They say that any deposing and, with still greater cause, any degrading of a priest should be done with cognisance of the case, and that the secular judge can ordain nothing concerning the sacrament of [the accused's] order. So, when one seeks justice against a priest, everything has to be begun again. If that were allowed, ecclesiastical justice would constitute a new jurisdiction after the final jurisdiction of secular justice; and the bishop or his official would control the decrees of a *parlement*.

43. Now it is true enough that every deposing or degrading ought to be done with cognisance of the case. But is it not sufficient cognisance of the case when a *parlement* has dealt with it? As for saying that it can do nothing touching the order of priesthood, it does not pronounce on that. It only condemns the priest to death after declaring him convicted of a capital crime. When the bishop degrades him before the decree is executed, this is not in order to obey the secular judge, but for fear that to deliver the priest into the executioner's hands will be to injure the order. So, the bishop's refusal to degrade him is a refusal to preserve the order from injury. For the condemned man must always be executed, whether with or without degradation. In the latter event the secular judge releases him from his order, in the same way that Alexander set the Gordian knot at nought, cutting it as he could not untie it.

44. But if it should be the case that a priest cannot be executed without prior degradation, is it not reasonable that these two justices,

[66] Session 13 [11 October 1551], *decretum 'De reformatione'* cap. iv [Mansi, XXXIII, col. 87].

these two earthly powers, the ecclesiastic and the secular, should assist each other? Is it not evident that the secular judge does not refuse to execute the sentence of the ecclesiastical judge by arresting [the condemned party] and seizing his goods without fresh cognisance of the case and without judging 'the self-same issue twice' when, by way of commission of inquiry, the ecclesiastical judge comes to implore the aid of the secular arm? So the church ought likewise to facilitate the execution of the sentences of temporal judges. As Optatus Milevitanus says,[67] the church is in the kingdom, not the kingdom in the church.[68]

45. In fact, the only passage of our law which prohibits the execution of priests without degradation – the one cited above[69] – plainly presupposes that such degradation be done without fresh cognisance of the case. For Justinian, deciding in the same passage by whom ecclesiastics should be judged, ordains that in ordinary offences they shall be judged by ordinary judges, to wit the presiding judges of the provinces: provided nevertheless (says he almost in passing) that they shall not suffer the death penalty before being degraded by the bishop; but that in respect of ecclesiastical offences they shall be judged by the bishops and their council – with neither encroaching upon the other, says he.

46. Even so, ecclesiastics fancy it to be grounded in antiquity that the secular magistrate cannot judge priests unless the bishop has sent them back to the secular court. In this they have corrupted the fine term 'to consign to the court' which is often read in our lawbooks. They say that at the moment when bishops have degraded a priest 'they consign him to the secular court for punishment'. This is explained in the law,[70] and was formerly interpreted by Gratian[71] in a signal error which well deserves to be exposed in passing.

47. I said in the last book of my *Officae*,[72] when I was discussing the officers of towns, that the position of the decurions or curials of the

---

[67] [*PL*, XI, col. 999.]

[68] [1701 adds: Further, it is a rule of law and of legal practice, indeed of the law of nations, that the judge to whom one applies for the execution of a sentence 'ought not to try the ruling of the law: otherwise he will be acting ineffectually', especially if his finding should contradict the ruling.]

[69] [Above, section 30, at note 54.]

[70] *Decretales* 5.40.27.

[71] *Decretum* 11 q.1 c.11 *s.v.* 'Sicut [enim impietatio' (*Decreti divi Gratiani* (Lyon, 1572), cols. 898–9)].

[72] v.[vii.13].

towns of the Roman Empire became so burdensome that everyone spurned and avoided it until at last it was imposed as a penalty, as may be seen in several laws.[73] Valentinian afterwards prohibited this;[74] and it seems that this prohibition was then restricted by Gratian 'only to the officials, that is the apparitors of the presiding judges', as Cujas interprets him.[75] The grounds for the prohibitions were that it was not reasonable, according to these laws, for the order of decurion, which was honourable, to be given as a penalty, and for a man to be placed in this order as a consequence of something for which he should have been driven from it.

48. But, as the difficulty of finding decurions continued to increase so that men had to be placed in that position by compulsion, an expedient was found to continue to place them there as a punishment whilst none the less not acting counter to the reason of these laws. It was that persons placed there as a punishment should have the duties and inconveniences of the decurionate, but not its honours and advantages. Callistratus finds the laws compatible in this,[76] and Justinian ordained[77] to the same effect in respect of Jews, Samaritans and heretics.

49. Likewise the Emperor Arcadius ordained[78] that anyone expelled from the clergy should immediately be singled out to be a decurion or a gildsman: that is, of the number of those who in every city were chosen from among the artisans to attend to the town's necessities, which was a toilsome and shameful situation:

50.

> Any cleric whom the bishop shall have judged unworthy of his office and separated from the ministry of the church, or anyone who shall have deserted of his own accord the profession of holy religion, shall immediately be claimed by a city court; and according to the legal status of the man and the amount of his patrimony, he shall be joined either to an order or to a gild (*collegio*) of the city.

This shows in passing that a modern scholar is mistaken, confusing 'consigned to a court' with 'to a gild'. The difference is still better

---

[73] *Code Theod.* 6.35.14; 8.5.1.
[74] *Code Theod.* 12.1.66.
[75] [*Operum C*, III, col. 1397] on *Code J* 10.31.38.
[76] *Digest* 48.12.7.20; cf. *Code J* 10.59.
[77] *Nov. J* 45.
[78] [*Const. Sirm.* 9.]

elucidated in a Novel of Majorian;[79] and the word *collegiatus* is explained by M. Brisson.[80]

51. There are also several passages in the ancient authors to show that this custom persisted, that ecclesiastics expelled from the church 'were consigned to city courts'. Thus in St Ambrose,[81] in Ammianus Marcellinus,[82] in Sozomenus,[83] in Nicephorus,[84] in Theoderet.[85] The reason for this is given in the Novel:[86] 'As one who has despised the sacred ministry, he shall serve an earthly tribunal'; and in [another] Novel[87] it is said that a married priest or one who keeps a concubine 'ought to be removed from the clergy according to the ancient canons, and consigned to the court of the city where he was a cleric'.

52. Now the ancient canons to which this Novel alludes may be those recorded by Gratian[88] where it is said that the cleric who will not obey his bishop 'should be deposed from the clerical order and be consigned as a servant to the secular court and serve it throughout his life'. The canonists have corrupted this both in the decretals and in the style of their sentences, substituting 'as a punishment' for 'as a servant'. Furthermore, they are deceived by the ambiguity of the word 'court' which nowadays means 'jurisdiction' and anciently meant the council or senate of the towns of the Roman Empire, as I have said elsewhere.

53. Also, an ecclesiastic is these days never degraded unless he has committed a capital crime and, furthermore, is considered incorrigible, degradation being the greatest penalty that the church can inflict.[89] That is why the church, 'which cannot impose the death sentence', refers the cleric who has committed a capital crime to the secular jurisdiction, to be punished there. None the less it begs that jurisdiction (in accordance with mercy and goodwill, and also to avoid irregularity if the death penalty is intended) to deal mildly with the

---

[79] [*Leg. Nov.*, Nov. Majorian 7.7.]
[80] [Barnabé] Brisson, *Lexicon iuridicum* [(Cologne, 1615), p. 272].
[81] *Omnia opera* [(Paris, 1539)], fos. 154ʳᵒ–155ʳᵒ.
[82] [Cf.] *Rerum gestarum* [xv.vii.6–10].
[83] *PG*, LXVII, col. 1311–12.
[84] *PG*, CXLVI, col. 476–7.
[85] 'liv. 1, chap. 9, & liv. 7, chap. 7' [untraced in Theodoret, *Ecclesiasticae historiae libri quinque* (*PL*, LXXXII, cols. 881–1280)].
[86] *Nov. J* 5.6.
[87] *Nov. J* 123.29.
[88] *Decretum* 3 q.4 c.8; 11 q.1 cc.18, 31.
[89] *Decretales* 2.1.10.

man and not to punish him according to the full rigour of the law.[90]
54. But anciently clerics were deposed for many lesser causes, to wit, for plain disobedience.[91] That is why he was thereafter liable to no other punishment, except that, through the ordinances of Arcadius[92] and Justinian,[93] as soon as he was expelled from the church he was claimed to belong to the court, but not that he was referred to the secular judges to be judged and punished afresh.
55. So, to complete this account of the form and ceremonies of the degradation of priests, the following extract will suffice:[94]

> A cleric to be degraded, wearing his consecrated garments and having in his hands a book, a vessel or other instrument or ornament appertaining to his order and, if necessary, to the solemn ministry of his office, shall be brought into the presence of the bishop; and the bishop shall publicly remove from him each of those things, whether garments, chalice or book, which severally and until the deaths of ordained clerics were given to or conferred upon him by the bishop upon his ordination, beginning with that vestment or ornament which was given last, and continuing the degradation by degrees unto the first garment given with the conferment of the tonsure; and then his head shall be shaved or sheared so that no trace of the tonsure shall remain. In a degradation of this kind the bishop may also use words to strike dread in those brought forward for conferment of orders, saying, etc.

56. Such was, more or less, the ceremony of degradation of Roman vestal virgins which Plutarch[95] and Alessandro Alessandri[96] record. The condemned vestal was taken to the place of execution in an open coffin; her sacred veils were removed, and then the pontiff, with his arms raised towards the heavens, pronounced certain solemn prayers, covered her head, and had her borne to the top of the ladder which was positioned for her descent into the prepared ditch. Those who placed her in it turned their backs upon her; the ladder was withdrawn, and so she was buried alive.

---

[90] *Decretales* 5.40.27.
[91] *Decretum* 15 q.7 c.3; 11 q.1 cc.18,31.
[92] [*Code Theod.* 16.2.39.]
[93] [*Nov. J* 83. *Preface* 2.]
[94] *Sext* 5.9.2.
[95] *Numa* x.4–7.
[96] [*Genialium dierum libri sex* (Paris, 1586), fos. 270vo–271vo.]

57. The ceremony was very like the deconsecrating of Roman priests in the pagan era. Capitolinus says[97] that, being pontiff before becoming emperor, Marcus Antoninus 'both initiated and dismissed many persons according to no one's dictation, for he had learned all the incantations himself'; calling 'incantation' 'that solemn formula of prayer which is pronounced by the pontiff, as laid down beforehand, lest any word be omitted or said out of place', says Pliny.[98]

58. Finally, in order to understand the effects of deprivation of ecclesiastical orders, we must distinguish from each other the three kinds of deprivation – to wit, suspension, deposition and degradation – and briefly and firmly determine the effects of each according to the most common opinion of the theologians, without spending time on recording diversities of opinion.

59. Suspension is not by nature perpetual, even though it may be pronounced without indication of time; for in this case there is always hope of ending and lifting it by common law and without dispensation. It is noteworthy that suspension prohibits the ecclesiastic from performing the function from which he is suspended, on pain of disqualification.

60. But its terms must be precisely considered, for there are several sorts of it. Suspension of order prohibits only the performance of the order and not of office, or of benefice. Again, if it is limited to a certain order it does not apply to lesser ones, though it does to greater ones. For example, a bishop suspended from the episcopal order can say mass, even with pontifical ornaments, because they relate to the office and not to the order. He can also exercise his jurisdiction and every other temporal administration of his bishopric, because he is not suspended from office and benefice. Yet, conversely, a bishop suspended from the order of priesthood cannot confer orders nor do all that appertains to the episcopal order, for one must freely enjoy the order of priesthood in order to exercise that of a bishop.

61. But suspension from office, formerly called suspension 'from the gods', includes the office as much of the order as of the benefice or ecclesiastical charge.

62. Sometimes it even embraces the benefice itself – that is to say, the administration of ecclesiastical revenue – as when it is imposed

---

[97] *Marcus Antoninus* [iv.4].
[98] [*Nat. hist.*] XXVIII. [iii.10–11].

for a crime. Yet if it is ordained for a trifling offence or for simple default, or if it should be pronounced with this restrictive term 'only', it does not include the administration of the benefice. On the other hand, suspension of benefice concerns only the administration of its temporal revenue and not the office or spiritual administration which is not accessory to the temporal; on the contrary, it is the temporal that is accessory to the spiritual, and the benefice to the office.

63. As for deposition, 'for which the term *degradatio* is used', it is by nature perpetual and without hope of reinstatement, at least by common law and without dispensation. However, in respect of order the bishop can grant dispensation. In respect of benefice, deposition automatically renders it vacant and it is lost absolutely, without awaiting degradation which concerns only the dignity of ecclesiastical order. And the benefice is hardly ever recovered because it does not often happen that someone else is not appointed there before the reinstatement or dispensation of the deposed person. In any case, the latter must be appointed anew because through deposition he has quite lost his appointment. Yet, as order is more inherent to the person than office and benefice, simple deposition does not deprive one of the order nor of everything that depends from it, but only of its performance. The deposed priest retains both his dignity – that is, the rank and title of priest – and the privileges, 'namely public and canonical'; but above all there is no doubt that he retains the character of priesthood.

64. Finally, according to the most common opinion amongst the theologians and the canonists, actual and solemn degradation does not remove order altogether, because it is engraved and imprinted upon the very soul, and because sacred things are by their nature eternal and incorruptible. So, to know what effect it has, we must distinguish between two divers parts of sacred order.

65. The one is external: the dignities and privileges which depend from it. The other is internal: the character of the consecration. As for dignity and privileges, it cannot be doubted that degradation removes them, so that the degraded priest can no longer be called priest, nor hold the rank of priest, and no longer falls within the ecclesiastical jurisdiction, and whoever strikes him is not excommunicated.

66. But as for the character imprinted upon consecration, it cannot be obliterated, 'neither by means of authority' because it is sacred

and thus irremovable and incorruptible, 'nor by the subject's means' because it is imprinted on the soul which is immortal and impenetrable. There is therefore no doubt that a degraded priest can efficaciously and really consecrate, 'that he may prepare the real body of Christ': which is St Thomas's conclusion.[99]

---

[99] [*Summa theologiae*] III.[82].8.

CHAPTER TEN

Of the plain dignities of Rome

1. I call plain dignities all the titles and qualities with which one can be titled and qualified solely by honour without their being in effect true orders, offices or lordships.

2. Now there are two kinds of them: to wit, honorary dignities which are plain titles of honorary orders, offices or lordships, and 'held by title', but otherwise without performance or practice or reality; and epithets of honour, that is, the honourable qualities ascribed to every dignity, whether order, office or lordship.

3. And there is this difference between them: that an honorary dignity is a substantive name ascribed immediately to the person and because of himself; and an epithet is an adjectival name ascribed mediately to him because of some real dignity of order or of office or of lordship.

4. Let us begin, according to our custom, with the custom of the Romans. Let us speak first of their honorary dignities, then of their epithets. For, as they had only two kinds of dignities, to wit, orders and offices, and did not have the use of lordships, it is true that they had various orders, and above all various honorary and nominal offices.

5. As for orders, first they had nominal senators: to wit, all those who had exercised great offices, called 'curule magistrates or magistrates of the Roman people', and thereafter had entry and voice in the senate and had also the senatorial ornaments, so that only the name of senators remained any longer to them. For they could [not] be true senators until they had been enrolled by the censors, consuls or emperors, as I said in the second chapter.[1]

---

[1] [Section 89.]

6. They also had honorary knights: to wit, those who, being unable to become real knights through not having the requisite means or skill, obtained from the emperor the right of gold rings which was the public ornament and insignia of the knights. By these means they ranked with the real knights and had the right to sit in the theatre in the fourteen degrees reserved for the latter, as I said in the same chapter.[2] But it must be noted that these two species of honorary dignities (if such they must be called) were quite the reverse of the others: for they had the effect of the dignity and not the title, whereas honorary dignities generally have only the title and not the effect.

7. The Romans likewise had honorary citizens of various kinds. For although no one could be a true and perfect citizen of a town or city unless he actually resided and lived there, nevertheless the Romans, being clever at increasing their power together with the honour of their town, found a way of giving the rights and privileges of a Roman citizen to those who lived outside Rome, even in distant countries. Just as Aristotle says[3] that there can be various degrees of citizen, so we observe in the history of Rome four kinds or degrees of Roman citizens. In order to distinguish more easily between them (for I must say that this is among the most obscure points of Roman antiquity), I will give to each of them a particular name of my own devising. I shall call the first true and perfect citizens; the second, citizens solely in law; the third, citizens solely of honour; and the fourth, imperfect citizens.

8. True and perfect citizens, 'who were said in law to be the best citizens', were the free-born living in Rome and the surrounding territory. They 'were properly called Quirites, and they had power of abode, tribe and honour', concurrence of which three things made the true citizen. Domicile distinguished him from citizens in law, the tribe or parish from citizens of honour, and capacity for honours from imperfect citizens.

9. Citizens in law were those who resided 'beyond the territory of Rome' and nevertheless had the name and the rights of Roman citizens, either as they were severally 'given citizenship', or as they resided 'among those inhabitants of free towns or settlements which had obtained the rights of Roman citizenship'. These 'had the power

---

[2] [Section 62.]
[3] [*Politics* 1278ª15.]

of the tribe and of honour (indeed, they were rated in one of the thirty-five tribes of the Roman people) and all the rights of Roman citizenship, certainly of command, of civil freedom, of intermarriage, of paternal power, of inheritance, of property, of usucapion, of last will and testament, of legal guardianship, of military service, etc.'.

10. Otherwise, they did not have those rights which depended upon residence at Rome. These are the main ones:

> Certainly the rights of sacrifices, of public games, of festivals, of suffrages, of courts and of the forum. Indeed, they observed and followed the sacred festivals of the games and decisions in accordance with the curiae. While the curial privilege remained throughout Roman territory, they did not have the privilege of the forum, great as it was in Roman affairs, unless they spent time in Rome.

This would well merit a separate treatise if Sigonius had not explained it[4] very learnedly.

11. It is true that these citizens in law could come to reside in Rome when they wished to do so, and they then enjoyed all the latter rights and privileges. But while they remained 'in their free towns, they were said strictly to be inhabitants of those towns, not citizens of Rome'. It was said of them that they had two countries, the one by nature, the other by law; as Cicero says,[5] 'I think that I with my fellow citizens have two fatherlands, one by nature, the other by law'.

12. Honorary citizens were those of free towns which had voluntarily joined the Roman state solely in recognition of its sovereignty and not in respect of the city. They wished to have their city apart: that is, their particular laws, their own officers, and also their liberty; 'for they were not made with the approval of the people of Rome'. In a word, they were joined and not quite united to the Roman state; and so they were Roman citizens solely by honour.

13. But, as they were not true citizens nor citizens in law, 'they did not have a tribe' nor, consequently, anything which depended from it, such as suffrage and aptitude for Roman magistracies – nor, particularly,'quiritary rights, certainly of authority, of paternal power, of lawful ownership, of inheritance, of usucapion, of guardianship'.

---

[4] *De antiq. jur.*, I *passim*.
[5] *De legibus* [II.ii.5].

They had only the right of freedom which was of not recognising another sovereignty than that of the Roman people, interchange of marriages and wills with true Roman citizens – and, above all, military service, for they were enrolled in the legions [and not] among the auxiliary or relief forces, which was greatly valued.

14. On this kind of Roman citizen, attention should be paid to Aulus Gellius's book where it is said[6] that 'they were merely participants with the Roman people in an honorary privilege, from the enjoyment of which they seem to derive their name'. Sigonius interprets it thus:[7]

> They were not chosen for Roman magistrates, but merely entered upon a privilege of honour, that is, to perform honorary military service in a legion as citizens, not as associates in the auxiliary troops.

15. And in fact Aulus Gellius, continuing his discourse,[8] says that the Caerites were the first to be made citizens of this kind, 'being accepted and made guardians of sacred Roman rites in the Gallic war'. Speaking of this, Strabo says[9] that they were Roman citizens in name and not in fact, having their commonwealth separate from that of the Romans.

16. Livy says as much[10] 'of the Campanian horsemen to whom honorary citizenship without suffrage was given because they would not rebel with the Latins'. And this right of suffrage was what constituted the principal difference between citizens in law and those of honour: the ones, 'free townsmen with right of suffrage'; the others, 'without right of suffrage', as Sigonius fully explains.[11]

17. Finally, imperfect citizens were freedmen who, 'although they were Roman citizens and Roman by domicile and tribe, yet they did not have the possibility of honour'. For they were capable neither of choosing nor of being chosen magistrates, as I said in the second chapter;[12] while under the emperors most freedmen did not have 'a tribe, although they had domicile'. They had only 'the Latin law, by

---

[6] *Noct. Attic.* XVI.xiii.[6].
[7] [*De antiq. jur.*, p. 194.]
[8] *Noct. Attic.* XVI.xiii.[7].
[9] [*Geographia* V.ii.3.]
[10] [Cf.*Hist.* VIII.xiv.10.]
[11] *De antiq. jur.*, pp. 193–5.
[12] [Section 76.]

the *lex Aelia Sentia*[13] and *lex Ju[n]ia Norbana*',[14] as I said in my *Offices*.[15]
18. These, more or less, are the honorary orders which the Romans had in the Republic. But under the emperors the orders were confused and ultimately abolished altogether.

19. For, first, the ordinary authority of the senators was taken from them, because the later emperors wanted to have the council of their choice and from their retinue; and then the condition of senator became burdensome, as did that of decurion, as was said in *Offices*.[16]

20. The knights were no longer recognised, no longer having any function nor censors to choose them; and above all, there were only freedmen who were of this order, by the right of gold rings which the emperors gave them too readily.

21. In a word, that difference between the four kinds of Roman citizens, even between Roman citizens in general and the other subjects of the Empire, was entirely abolished by edict of the Emperor Antoninus Pius[17] who made all the subjects of the Empire into Roman citizens.

22. So, when the dignity of senator had been brought so low, an order was invented above them to satisfy the ambition of the emperor's principal courtiers. This was the order of patricians, which was quite another matter under the emperors than in the Republic.

23. For in the Republic the patricians were the descendants of the one hundred – or, as some say, two hundred – first senators chosen by Romulus, whom he called 'Fathers': so that the patriciate was then the ancient nobility.

24. But proof and knowledge of these ancient lineages were quite lost, as much through such a long passage of time as through the great changes which happened under the emperors, and especially when the seat of the Empire was transferred to Greece. According to Zosimus,[18] Constantine the Great was the one who invented the new patricians in order to replace those old ones. New ones came

---

[13] [Proposed by the consuls Sextus Aelius and Gaius Sextus, AD 4, with comprehensive regulations governing manumission: see W. Buckland, *A Textbook of Roman Law* (3rd edn., Cambridge, 1963), pp. 78 *et seq.*]

[14] [Proposed *c.* AD 19, or perhaps earlier, creating a stratum of manumitted slaves with inferior status and subject to severe restrictions: see Buckland, *Textbook*, p. 93.]

[15] I.i.[87].

[16] [v.vii.13.]

[17] *Digest* 1.5.17.

[18] [*Historia nova*] II. [xxxii.2–xxxiii.4].

about no longer by lineage, but only by his favour; and he made of these so high and so excellent a dignity that it surpassed all the other dignities. Theodoric says, in Cassiodorus,[19] that 'by the formula of the patriciate so much is granted in one act of splendour as we are resolved to confer': meaning the consulate which, says Claudian,[20] 'was always the harbour of honours'.

25. There is no doubt that these patricians were so called not as fathers of the commonalty – 'fathers of the state', as Suidas has defined them[21] – but, rather, as fathers of the emperor, 'whom the emperor made his fathers', says Theophilus.[22] So much is said in the *Code*;[23] and there is a fine hit in Claudian who, consoling the patrician Eutropius on his condemnation and confiscation of his wealth, says to him:[24]

> Why do you bemoan the plundered riches which your son
> will have?
> Not otherwise could you have been the father of an emperor.

26. This title of patrician, with the consular ornaments, was sent to King Clovis by the Emperor Anastasius after the defeat of the Visigoths. Here is his ambassadors' speech, recorded by Paolo Emilio:[25]

> Augustus salutes you as consul and patrician, than which splen
> did title there is no greater nor more exalted rank after that of
> Caesar. The royal appellation is indeed sacred, but it is common
> to you and many others; your greatness surely exceeds other
> kings and demands new glory. Therefore accept these insignia
> of the consulate and the name of patrician.

27. It is noteworthy that this patrician dignity was granted only to those who had actually been consuls or prefects or military commanders, the three greatest offices of the Empire, all three equal in dignity.[26]

---

[19] [*PL*, LXIX, col. 681.]
[20] [*In primum consulatum Fl. Stilichonis* II. 314–15.]
[21] [Cf.]*Suidae* [*Lexicon*, ed. A. Adler (Leipzig, 1931), part IV, p. 67].
[22] [Cf.] Theophilus [Antecessor, *Institutiones iuris civilis in graecam linguam . . . olim traductae* (Paris, 1534), pp. 120–1: on *Inst. J* 1.12.4.]
[23] *Code J* 12.3.5.
[24] *In Eutropium* [II.49–50].
[25] [*De rebus gestis Francorum* (Basle, 1601), pt. i. p. 12.]
[26] *Code J* 12.3.3.

28. Hence I hold unshakably that the title of patrician was higher than that of a person of consular rank – that, as this law says, 'the high rank of patrician takes precedence over all others'. In fact, in one Novel it is said[27] that the patricians ought to sit before the consuls in the senate. This seems contrary to the passages in Cassiodorus and Claudian cited earlier,[28] and to the law where it is said[29] that 'the consulate is set above all other exalted ranks of dignity, and in all acts, judgements and assemblies of the senatorial court'. These passages have prompted the learned President Faber to hold indiscriminately[30] that the consular dignity was higher than the patrician. 29. Yet nothing is easier than to reconcile these laws and authorities. The office of consul must undoubtedly be distinguished from the consular dignity: that is, the consul in function from the person of consular rank. Whilst in office and during the time of his function, the consul took precedence over all the patricians. But when this time was past and he was no more than ex-consul and in plain dignity and not in office, he was thereafter preceded by the patricians whose dignity was always permanent, says Cassiodorus in the same place. This was mainly because, before the Novel in question, he had to have been consul or to have had an office of the same rank in order to be a patrician; and so two dignities joined together surpassed a single one.[31]

30. So much for what was the patrician dignity, to which some of our modern writers have sought irrelevantly to trace the origin of our peerdoms. References to patricians in the ancient books have to do with countries, mainly Burgundy and Languedoc, where there really were patricians such as those of the Empire of Constantinople where the custom was eventually to give the government of distant provinces to patricians. Thus that great Aetius who fought Attila on the Catalaunian plains is called the last patrician of the Gauls.

31. Likewise, during the troubles of the Empire of Greece, there were those who occupied Italy and, not daring openly to dub themselves emperors, called themselves patricians of Rome: such as Avitus, Majorian, and others as far as Augustulus who expelled Odo-

---

[27] *Nov. J* 62.2.
[28] [Above, section 24.]
[29] *Code Theod.* 6.6.
[30] *Semestrium*, pp. 23–7.
[31] *Code J* 12.3.1.

vacar, king of the Heruli. However, when our French occupied [the territory of] the Gauls and found this dignity of patrician established in many places, they continued it for some time, as their custom was to change or to alter ancient practices as little as they could.

32. M. Pasquier has discussed this fully.[32] Nevertheless, I cannot be of his view, given that he wants to derive our peers from these patricians. It seems to me, as to Du Tillet,[33] that the invention of our peerdoms came from the practice of fiefs, of which neither the Romans nor the Greeks had any knowledge.

33. But the same Constantine who invented the patricians, having transferred the Roman Empire to Greece – a nation still more vain and ambitious than the Italian – wanted, in conjunction with this decision, to accommodate himself to the humour of the new country. So he invented the dignity of count as well, and with it honoured those who had accompanied him in this change of country. With the passage of time courtiers, or the principal members of the emperor's retinue, were commonly honoured in this way.

34. Likewise, the word *comites*, being linked to the emperor, properly signifies those of his retinue and company whom we call courtiers because we call the prince's company the court, which the Latins call *comitatum principis*.

35. In the emperor's household and retinue there were persons of divers merits and qualities. So the counts or courtiers were distributed into three ranks or orders, called 'counts of the first, second or third order'. 'Of courtiers', says Eusebius in his life of Constantine,[34] 'some were thought worthy to belong to the first rank, and some to the second, and some to the third'. However, it must be noted that when the title simply of count is expressed it signifies above all counts of the first rank.

36. These, amongst others, were the heads of offices of the emperor's household, called 'superintendents, or tribunes of the *scholae*'. (For, as was said earlier,[35] the companies or bands of minor domestic officers of the emperor were called *scholae*.) And some of those heads of offices bore the title of count with the name of their

---

[32] *Recherches*, II.viii, ix [in *Les Oeuvres d'Estienne Pasquier* (Amsterdam, 1723), I, cols. 95–9, esp. 97].

[33] [*Recueil*, p. 252.]

[34] *PG*, xx [col. 1152].

[35] [Cf. *Offices*, IV.iii.]

charge, such as 'counts of the public treasury, of the household slaves, of the granaries, of the public chest, of the sacred garments', and others.

37. In this connection the word 'count' signifies very nearly what we call in France *intendant* of such and such a charge. As for other heads of offices whose posts did not afterwards bear the title of count, they nevertheless had the right to call themselves counts because of their offices. So much may be seen in innumerable passages of the last three books of the *Code* which are carefully recorded by M. Brisson,[36] to whose book I refer the curious reader.

38. But above all the councillors of state were the true and, as we are to believe, the first counts. So, also, are they usually called in law 'counts of the emperor's cabinet'. Even before the name of 'count' had been used as a title of dignity, it seems that the emperor's counsellors were called by it: witness this passage from Spartianus,[37] that 'when [Hadrian] tried cases he had in his council not only his friends the counts, but [also] jurists'. Likewise, in many passages of law the assessor of a provincial governor is called 'count'.

39. In the imperial household there were also other lesser offices to which this dignity of count did not naturally appertain, but was sometimes especially conferred by the emperor to the greater honour of those appointed. Thus, in the *Theodosian Code*,[38] the office of 'master of the archives was especially granted the honour of count'. As much is said of the 'tribune of the soldiers' who was then called 'count of military affairs'.[39]

40. Likewise with provincial governors,[40] which is very noteworthy because from this it has followed in the course of time that most governors of provinces have been called 'counts'.

41. Others at last obtained the title and dignity of count, after having served the public for some time with lesser status. Thus, advocates of twenty years' standing;[41] also, professors of certain sciences, and

---

[36] [Barnabé] Brisson[*De verborum quae ad ius pertinent significatione* (Paris, 1596), fos. 93vo–94vo].

[37] *Hadrian* [xviii.1].

[38] [Cf.] *Code Theod.* 11.16.14.

[39] [Cf.] *Code J* 12.12; *Code Theod.* 6.10.4.

[40] *Code J* 12.14.1.

[41] [Cf.] *Code J* 2.7.20.

notably of jurisprudence.[42] Our doctors regent of the universities
have not forgotten this. Even the learned Cujas persuades himself[43]
that they are counts after they have taught for twenty years – as if
the dignities of the Empire of Greece were like ours, and as if their
laws and customs bound us in France.

42. However that may be, from the first the title of count was
ascribed only to those who had some great office or who had given
long service to the public. But in the end it was given to those who
had never held office nor done service; and these were called 'counts
vacant'.[44]

43. As for counts of the second rank, these were certain lesser
officers of the court who had heads above them; they are mentioned
in several laws.[45]

44. Lastly, those of the third rank were of still lower condition. They
too are mentioned in various laws.[46] I will not spend time on going
into detail because these qualities of counts of the second and third
rank were eventually so despised that they abolished themselves, so
they do not figure in Justinian's *Code*.

45. So much for the honorary orders of the Romans. Yet, especially
in respect of offices, they had numerous honorary and nominal ones
in the later period.

46. Let us begin with the consuls. There were more than four or
five kinds of these, the premier office of their commonwealth.

47. From the time of the Republic there were, however rarely, extraordinary ones which they called 'substitute or minor consuls'. The
disorder was begun by the ten commissioners called Decemvirs who,
after Sulla's dictatorship, were deputed to re-establish the Republic.
Having power from the people to create annual consuls, and in order
to make many friends, they created not only two as was customary,
but many more, to be consuls one after the other at certain times of
the year, says Dio.[47] The same author says[48] that Caesar adopted the
same practice in his dictatorship.

---

[42] *Code J* 12.15.
[43] [*Operum C*, III, col. 1561.]
[44] *Code Theod.* 6.18.
[45] *Code Theod.* 6.14.2; 6.26.17, 18.
[46] *Code Theod.* 14.4.9, 10; 12.1.127; 6.26.17.
[47] [*Rom. hist.*] XLVIII.[xxxv.2–3; liii.1. Both references are in fact to Caesar's time.]
[48] *Ibid.* XLIII.[xlvi.2–xlvii.3].

48. Witness that Gaius Caninius who was consul for only one day; and so vigilant was he, says Cicero in jest,[49] that he did not sleep during his consulship. This disorder continued under successive emperors until the Emperor Commodus made twenty-five of them in one year.

49. Amid this diversity of consuls, those who had been such at the beginning of each year were called the great consuls, or ordinary consuls, so that the year was always reckoned by their names. During that entire year they were always called consuls. The others were called 'lesser and substitute consuls', and were not recognised outside Italy. So says Dio,[50] and Rosinus has explained it very well.[51]

50. This discourse serves to remove a great doubt that sometimes occurs in our laws. There one sometimes finds, mainly in decrees of the senate, denominated consuls which are not found in the registers of the higher magistrates: for example, those termed Pegasian and Trebellian in decrees of the senate are not found there. The reason is that in the registers there are only ordinary consuls, and in the decrees extraordinary consuls are named who were in function at that time.

51. But apart from these extraordinary consuls who functioned in some part of the year, for two months at most according to Dio,[52] a further device was found under the emperors of making plain honorary or nominal consuls who had never functioned as consuls. These are mentioned in various laws.[53]

52. Even women of illustrious houses who married men of lesser quality obtained consular rank and ornaments from the emperors. So much may be seen in Lampridius:[54]

> A congress of matrons was held, at least on certain festivals or whenever a matron was presented with the insignia of a consular marriage which early emperors had bestowed upon those connected to them by marriage, especially upon those who did not have noble husbands, lest they be bereft of noble rank.

[49] [Cf.] Cicero [*Epistulae ad familiares* VII.xxx.1. Cicero's jest is in fact that, during Caninius's consulship, 'I would have you know that nobody broke his fast' (*scito neminem prandisse*).]

[50] [*Rom. hist*] XLVIII.[xxxv.3].

[51] [*Rom. antiq.*] VII.ix [pp. [2]83–4)].

[52] [*Rom. hist.* XLIII.xlvi.5.]

[53] [E.g.] *Code J* 12.3.4; *Code Theod.* 6.22.7.

[54] *Antoninus Elagabalus* [iv.3].

The law contains another fine observation on this:[55]

> Women who previously have been married to a man of consular
> rank generally try to prevail upon the emperor to let them keep
> their consular rank despite a subsequent marriage to a man of
> lower rank: as I know the Emperor Antoninus gave this indul-
> gence to his cousin Julia Mamaca.

53. Now let us revert to men. Those who had obtained the consular
ornaments without ever having functioned as consuls were specifically
called 'persons of consular rank', being manifestly distinguished in
law [56] from consuls: 'If anyone should be distinguished with the
insignia of ordinary or honorary consul so as to be made either a
consul or a man of consular rank, etc.'. The point is made still better
in the law where it is said that[57]

> Men of consular rank, made consuls after an earlier advancement
> to the dignity of consul (as we must read with Cujas, and not 'to
> the consulate'), have a proper claim to the order. It must also be
> observed that a man who, being of consular rank, tendered a
> hundred gold pounds for the aqueducts shall not be required to
> pay them again if he should afterwards be made consul.

That was a tax imposed on ordinary, extraordinary and honorary
consuls alike, with an intention to reduce the great number of them
and in any case to profit by the ambition of courtiers, selling them
dearly this vain title of honour.

54. 'Persons of consular rank' thus means three things in our law.
First, it means someone who has actually been consul, whether great
or little. This is its first meaning in which it is always taken in the
Digest[58] and also in a law of the *Code*.[59] Afterwards it meant, as has
just been said, someone who 'had obtained an honorary consulship:
so *consularitas* is the dignity of honorary consul', says M. Brisson.[60]

55. Finally (and this is highly noteworthy for understanding many
passages in the ancient books) *consularis* signified certain provincial

---

[55] *Digest* 1.9.12.
[56] *Code J* 10.32.67.1.
[57] [Cf.] *Code J* 12.3.4; *Opera C*, II, pt. ii, col. 280.
[58] *Digest* 4.3.11; 1.9.12. [Loyscau also alludes to] *Digest* 4.6.35–6; [cf. 4.8.3, where the Accursian gloss on 'consul' goes directly against his argument (*Digestum vetus* (Paris, 1576), I, col. 626, *gl. ord. s.l.* 'o')].
[59] *Code J* 12.3.1.
[60] *De verborum*, [fo. 115ʳᵒ].

governors. It is in this sense that the word is taken in a number of laws,[61] and especially in the Novel[62] where, having recorded the various titles of governors of provinces and having styled 'ministerial, proconsular and presidial offices', it is added that 'these are said to be of consular and gubernatorial rank'. The same formula for this dignity is found in Cassiodorus[63] where the relevant ornaments and function are shown. Hence we often find in law[64] *exconsularis* and *exconsularitas* to signify those who had had this dignity.

56. These words cannot signify someone who had been consul and 'who is said to be of consular rank or an ex-consul, but not *exconsularis*'; nor the honorary consul who, having never been in function, could not be said to be either 'ex-consul' nor *exconsularis*, but simply *consularis* – that is, adorned with the same dignity as the consuls had when their term of office was over.

57. The origin of this last consulary lies in the Emperor Hadrian's instituting four officers to dispense justice in Italy. He called them 'consularies' because they were taken from the number of those who had been consuls. So says Spartianus;[65] and Capitolinus mentions[66] that Antoninus Pius had had one of these offices. This device multiplied to such an extent that in the *Notice*[67] there are recorded more than fifty [*sic*] provinces administered by governors called 'consularies': to wit, fifteen in the east and twenty-two in the west, of which seven were in Gaul.

58. Hence we gather that this kind of consulary was in the end so common that it entirely abolished the two others, so that *exconsularis* and in time *consularis* signified no longer those who had been consuls or who had obtained the honorary consulship, but those who had had such provincial governorships. So *consularitas* was in the end a kind of honorary dignity conferred upon mediocre persons and much less than the ancient consular dignity.

59. Otherwise, when we read in the law[68] of 'servants in the imperial scriptoria' becoming consularies after twenty years, how likely is it

---

[61] *Code J* 1.49; *Code Theod.* 6.22.7, 7.10.1, 6.18.
[62] *Nov. J* 8.[1].
[63] *PL.* LXIX, col. 701.
[64] *Code Theod.* 6.24.8, 9; 6.30.19, 24.
[65] *Hadrian* [xxii.13].
[66] *Antoninus Pius* [ii.9].
[67] *Notitia* [*utraque dignitatum cum orientis tum occidentis ultra Arcadii Honoriique tempora* (Venice, 1593), pp. 69 *et seq.*, 149 *et seq.*].
[68] *Code Theod.* 6.26.7.

that this relates to honorary consulships – the greatest dignity of the Empire after the patriciate, even greater than the prefectorial dignity? Further, the following law[69] explains the matter clearly when, having ordained that after twenty years' service the plain 'servants in the imperial scriptoria should be supported among those chosen for consular honour', it adds that 'they should have the same honour of dignity in the senate as was accustomed to be granted to ex-consularies'. For it is certain that 'ex-consuls' and 'ex-consularies' are distinct dignities. Ex-consuls were those 'who sustained the charge of the consulship, who are also called "consular" in the books of the *Digest*'; while 'ex-consularies' are those 'who bore the charge of consulary offices, that is, of such a kind as provincial administration, who were wont to be called consularies'. Elsewhere it is said[70] that 'members of the secret service shall be ranked as consularies'. But their principals had only the proconsular dignity, which was less than the ancient consular dignity.[71]

60. For it was a common practice in the Roman Empire, where the officers were temporary, that after the time of their active tenure there always remained a rank and a title of honour to those who had exercised it; and even so this was less by one degree than that of those who were actually in office. This title of honour was coined by means of a derivative from the original name of the office – *consularis* from 'consul', *praetorius* from 'praetor', *censorius* from 'censor', and others likewise; or else by placing the preposition 'ex' before the name of the office – 'ex-consul', 'ex-president', 'ex-quaestor', or, as the oldest authors said, *ex consule, ex magistro, ex quaestore*.

61. But, beyond that, honorary and nominal offices were made out of all offices. Owing to the vanity of the Greeks, everyone wanted to be an officer. The emperors did not have offices for all, and so they devised a way of satisfying these ambitious persons with certain nominal dignities of offices which they did not want actually to confer upon them, similar to those that remained to real officers after the time of their office. Thus, beyond the title of honour, they would also have by these means the rank and even the privileges of those offices. These dignities were also called 'by imperial mandate' because they consisted not in any actual practice, but in simple letters or provision by the emperor which are termed *codicilli* or 'honorary

---

[69] *Code Theod.* 6.26.8.
[70] *Code Theod.* 6.27.5.
[71] *Code J* 12.21.3.

imperial mandates'. There is an express section on this in the *Theodo-sian Code*.[72]

62. There were three kinds of these officers by letters without exercise: to wit, 'vacant', 'honorary' and 'supernumerary', without including those called 'assistants' who were 'employed to carry administrative measures through'[73] – that is, former officers after their time had elapsed. The name 'assistants' has a broader signific-ance, however, embracing all those who had had some notable public responsibility, in recompense for which they had obtained imperial mandates or honorary letters for some dignity by a name other than that of the office which they had exercised.[74] These took precedence indiscriminately over the other kinds of honorary dignities.

63. Those called 'vacant' (which signifies quite the contrary of that which we term *vaquer* [to attend to] in French) were those who, 'not by merit of carrying administrative measures through, deserved the girdle of honourable dignity'.[75] That is to say, not only had they been honoured by the emperor with the title of some office by plain title, but its ornaments and insignia had actually been conferred upon them, so that only the exercise remained; and 'they were also called enrolled or chosen members, and interagents'. Thus they enjoyed all the privileges of the office, as Cujas proves.[76] Capitolinus says of this kind of officers:[77]

> As Commodus had thrown the praetorian rank into confusion by innumerable appointments, Pertinax carried out a decree of the senate and ordered that those who had not borne the responsibil-ity of praetor but had received [the status] by appointment should be ranked below those who had really been praetors.

Such, it seems, are the ones of which Lampridius speaks:[78]

> He appointed by imperial mandates to the office of pontiff, to the College of Fifteen and to the augurship, on condition that they should be endorsed (*allegerentur*) by the senate.

---

[72] [6.22.]
[73] *Code J* 12.8.2.
[74] *Code J* 12.8.2; 7.2.5.
[75] *Code J* 12.8.2.
[76] [*Opera C*, II, pt. ii, cols. 289–90.]
[77] *Helvetius Pertinax* [vi.10].
[78] *Alexander Severus* [xlix.2].

This should be read *allegerentur* and not, as in the vulgar form, *allegarentur*. In another place he says:[79]

> Severus swore that he would not have any enrolled persons, that is, holders of vacant places (*vagantium*), lest he burden the commonwealth with their maintenance,

where we must undoubtedly read, with Cujas, *vacantium*.[80] It may be inferred from this passage that holders of such places, like real officers, received pay.

64. 'Honorary or nominal officers', who also are often called 'appointees by imperial mandate', are defined in the law[81] as those 'upon whom, apart from the girdle, dignity is conferred solely for the sake of honour'; or, as Ausonius says,[82]

> Free from the duties, participants in the name,

or, finally, as in the law,[83]

> Those stationed outside the imperial palace, having no part in public offices, if they enjoy the shade of a secluded repose and have acquired the semblance of all their honours by patronage rather than by merit.

Further, they had only their letters of retainer and not the insignia of office. Consequently, they did not have the privileges, but only the title and the rank. That is why they are called in law[84] 'empty forms and futile semblances of dignities'; and in a Novel[85] it is said that they are called honorary 'because they contain nothing other than pure honour'.

65. Finally, 'supernumeraries' were those who in the militia or associations 'were over and above the prescribed number', and yet were retained to take up the first place vacated by ordinary members, and meanwhile took the title and quality of the office. So say various laws.[86] The law which is the key to the matter[87] does not mention

---

[79] *Ibid.* [xv.3]
[80] [*Opera C*, II, pt. ii, col. 289.]
[81] *Code J* 12.40.9.2.
[82] [*PL*, XIX, col. 878.]
[83] *Code Theod.* 6.22.5, 6.
[84] [*Code Theod.* 12.1.74.]
[85] *Nov J* 70 [preface].
[86] [E.g.] *Code J* 12.19.7.3.
[87] *Code J* 12.8.2.

this, because it deals only with illustrious dignities, whereas 'supernumeraries' were only plain militiamen or bands of domestic officers to the emperor or to provincial governors. It seems very likely that they are those whom Antonius Augustinus and Laelius Taurellus were so hindered from finding, to interpret this passage in Suetonius:[88] 'He instituted a kind of imaginary soldiery which was called supernumerary and could be performed *in absentia* and in name only'.

66. Thus it appears in canon law[89] that the pope sometimes creates canons 'in expectation of a prebend, who have a stall in the choir and voice in the chapter, but do not yet have a prebend'. Nowadays this is no longer done 'for the purpose of obtaining the first vacant prebend', as it formerly was, because it was a kind of reservation, which is in general prohibited by the Council of Trent. But I have heard tell that they still create them 'for the purpose of obtaining dignities', because ordinarily the dignities of chapters are assigned only to canons, so that in order to be capable of them one has oneself made by the pope a canon without prebend.

67. So much for the honorary dignities used amongst the Romans. As for epithets – that is, the titles of honour which they ascribed to each one of their dignities, whether actual or honorary – here they are, in accordance with their order and rank: *illustres, spectabiles, clarissimi, equites, perfectissimi*, and *egregii*, on which Alciato has a chapter.[90] But I consider that they can only be discussed by guesswork, the precise meaning of these terms having been lost through the lapse of time and changes which occurred in the Roman Empire. However, we can say with Cujas[91] that the first three epithets, *illustres, spectabiles* and *clarissimi*, applied to senators according to the various magisterial offices which they had held. The fourth was that of the knights, and the last two were ascribed to the most notable plebeians.

68. Even before Justinian there were some officers who did not content themselves with the title and epithet of 'illustrious', but took the rank above it: to wit, consuls, legal practitioners and even the ancient consulars as well. Nevertheless, no other epithet, neither Greek nor Latin, was devised for them, except that in our books they are speci-

---

[88] *Divus Claudius* xxv.[1. Loyseau's allusions are to the sixteenth-century Italian scholars Antonio Augustín and Lelio Torelli.]

[89] *Decretales* 3.5.9, 19.

[90] *Dispunctionum lib. IIII* [(Basle, 1531), fos. 73ʳᵒ–74ᵛᵒ].

[91] [*Opera C*, II, pt. ii, cols. 269–70.]

fied by these words, 'who are above the *illustres*', 'have surpassed the illustrious'.[92] I have followed Cujas[93] in placing *illustres* as the first epithet, although Accursius and the ancient doctors have coined another in respect of these texts, to wit, *superillustres*.

69. Such, from the first, were the epithets of dignities. But as for particularising to which offices each of them was ascribed beyond what the *Notice* tells us, this is, for the rest, impossible. They have changed from time to time; and there is nothing decreed in such a business where ambition, which resides in the fancy of the great, overcomes all reason and custom. Everyone always tries to usurp the highest titles. When the lesser have usurped the honours of the greater, the greater have to seek still higher ones in order to be raised above those who have made themselves their equals; and so, by degrees, there is always increase. Thus in the ancient Empire it was necessary in the end to find other epithets of dignity, beyond the six which I have just recorded. For the great disdained thenceforth to title themselves with these epithets different from the names of offices, and so titles derived from those of offices were generated. Thus, in the twelfth book of Justinian's *Code* and in the sixth of the *Theodosian Code*, which deal with dignities then recognised in the Empire, there is scarcely mention of those ancient epithets, any more than in Cassiodorus.

70. But in as much as a diligent reading of these books has enabled me to understand the matter, I have found that the great dignities were then divided into four classes or ranks: to wit,[94] *praefectorum, proconsulum, vicariorum* and *exconsularium inter allectos*. Each of these comprised several offices, whether actual or honorary, which therefore converged upon the same rank and position, bearing the same dignity; and those who were honoured were not ordered amongst themselves otherwise than by seniority of advancement.

71. The first rank was thus 'of the prefectorial dignity'. It is therefore called in the laws[95] 'the lofty summit' and 'the most exalted rank'. To this belonged 'consuls, patricians, prefects (praetorian and city alike), military commanders whether of cavalry or of foot, and provosts of the imperial chamber'.

---

[92] *Inst. J* 4.4.10; *Code J* 4.32.26.2, 7.62.38, 4.20.16.
[93] [*Opera C,* II, pt. ii, cols. 269–70.]
[94] *Code Theod.* 6.22.7.
[95] *Code Theod.* 6.22.7, 8.

72. The second rank was the proconsular, in which were 'quaestors, masters of the officers, officers of public finances, the chief of the secretaries, officers of the cabinet, provosts and tribunes of the imperial guard having the title of count (otherwise not), officers of military affairs, and the chiefs of the secret service' in the later period.

73. Of the third rank, called 'the dignity of deputy', were 'counts of the provinces, consularies, presidents and other rectors of the provinces, sinecure countships, all countships of the first order, assistant masters of the imperial archives, and masters of depositions'.

74. Finally, of the fourth rank 'of ex-consularies among the élites, who also were called *clarissimi*', were, after their time of service, 'decurions and silentiaries, household servants such as imperial body-guards, provosts of the imperial standards, servants in the imperial archives' and, formerly, 'chiefs of the secret service' to whom the proconsular dignity was afterwards granted by Honorius and Theodosius.[96] It is noteworthy that those who had this dignity had entry and voice in the Roman senate.

75. As for the dignity of knight, it was given[97] only to townsmen and not to courtiers.

76. Finally, the dignity of *perfectissimus* applied only to those of the common people who were employed in the mechanic arts and were free-born.[98]

77. Now it is very difficult to decipher and to specify the order of dignities more precisely, because the law of the Emperor Valentinian, who made this specification and is mentioned in the above law,[99] is not to be found in its entirety. There remain to us only some fragments which Cujas indicates.[100] Even so, in the same class or rank of dignity there were not only several offices of divers names, but also several of the same name and different kinds – to wit, actual on the one hand, honorary on the other, of three or four kinds which have just been recorded. For the curious reader's satisfaction, it is appropriate that I rehearse here some rules of rank which applied to them all.

---

[96] *Code Theod.* 6.28.7.
[97] *Code Theod.* 6.36.
[98] *Code Theod.* 6.37 [cf. *Code J* 12.32.1].
[99] *Code J* 12.8.2.
[100] [*Opera C*, ii, pt. ii, col. 288.]

78. First, it is true enough that officers in function took precedence over all others of the same dignity whose function had ended. Again, officers of the next rank of dignity took precedence during their term of office over all officers, honorary and ancient alike, of the rank immediately above. For example, proconsuls in function preceded ex-consuls or ex-prefects and, with still more reason, all kinds of honorary consuls or prefects.[101]

79. After the officers in function came former officers – that is, those who had previously exercised the same office or another of the same dignity. They themselves walked according to the seniority of their advancement. This is a general rule among all officers, even when the last appointee has exercised the office twice. 'Where the official insignia are repeatedly obtained they prove merit, but do not increase it', says the law.[102] It is true, as the law says,[103] that someone who had exercised two offices of the same status always took precedence over someone who had held only one, and someone who had had three took precedence over someone who had held only two of them.

80. And after those who had exercised an office of the first rank came those who had exercised one of the second rank, who thereby took precedence over the three kinds of honorary officers of the first rank. Even so, if those who had exercised an office of the third rank had obtained letters of honorary office of the first rank, they walked alongside former officers of the second.[104]

81. Finally, after former officers of the second rank came honorary dignities of the first rank, in this order: first, those upon whom the insignia and ornaments of the first dignity had been conferred in court; then, those to whom they had been sent *in absentia*; thirdly, those who had obtained in court plain letters of dignity; and at the end, those to whom these letters had been issued or sent in their absence.[105]

---

[101] *Code Theod.* 6.22.8.
[102] *Code J.* 12.3.1.2.
[103] *Code Theod.* 6.6.
[104] *Code Theod.* 6.22.7, 8.
[105] *Code J* 12.8.2.

CHAPTER ELEVEN

Of the plain dignities of France

1. I remember that in my youth, at the time of the death of the late Monsieur the Chancellor de Birague, it was said that he had died a cardinal without title, a chancellor without seals, a bishop without a diocese, a knight without an order, and a priest without a benefice. I do not know whether this was true, and I say it not in order to carp at his memory, but rather to honour him for not having aggrandised himself further by means of such dignities. Yet this common saying can serve us as a notable example of the honorary dignities of France. For, while we do not have quite as many of them as there were at the end of the Eastern Empire, we do have some, in the shape of offices, orders and even lordships.

2. Let us begin with orders, and indeed with ecclesiastical orders. It is true enough that there are not only cardinals of Rome without title, as I said earlier,[1] but also certain cathedral churches whose canons are called cardinals – to wit, those of Ravenna and Compostella, according to Duaren.[2]

3. Admittedly, in one gloss[3] the cardinals of Ravenna are derisively compared with the king of Yvetot in France. However, it is also true that priests having leave of the incumbents to officiate for them in cathedral churches (whom we now call canons) were formerly called

---

[1] Above, ch. 3 [section 29].

[2] [François] Duaren, *De sacris ecclesiae ministeriis* [*ac beneficiis libri* VIII (Paris, 1551)], p. 70.

[3] *Decretum* 32 q.2. c.1: *gl. ord. s.vv.* 'principem mundi' [cf. above, ch. 3 section 40 (note 31)].

cardinals – that is, principals.[4] And they are in cathedral churches what the cardinals of Rome are in the universal church.

4. Likewise, in several places in the *Decretum* bishops are called cardinal priests.[5] This is found more than twenty times in the epistles of St Gregory the Great. In all these passages I have noticed that bishops are there called cardinal priests only when they hold a second bishopric *in commendam*, for it is not licit to call them bishops of two places, but only to call them principal priests of the second bishopric.

5. To be brief, we see that the priest of the Trinité of Vendôme is commonly called 'cardinal priest', a title that would better suit the heads of an order who have several abbeys and monasteries under them. However, I know of only the one of Vendôme who takes this title; and in this quality he bears at the crest of his arms a green hat in the form of that of the cardinals of Rome. And perhaps it is to distinguish themselves from all these honorary cardinals that those of Rome call themselves not plain cardinals, but cardinals of the Roman church.

6. As for bishops, there are no honorary ones of these unless we would hold to be such those whom we call, vulgarly, 'portable bishops'. These are preferred to bishoprics in the hands of infidels or heretics; or else, have resigned their bishoprics whilst none the less remaining bishops in respect of the episcopal order, as was said before;[6] or else again, the coadjutors given to decrepit or sickly bishops, which was very common in the early church, as I have said elsewhere.[7]

7. Finally, in respect of priests, deacons and sub-deacons, no honorary ones are made of these because as many are made as are desired. True, it can be said that all those of the present time are only honorary as they are ordained without title – that is, without certifying any ecclesiastical post, as was done in the early church. But they are almost all ordained with the title of their patrimony, as I said in the third chapter.[8]

8. Let us come, then, to the orders of nobility. The same can be said of the order of princes, that they are all honorary, as the only

---

[4] *Decretales* 1.24.2.
[5] *Decretum* 7 q.1. c.42; *Decretum* D.71 c.5.
[6] [Above, ch. 3 section 25.]
[7] [*Offices*, I.v.10–20.]
[8] [Sections 20, 21.]

true and perfect prince is the sovereign who, furthermore, is called in all languages 'the prince', without qualification. However, it can also be said that royal bastards and their descendants, together with the kinsmen of foreign princes, are honorary princes; albeit that only the princes of the blood are true princes, because they alone are capable of true princedom and sovereignty. In a word, if all those sprung from a sovereign house were held to be true princes, honorary princes could still be found: to wit, those who possess a lordship erected into a principality.

9. But there is no doubt that in respect of knights there are more honorary ones than there are of those who have actually received the order of chivalry. The latter unquestionably are the true knights whom we call 'knights of the order'; the others are called plain knights, without mention of order. Yet it remains the case that no one can be a true knight unless the order of chivalry has been conferred upon him: given, as was proved above,[9] that even the king's sons are not born knights.

10. Nevertheless, in these latter times the title of knight is ordinarily taken to be a plain dignity with which all those of the high nobility title and qualify themselves, even though they have never been knighted. Thus great lords, such as dukes, marquises, counts, lords of principalities, viscounts; and even barons and castellans usurp it, even though they may not be of the rank of great lords, as I said in my *Seigneuries*.[10] However, barons have some claim to it given that in former times the title common to all great lords was to call them 'barons of France', as Du Tillet says.[11] So it seems that the title of baron is the limit and last dignity of the high nobility, and that the castellan is thus of the rank of plain gentlemen and not of the great lords – nor, consequently, of the knights, unless he has received the order of chivalry.

11. Likewise, the great officers who are also of the high nobility call themselves knights: the officers of the crown, the heads of offices in the royal household and all those who are of the council of state. I include amongst them the presidents and the representatives of the king's interests in the *parlement* of Paris and the heads of the other sovereign courts, and some other notable officers. Here is my reason:

[9] [Above, ch. 6 section 33.]
[10] [viii.12.]
[11] [*Recueil*, p. 341.]

it is very likely that the honorary title of knight relates to that of
'count' or 'friend' in Roman law.

12. I said in the last chapter[12] that the principal officers of the
Empire, and especially the heads of offices of the emperor's household and, above all, those of the sacred consistory – that is, of his
privy council – were counts of the first order: that is to say, they were
companions of the emperor. Likewise in France, those who are in
similar posts can call themselves knights: that is, honoured with the
accolade and friendship, and, as it were, collaterals of the prince. For
I said before[13] that the first origin of the knights was that the kings
publicly accolled and embraced those whom they wished to raise in
honour; and this accolade served them thereafter as a public testimony to their being recognised among the king's principal friends
and favourites. However, with the passage of time those who had not
received this princely accolade, but had received other public evid-
ences of his favour, such as those whom he appointed to great offices
or invested with high lordships, were recognised as principal officers
or vassals of the kingdom, and took this title of knight.

13. As for plain nobility, it can be said that there is also an honorary
and a simply nominal form of this: to wit, that by which judicial
officers, advocates, and others who are not noble by lineage and have
no ennobling office, call themselves. This nobility is commonly called
'town nobility'. It entails only the honorary title of 'noble man' for
the husband and 'damoiselle' for the wife, as was proved in the fifth
chapter,[14] and not the franchises and privileges of nobility such as
exemption from direct taxes: though Guy Pape says[15] it to have been
adjudicated in Grenoble that advocates were not liable to direct taxes.

14. As for the orders of the third estate, I know of no honorary ones.
However, Guy Pape[16] and Rebuffi[17] tell us that in their time there
were certain graduates by bull or letters patent who obtained the
degree of doctor simply by letters of princes and sovereign lords.
The gloss on a rule of chancery of Julius II says of these that 'they
are not of greater importance than the bull'. This is how the same

---

[12] [Sections 36–8.]
[13] [Above, ch. 6 sections 15–16.]
[14] [Cf. above, ch. 5, section 20.]
[15] [*Decisiones parlamenti Dalphinalis* (Lyon, 1593)] p. 584.
[16] [As note 15.]
[17] [Pierre] Rebuffi, *Tractatus nominationum* [(Paris, 1538)], p. 51; *Concordata* [(Paris, 1538)], pp. 27–31.

Rebuffi resolves the matter, that they have no privilege or right in France and are not recognised there at all: a reason why they are no longer seen there. The ordinances of France also direct[18] that graduates made in the privileged universities of the realm without the rigour of public examination and other requisite and accustomed solemnities (vulgarly said to have passed by stealth, that is, privately, and not in the university's public hall) should not enjoy the rights and privileges ascribed to those who have passed publicly and with the rigour of the examination.

15. Likewise among the artisans, there are masters by letters. They are those who, upon royal entries and marriages, the birth of Monseigneur the Dauphin of France and the declaration of the first prince of the blood, obtain letters to be received master of a trade or craft without making a masterpiece or holding a festive entertainment or incurring other costs which arise upon the reception of other masters. The latter are called 'masters by masterpiece', to distinguish them from these masters by letters.

16. There used to be a great difference between the former and the latter. Masters by letters, as simple 'codicillaries', were neither summoned nor admitted to assemblies, nor enrolled in the confraternity, nor, by consequence, elected to the offices of the trade or craft. Their widows and children did not enjoy the exercise of the trade after their deaths, as did those of masters by masterpiece. This was quite reasonable, so that money should not have as much power as art. However, modern edicts[19] have curtailed these differences in favour of the contractors who buy such letters of mastership in order to re-sell them, so that nowadays masters by letters are equal in all respects to those by masterpiece.

17. So much for orders. As for offices which at present are sold so dear, so great account is made of them that it is not reasonable that there should be plain honorary ones. However, such there formerly were: witness the extraordinary masters of requests who were suppressed by the ordinance of Orléans.[20] In order to distinguish themselves from these, the real masters of requests still call themselves today ordinary masters of requests. I remember that at the time of

---

[18] [Cf. L.W.B. Brockliss, *French Higher Education in the Seventeenth and Eighteenth centuries: a Cultural History* (Oxford, 1987), pp. 71–82, especially 77–8.]

[19] [Cf., for example, Fontanon, I, pp. 1085–96, 1101–12.]

[20] [1561,] art. 33 [Fontanon, I, p. 135].

the reduction of the towns of the League several officers of our [long] robe were deceived. They had, as is said, good assurances, because the king had promised them that he would make them masters of requests so that they would bring about the said reductions. Afterwards they were much taken aback when they were given only letters of offices of extraordinary masters of requests.

18. Likewise in respect of household offices of the king and privileged princes, there are several offices which are neither ordinary nor specified in their household establishments, but simply have letters called 'retainers'. None the less, these are altogether similar to those of officers actually serving, except that the term 'ordinary' does not apply to them. So these are properly such as are called 'supernumerary' in Roman law, as I discussed in the last chapter.[21]

19. These extraordinary officers do not have the privileges which are enjoyed by real household officers of the king and privileged princes who actually serve and are specified in their household establishments. Yet, according to the ordinance of Orléans[22] it is not enough actually to serve and to be specified in the establishment. It is necessary to have at least twenty crowns in wages and to be paid them, and that this should appear by certificate of the treasurer of the household. But this was changed by the order of 1598.[23] Instead of the treasurer's certificate, which could easily be counterfeited, the king willed that the establishments of privileged princes be verified in the *cour des aides*. This being done, persons specified and named in these establishments are thereafter exempt by decree, however meagre their wages and whether they are paid or not, provided only that they have actually served. This is always necessary to distinguish true officers from honorary ones.

20. But in respect of officers who have resigned their offices, I said in my first book[24] that they no longer retain any privileges thereof, not even the title and rank, unless they have obtained the letters of a veteran. Even so, persons of honour are given by courtesy some rank in memory of their former dignity. Therefore, and also in order that they may call themselves late officers, they can be placed in the rank of honorary officers.

---

[21] [Section 65.]
[22] [Article 125.]
[23] *Règlement des tailles* [Fontanon, II, p. 877].
[24] *Offices* [I.ix.35–8].

21. It must still be observed that there is a certain honorary title which is ascribed to several officers of France: to wit, that of 'king's counsellor'. This perhaps has taken its origin from Roman law where we find that jurisconsults were often summoned to the prince's company and retinue, to be of his council. I proved this above,[25] notably through the example of the jurisconsult Menander who is called 'Counsellor Menander'.

22. These councillors of state of the emperor were also called 'friends of the prince': witness the passage in Spartianus,[26] that 'in his council he had not only his friends or counts'; and this fine sentence of Marius Maximus, recorded by Lampridius,[27] that 'the commonwealth in which the prince is evil is happier and more secure than that in which the prince's friends are evil'. For this reason the title is commonly ascribed in law[28] to jurisconsults, as may be seen in these words: 'Volusius Maecianus, our friend'; and, a little further on, 'You will communicate with the said Maecianus and others of our learned friends'. Thus in letters of the chancery the king readily gives this quality of 'friend' or 'beloved' to those who bear the title of his councillors, saying 'Our beloved and trusty counsellor, etc.'.

23. Hence it follows that this title of 'king's counsellor' is more elevated than one thinks. For properly, and originally, it appertained only to councillors of state; and yet it has justly been retained by the officers of the *parlement* of Paris and of the *grand conseil*, as much because they were councillors of state from their first foundation as because the king speaks in their decrees. This last reason is why the other *parlements* have also retained it, besides that they were erected in the same manner as the *parlement* of Paris and with the same honours and prerogatives. Likewise the other sovereign bodies which judge in the king's name have taken this title, even though the proper title of the officers of the accounts should not be 'king's counsellors', but 'masters' or 'clerks of the accounts', and those of the *cour des aides* were originally called 'generals' (*généraux*).

24. In the same way, bailiffs and seneschals have taken the same title of 'king's counsellors' since they had the administration of provinces. They were then notable personages, and usually councillors of state,

---

[25] viii.[26].
[26] *Hadrian* [xviii.1; above, ch. 8, section 26 and ch. 10, section 38].
[27] *Alexander Severus* [lxv.4].
[28] *Digest* 37.14.17.

who were sent by turns to the provinces to govern them and to dispense justice there, rather by virtue of commission assigned to councillors of state than by virtue of office: just like the counts in the Roman Empire, so called 'because they were sent by the court of the prince to govern the provinces'. That is why they were at first called in France *missi dominici*, and then 'bailiffs' (that is, guardians of the people) and 'seneschals' (that is, household officers of the king). Hence it is that provincial governors who have succeeded to the most noble part of their charges still have the right of sitting in the *parlement*.

25. As for lieutenants of the bailiffs and seneschals, when the king made them his officers (whereas previously they were appointed by the bailiffs and seneschals) he wished them to be called his counsellors in order to distinguish them from those former appointees or assessors and to give them a public mark as royal officers and magistrates.

26. There are no other judicial officers to whom this title rightly belongs. Counsellors of the presidial, bailiwick and provostal courts do not have it. Presidial counsellors are called only 'counsellor magistrates' to distinguish them from their principals or from ancient advocates instead of whom they were appointed to act as counsellors to bailiffs, seneschals and their lieutenants. For that reason those advocates were formerly called 'counsellors' both in the law and in France, as I have proved elsewhere. It is quite true that often enough there have been attempts to ascribe the title of 'king's counsellor' to presidial counsellors in return for money; but they have not wanted it for the price and have found means of exempting themselves.

27. Let us turn to financial officers. In former times the treasurers of France were in number only one, then two, then four. These, as heads of finance, were councillors of state. Afterwards they were dispersed in the provinces and even multiplied in bureaux[29] established in each province, the new ones always being raised to the same honours and prerogatives as the old ones. On the pretext of the former arrangements they have gained this point, not of being in effect councillors of state, but of having the honorary title of king's counsellor, which was the ancient title of councillors of state. After their example, this same title has been ascribed to the other treasurers

---

[29] [*berceaux* (cradles) in 1610, corrected to *bureaux* in 1701.]

at the time of their erection. In the end it was given perforce to the *élus* procuring finance, and again to a crew of vile financiers (more capable of robbing than of counselling the king), either when their offices were instituted (to embellish them so as to sell them more easily), or by particular concession made subsequently in return for money; our kings having learned from the Eastern emperors to sell these empty titles of honour as well as real offices. For, in effect, this title of 'king's counsellor' ascribes no right of privilege nor even any rank to those who have it, but is a plain quality of honour. Those emperors gave titles of honour only to those who wanted to buy them; but in France those who do not want them are made to buy them.

28. Finally, in respect of lordships, these are dignities which are almost only honorary: that is, consisting only in honour, with no public power other than that of their justice, which power resides in effect in their officers and not in them. Nevertheless, there are still a few which are plain honorary lordships: to wit, modern counties and baronies, erected by royal letters and yet depending upon another than the king, notably those which depend from a lordship of lesser title. For example, the barony of Lucé has been judged a plain honorary barony in the decree of verification of the letters of its erection in 1540, because it depends from the lordship of Château-du-Loir, as Choppin tells us.[30].

29. There is also another kind of honorary lordship which was formerly more usual than it is at present. The explanation of this will serve to remind us of several fine antiquities on this matter. The title and all other rights of a lordship are indivisible and apply to the whole, and thus they reside inseparably throughout the seigneurial land and in every part of it. Formerly, then, the younger sons of houses to whom some member or portion of a barony, castellany or other seigneurial land was given partibly claimed with much probability of proof that because of this they were barons or castellans; or at least, that they held their share with equal right to their elder brother's tenure of the principal manor. On this we have a very fine observation in the custom of Anjou[31] and that of Maine:[32]

---

[30] Choppin, I [pt. i, p. 310].

[31] Art. 63: *Coustumes du pays et duché d'Anjou* [ed. C. Pocquet de Livonnière (Paris, 1725)], I, cols. 148–9.

[32] Art. 72: *Les coustumes du pays et comté du Maine* [eds. Thibault Baillet and Jehan le Lieure (Le Mans, 1581)], fos. 19ᵛᵒ–20ʳᵒ.

There are lords (say these customs) who are not counts, viscounts, barons nor castellans; and these are called bachelors, and they have such and similar justice as those of which they are part.

30. This is properly and originally what the same customs and several [others] call holding 'in parage': that is, with equal right. In fact, in the custom of Anjou it is said[33] that 'he who holds in parage has such and similar justice as his elder, and holds as nobly as he'. That is why in the *Book of Fiefs* it is said[34] that those who have a fief for life 'do not have *paragium*' (for thus it should be read, and not *paradogium*, with the old interpreters, or *pedagium*, with the vulgar), because a fief which is not heritable is not subject to being divided. That is also why among the feudists *paragium* – or, as they say, *paradogium* – sometimes signifies the nobility, as Tiraqueau says,[35] following Iserni. In fact, places are to be found in the ancient books[36] where 'parage' is taken in this sense: such as 'to endow a daughter with a parage', and 'to marry a daughter according to parage', which is what our customs call 'to apparage' or 'to emparage' nobly.

31. But in my opinion Cujas above all interprets this term best, saying[37] that these words, 'They have no parage', signify, 'Lesser lords are not reckoned to be peers, because only nobles have the dignity of peerdom'. In fact it is very likely that originally, and at the time of first antiquity, peers by fief were those who held with equal right to the chief lord's, and thus were his peers and companions. That is why they ought to be called and summoned to judge disputes between vassals, as sharers in the justice and lordship of the fief. It is also why with the passage of time the principal vassals of the lordship, who were called 'peers of the fief' or 'peers of the lord's court', were placed among these peers or paragers.

32. The effect of these ancient parages was evidently observed among the children of our kings of the first dynasty. After the father's death the eldest of them was the head and principal lord of the realm,

---

[33] *Coustumes ... d'Anjou*, [I, cols. 540–1].
[34] [*Operum C*, III, cols. 1841–2; cf. above, ch. 6, note 62.]
[35] *De nobil.* [p. 38].
[36] *Statuta [et novae reformationes] urbis Romae* [(Rome, 1519)], I, p. 25; *Constitutionum neapolitanarum [sive sicularum, libre tres, in Codex legum antiquarum*, ed. F. Lindenbrog (Frankfurt, 1613)], p. 799.
[37] [*Opera C*, II, pt. ii, col. 664.]

always having its chief town, which is Paris and the adjacent country. But the younger had their shares with equal right to his: to wit, as kingdoms and in equal sovereignty. We even read in our annals that long afterwards Charles, king of Navarre, obtained by force of arms [the right] to hold Normandy in parage (thus must we read in our old annals, and not *en paroye*); and this signified a kind of sovereignty.

33. Today the great German lords still observe parages better than we. The younger sons of their dukes, marquises, counts or other potentates claim to hold their shares with equal title, rights and prerogatives to their brother's. That is why all the children of German dukes and counts call themselves dukes and counts, not with addition of the name of the family duchy or county as their eldest brother does, but with addition of their forenames or proper names: the Archduke Matthias, the Count Charles, and so on.

34. This was observed in France until well into the third dynasty in respect only of our kings' daughters who were called queens with addition of their proper names: witness Queen Constance, daughter of King Louis the Fat and wife of the count of Toulouse. Du Tillet says[38] that in 1245 an inquest was made to prove this custom, and it is still in the royal Trésor des Chartes. Nevertheless, the custom has not persisted because, as he says, it became absurd; though Bartolus says[39] that it is grounded in law.

35. However, it has recently been renewed in the person of Madame Marguerite of France who, being the daughter of a king and sister to three kings, bore with good right this title of Queen Marguerite.

36. In this connection Tiraqueau[40] conducts a discussion to show that the king's children can be called 'kings', adducing amongst several other authorities the canon law[41] where a king's son is called 'king' by way of honour in his father's lifetime; and that vulgar passage in Vergil, speaking of Ascanius, son of Aeneas, 'They seek the king', where Servius has annotated it.[42]

37. So much for honorary dignities. But no more than the Romans and the Greeks do we in France lack epithets of honour. We always

---

[38] [*Recueil*, p. 216.]
[39] [Cf. *Super postremis tribus libris codicis commentaria*, in *Operae ... omnia* (Basle, 1588–9), IV, pt. iii, pp. 118–19.]
[40] [*De iure prim.*, pp. 392–4.]
[41] *Decretum* 24 q.1 c.42.
[42] *Comm. in Aeneidos*, [I.267 et seq.].

place them before the name, while the Romans and the Greeks placed them immediately afterwards, like real orders. These epithets are that we call sovereign princes 'most illustrious', 'most powerful' and 'most victorious', and other such superlatives of honour which by custom are variously ascribed to every monarch. We call princes 'illustrious' and 'excellent'; knights and great lords, 'high and powerful lords'; cardinals, 'most illustrious'; bishops, 'most reverend'; abbots, 'reverend fathers in God', and lesser ecclesiastics, 'venerable and discreet persons'; priors and others, 'religious' or 'devout persons'; officers, 'noble men'; burgesses, 'honourable men' or 'honest persons'; while to men of learning, beyond the ordinary epithet there was formerly added that of 'wise' or 'scientifical'. In short, it is the art of secretaries to know how to sort out the epithets that must be ascribed to every order and quality of persons.

38. But again, beyond honorary dignities and epithets we have in France a third kind of plain dignity which neither the Greeks nor the Romans had. We place immediately before the names of persons an honourable term which I cannot call other than the forename: as when we call the king 'Sire'. It is true that in his case only, because of his Majesty's supreme excellence and because he is unique of his kind, we add at present neither name nor quality, as did our forefathers who said 'Sire God' and 'Sire King'. We call the prince 'Monseigneur'; the knight, 'Messire'; the plain noble, 'Monsieur'; the man of learning, 'Master'; the merchant or artisan, 'Sir so-and-so'; and even the religious, who have renounced the world's vanities, are called 'brothers', 'doms', or 'dams'. In the same way, this forename is imparted to women. The wife of a knight or other great lord is called 'Madame'; that of a noble, 'Mademoiselle'. A bourgeois's wife was formerly called 'Dame so-and-so'; but then, in order to be distinguished from an artisan's wife who is likewise called 'Dame so-and-so', the bourgeois's wife wanted to be called 'Madame'. So at present there is no longer a distinction between lady 'dames' and bourgeois 'dames' in respect of the forename, but only in respect of dress, at least in the provinces of this part of the realm. In Guyenne, however, the wife of a bourgeois is called 'Madone', and an artisan's 'Done so-and-so', to preserve distinction between them.

39. All these words, except 'master' and 'brother', can be translated into Greek only by the word κυριος, and into Latin only by *dominus*. From this, doubtless, come 'dom', 'dam', 'dame' and 'damoiselle'

233

which is the diminutive of 'dame'. It is to be presumed that from κυριος comes the word 'syre' which, for this reason, Robert Estienne spells 'çyre'. Hence, 'messire' – as it were, *mon syre*; or else, as some say, *my-syre*, and, according to Robert Estienne's orthography, *my çyre* – as it were, *demy-çyre*.[43] Hence also, according to some, the word 'sieur', either by transposition of letters or as a diminutive of 'syre'. In fact, 'syre' in Old French signifies 'seigneur'; and there still are great lordships which are called *syreries*, as I have said elsewhere.

40. We also observe that we qualify with this title of 'Sire' both the greatest lord, who is the king, and the basest of people – to wit, artisans. But this is because the king would not be sufficiently honoured by being called only 'Monseigneur' or 'Monsieur'. It could seem that he was called 'Seigneur' only of something bearing that name; but, as he is the universal lord of all, he is called 'Sire', without limitation 'and by use of antonomasia'. On the other hand, because one does not want so to submit to a merchant or artisan as to avow him for one's lord, he is called simply 'Sire so-and-so'.

41. True, it is very likely that the word 'sieur' comes from the possessive pronoun *sien*, and 'seigneur' from the Latin word *senior*, as I said in my *Seigneuries*[44] to which I refer the reader. However, it appears from the foregoing that priests of our time grumble without cause when they are called 'messires': for this is to avow them for one's lords and to equate them with knights, as indeed they are 'soldiers of the sacred army'. But when they are called 'Messire Jean' or 'Messire Guillaume' without adding their surname, that is to disparage them, comparing them with the artisan who is called 'Sire Jean' or 'Sire Guillaume'. Indeed, their sacred order well warrants that the priest be called 'monsieur'.

42. In order fully to explain these words κυριος and *dominus*, it must be understood that κυριος does not directly mean 'lord', δεσπότης, but it properly signifies the sovereign. In fact, in the Greek Empire the emperor was called κυριος and the second in dignity was called δεσπότης, like 'Monsieur' in France, as may be seen in Codinus.[45] This corresponds well enough to our usage. When we want to distinguish the lord paramount of an estate from the proprietor or lord beneficial, we call the former '*seigneur*', κυριος, who has the public

---

[43] [*Dictionnaire Françcois-Latin* (Paris, 1549)] *s.v.* under 'Messire'.
[44] i.[7–22].
[45] [*PG*, CLVII, cols. 113–16, 189.]

or paramount lordship such as justice, fief or manorial rights; and the latter the proprietor, δεσπότης, to whom the property and beneficial lordship of the estate belong.

43. As for the term *dominus*, private persons in Rome were from the first so far from calling themselves in this way that Suetonius records[46] how Augustus never wanted to be addressed by this name:

> He would not let himself be called *dominus* even by his children or grandchildren either in earnest or in jest, and forbade them that kind of flattery even amongst themselves.

He says, further,[47] that Tiberius 'warned someone who called him *dominus* not to address him again so insultingly'. Lampridius records[48] how Alexander Severus made an express edict to prohibit his being called *dominus*.

44. St Augustine writes[49] that Augustus's wishing not to be called *dominus* was a hidden miracle, because in his time the Lord of Lords was born. Yet the real reason is that the rule of the first emperors was a kind of plain principality, as I have said elsewhere, and not a true royal monarchy, and still less lordly as the ancient monarchies were. This is the remonstrance that [the younger] Pliny made to Trajan:[50] 'You occupy the place of prince, lest the place be for a lord'.

45. But the other emperors did not refuse this title. We see that Pliny,[51] Martial,[52] Symmachus[53] and other authors of the same century always call their emperors thus. Even Domitian,[54] and after him Diocletian,[55] made edicts to order that they be called *dominos*.

46. In the end, ambition or flattery was so great in the Roman Empire that this title was adapted to all persons without distinction of qualities, and until it became a joke. Witness this epigram of Martial's:[56]

---

[46] [*Divus Augustus* liii.1.]

[47] [*Tiberius* xxvii.]

[48] [*Alexander Severus* iv.1.]

[49] 'in the *City of God*' [cf. Paulus Orosius, *Adversus paganos (quos vocant) historiarum libri septem* (1562), VI.xxii (pp. 393–6) – a work dedicated to Augustine].

[50] [*Panegyricus ... dictu*] *Traiano*[*Imp.* lv.7].

[51] [*Epistularum* X.ii, v, vi, etc.].

[52] [Cf. *Epigrammata* X.lxxii.8–9.]

[53] [Quintus Aurelius] Symmachus [*Relationes* II, III, etc., in *Monumenta Germaniae Historica, Auctorum antiquissimorum*, VI(1) (Berlin, 1961), pp. 280 *et seq.*].

[54] [Suetonius, *Domitianus* xiii.2.]

[55] [Cf. Aurelius Victor, *Liber de Caesaribus* xxxix.4.]

[56] *Epigrammaton* [V.lvii.1–2].

Do not pride yourself, Cinna, when I call you *dominus*.
I often return even my slave's greeting in this way.

47. The custom upon meeting people was to greet them with this
title whether to do them honour or through failing to remember their
names. 'If the names of those we come across should not spring to
mind', says [the younger] Seneca,[57] 'we call them *dominos*'. Husbands
and wives addressed each other in this way, as we see in several of
our laws. Noteworthy in this connection is the passage in Epictetus[58]
which marks the time when this custom began: 'As soon as they are
fourteen, men call women ladies'.
48. Likewise, children called their fathers *dominos*, as is still done
amongst us in great families. Martial rightly derides this:[59]

> You know you were begotten by a slave, and you blandly
> confess it,
> Sosibianus, when you address your father as *dominum*.

49. We also read that upon meeting one another the early Christians
called each other brothers; but those who wanted to flatter someone
or to acknowledge him as a benefactor called him *domine frater*. This
pretty quatrain testifies as much:[60]

> If a friend receives a present he at once writes, beginning 'Lord
> brother';
> But if he gets nothing, he only says 'Brother',
> For these words are to be bought and sold.
> I at least desire no 'Lord', for I have nothing to give.

The title of 'brother' has remained in the end only to the religious;
and that of 'monsieur' indiscriminately to all persons of honour.
50. Lastly, as to the title of 'master', it applies to all those who have
pupils, clerks or apprentices under them, in relation to whom they are
called 'masters'. However, men of learning or officers have wanted in
respect of this title to be distinguished from tradesmen or craftsmen.
Men of learning call themselves 'masters' 'as a prefix', placing this
quality before their names as a forename. Tradesmen or craftsmen
are called 'masters' 'as a suffix', placing this word 'master' after their
names and relating it to the title of their trade or craft, like an order.

---

[57] [*Epistulae morales* III.I.]
[58] [*Encheiridion.* 40.]
[59] [*Epigrammaton* I.lxxxii. 1–2.]
[60] [*Greek Anthology* x.44.]

On the other hand, the title of nobility is considered more honourable after rather than before the name; when one says 'so-and-so Esquire', it signifies more than to say 'noble man so-and-so'. The former denotes true order and nobility by lineage; the latter, honorary order and the plain epithet of honour.

51. In France we do not only have these honorary dignities, epithets and forenames. We also have honorary names which we vulgarly call 'lordship name' or *nom de guerre*. On the pretext that French gentlemen took a title of honour from their lordships – which neither the Greeks nor the Romans did, as I have said elsewhere[61] – they are so pleased with this title that no longer are they known by any other name, and they themselves sign their letters with no other. Most of them use it in public contracts and judicial acts, quite abandoning their father's and ancestors' name in order to take that of their lands: to the point where some consider themselves slighted to be called by their fathers' names.

52. In this they are quite the reverse of the ancient Romans who made derivatives from their names and denominated their lands thereby: 'of this sort are the lands of Cornelian, Sempronian, Catullian' and others recorded at length by M. Brisson.[62] The custom was so ancient amongst the Hebrews that David records it elegantly in the psalm where, speaking of the great lords of this world, he says: 'They called their home from generation to generation by its name in their lands' – that is, by hypallage, 'they called their lands by their names', as Génébrard interprets it.[63]

53. The ancient French did likewise. Thus it is evident today that almost all the names of villages and lands are derived from the proper names of men, in a denominative form, adding to it the ending 'rie', 'ière' or 'ac', variously, according to country; or placing, either before or after the proper name, the word 'ville', 'bourg' or 'court' of N. This was indeed very honourable: for it was a sign that the land was in the family from antiquity, even that it had been built up and established by one's ancestors, as it bore the family's name.

54. On the other hand, our gentlemen at the present time are so attached to the land, or possessed by their lands, that they prefer to bear its name than that of their fathers which they unworthily sup-

---

[61] [Cf. *Seigneuries* xi. 10–11.]
[62] *De verborum* [*Quae ad ius pertinent* (Paris, 1596), fos. 222ʳᵒ *et seq.*, *s.v.* under 'familiae'].
[63] [Gilbert] Génébrard [*Psalmi Davidis* (Antwerp, 1592), pp. 268, 273].

press and abolish from the memory of men, as is sometimes ordained in law as a signal punishment of those who have perpetrated some dreadful offence. Moreover, it seems that by doing this they renounce their fathers and acknowledge themselves to be bastards, seeing that they take a new name as if they were the first of their line.

55. Even those who, in order to be heirs to someone else, undertake to bear his name and arms always retain with these their father's name. In as much as those who have no children give their possessions to strangers on condition that the latter bear their name, what an injury is done to fathers when their children want to have their substance without bearing their name! In Holy Scripture it is deemed such great felicity to leave children after us to perpetuate our name: 'Blessed be the Lord who has not left you without an inheritor of my family, that my name may be famous in Israel'; and, a little before, 'I must not mar the succeeding generations of my family'; and, a little later, 'to raise up the name of the dead upon his inheritance, that their name be not cut off from his family and brothers and people'.[64] I will thus conclude that someone who disdains to call himself his father's son through refusing to bear his name does not deserve his father's inheritance.

56. Furthermore, is it not a great shame that through this wild fancy the honour of fine deeds of times past, recorded in histories, is extinguished and removed from the family and posterity of valiant men, because of this change of names? As for fine deeds of the present time, the honour of these remains in lands and not in families: so that if the land by the name of which they were chronicled should change its master, the descendants of a stranger who buys it proceed with the passage of time to arrogate those deeds to themselves.

57. This inconvenience mainly concerns the interests of private families. But here is a public interest, and a very considerable one. It is that, through this ordinary change of names, lineages are no longer known so as to distinguish either ancient from new ones, or nobles from commoners, or kinsfolk from strangers. For when a gentleman who is named or known only by the name of his land, or who has appropriated this name to his family, sells his land, he still wants to keep the same name, and his descendants likewise. Similarly, the commoner who has purchased it takes the name and title as well and

---

[64] Ruth iv.[14, 6, 10].

appropriates them to his family. So in time the commoner descendants of that purchaser say that they are of the vendor's noble lineage. This is the inconvenience which the emperors remarked in the law[65] they made to prohibit changes of name, 'lest they should dare to place men of mean stock among the noble and free-born'.

58. All in all, just as first names (which the Latins called 'praenomens' and we call proper names) serve to distinguish persons of the same surname and family, so second names (which the Latins called 'cognomens' and we call surnames) are prescribed in order to distinguish families and to denote kinship.

59. The vanity of our modern sword-danglers is a little more excusable. Having no lordship whose name they can take, they only add *de* or *du* before their father's name; this is done after the manner of a lordship. Its purpose is to form a possessive genitive instead of the nominative. The Italians teach us this, and so do the Gascons with the names of men of learning, which they commonly end with an 'i', putting them into the Latin genitive. For example, in my time at Toulouse the learned President du Faur, who has written so well, was called the President Fabri. Now 'du Faur' in French is a genitive, as is 'Fabri' in Latin; and in saying 'Pierre du Faur' one must necessarily understand the name of lord, or some other, that can be linked to this genitive. Likewise, when 'Petrus Fabri' is said in Latin, the word '*Dominus*' must be added; otherwise it would be inconsistent with that rule of grammar which is called the rule of apposition.

60. Those who place these particles before their names want one to believe that their name comes from some lordship which was anciently in their family. This is still to attach oneself to the land and to prefer it to man, against the reason of the law,[66] and against Cicero's rule[67] that 'the owner should bring honour to his abode, not the abode to its owner'. But, so what? Our new nobility do not account persons to be gentlemen unless their names are ennobled by these articles or particles, even though the [chronicles] show us that in former times the most notable families of this kingdom did not have them. But that has happened by degrees, as ambition always grows.

61. At first only kings abandoned their surnames, because their majesty raised them above other men. Dukes and counts wanted to do

---

[65] [Cf.] *Code J* 9.25.1 [markedly milder in tone than Loyseau's rendering of it here].
[66] *Digest* 21.1.44.
[67] *De officiis* [I.xxxix.139].

the same when they usurped the rights of sovereignty. Barons and other, lesser lords have done as much with the passage of time. At last it has reached this height of absurdity that the pettiest lords have wanted to do it too, especially those who, having been poor or born of poor parents, have become rich and have tried to wipe out the memory of their former poverty by changing their names. Thus we read in Lucian[68] of a cobbler named Simon who, upon becoming rich, wanted to be called Simonides.

62. So much for names of lordships. As for *noms de guerre*, it is true that the poor soldier going on campaign does not want to leave his hands nor his feet at home, but he willingly leaves his real name there. He calls himself 'la Vigne', 'la Fontaine', 'la Pierre', 'la Haye', or some other *nom du guerre*; so that if by chance he is hanged on a tree his lineage should not be dishonoured. And if he should escape this hazard and bring his ears back home, resuming the name he left there, he will not find himself by that name on the provosts' charge-sheet.[69] Thus courtesans and women of pleasure, says Plautus,[70]

> today change their names,
> So that they may [not] disgrace their family by prostitution.

63. Nevertheless, soldiers ought strictly to be prohibited from this. For one thing, when they die in a place where they are known only by a false name, they leave their wives and their heirs in great uncertainty, from which great inconveniences ensue. For another, the impunity with which they conduct themselves under cover of that false name makes them much less restrained from evil doing. Beyond these considerations, it is certain that in warfare they are not so fond of honour nor so wary of dishonour as they would behave if, being well known by their real names, all their race and especially their posterity in their native country were to share in their glory or their shame.

64. Further, we read in Vegetius[71] that so far were Roman soldiers from having this licence to change their names that, on the contrary, they were bound to etch or write them on the backs of their shields

---

[68] Lucian [of Samosata, *The Dream, or the Cock*. 14].
[69] [I.e., singled out for punishment:] 'au papier rouge des Preuosts'.
[70] *Poenulus* [v.iii.1139–40].
[71] [Flavius] Vegetius [Renatus, *De re militari libri quatuor* (Lyon, 1592)], pp. 38–9.

so that, if they should abandon their shields, they would be dishonoured. This rule was renewed by Julian, commander of the Emperor Domitian's army, in his war in Dacia, as Dio observes.[72] Also, Festus and Cicero[73] tell us that 'in choosing soldiers, those who had beautiful names were called first'.

> Glory to God! May God make me mindful of Him
> as well at life's end as at book's end!

---

[72] [*Rom. hist.* LXVII.x.1.]
[73] [Cf.] Cicero, *De divinatione* [I.xlv.102].

Index

This index registers every person mentioned in the text, with identification; place names; significant institutions; and a selection of key words relating to major political concepts or to the defining, gaining, losing and especially the exhibiting of order. For obvious reasons it does not include terms, such as law, office, order or sub-sets of these, which in many instances pervade the entire work.

Index

Index

Index

Cambridge Texts in the History of Political Thought

Titles published in the series thus far